A FUNDER'S GUIDE *from*
Fieldstone Alliance & GEO

Power in Policy: A Funder's Guide to Advocacy and Civic Participation is one of a series
of works published by Fieldstone Alliance in collaboration with Grantmakers for
Effective Organizations (GEO). Together, we hope to strengthen nonprofit organizations, the communities they serve, and the nonprofit sector by helping grantmakers
in their work with nonprofits.

Chapter Authors *(listed alphabetically)*

David F. Arons, attorney-at-law, formerly Co-Director, Center for Lobbying in the Public Interest

Emmett D. Carson, PhD, CEO & President, Silicon Valley Community Foundation

Hodding Carter III, formerly President & CEO, John S. and James L. Knight Foundation (currently University Professor of Leadership and Public Policy, University of North Carolina)

Stuart Comstock-Gay, Director of the Democracy Program, Dēmos (formerly Vice President, New Hampshire Charitable Foundation)

Cynthia M. Gibson, PhD, Principal, Cynthesis Consulting (formerly Program Officer, Carnegie Corporation of New York)

Abby Levine, Foundation Advocacy Counsel, Alliance for Justice

Geri Mannion, Program Chair, Strengthening U.S. Democracy Program, Carnegie Corporation of New York

Lloyd H. Mayer, Esq., Associate Professor of Law, University of Notre Dame Law School and Of Counsel, Caplin & Drysdale, Chartered

Gayle Peterson, Senior Partner, The Headwaters Group Philanthropic Services

John Sherman, Senior Partner, The Headwaters Group Philanthropic Services

Kelly Shipp Simone, Senior Staff Attorney, Council on Foundations

Contributors *(listed alphabetically)*

David T. Abbott, Executive Director, The George Gund Foundation

Marcia Egbert, Senior Program Officer, The George Gund Foundation

Lenore M. Hanisch, Executive Director, Quixote Foundation

Jeff Krehely, formerly Deputy Director, National Committee for Responsive Philanthropy (currently with the LGBT Movement Advancement Project)

Gara LaMarche, Vice President and Director of U.S. Programs, Open Society Institute

Patti S. Lieberman, Chair, A.L. Mailman Family Foundation, Inc.

Maria Mottola, Executive Director, New York Foundation

Phil Nash, Vice President for Communications, Rose Community Foundation

Mary O'Connell, Director of Communications, The Joyce Foundation

Helen Davis Picher, Director, Evaluation and Research, William Penn Foundation

Jeffrey T. Pinzino, Program Officer, Woods Fund of Chicago

Tony Pipa, formerly Executive Director, Warner Foundation

William A. Schambra, Director, Bradley Center for Philanthropy and Civic Renewal and Senior Fellow, Hudson Institute

Brent Thompson, Director of Communications, William Penn Foundation

POWER IN POLICY

A FUNDER'S GUIDE TO ADVOCACY AND CIVIC PARTICIPATION

Edited by David F. Arons
Foreword by Hodding Carter III

FIELDSTONE
ALLIANCE

SAINT PAUL
MINNESOTA

Library of Congress Cataloging-in-Publication Data

Power in policy : a funder's guide to advocacy and civic participation / editor, David F. Arons ; chapter authors (listed alphabetically), David F. Arons ... [et al.].
    p. cm.
 Includes bibliographical references and index.
 ISBN-13: 978-0-940069-45-9
 ISBN-10: 0-940069-45-8
 1. Nonprofit organizations--United States--Political activity. 2. Social advocacy--United States. I. Arons, David F.
 HD2769.2.U6P69 2007
 361.7'632--dc22
                    2006036544

Contents

Acknowledgments

This book would not have been possible without the contributions of the authors and other contributors, most of whom work for a foundation or with foundations and believe in the important civic role foundations play in the United States and abroad. We appreciate the cosponsorship of Grantmakers for Effective Organizations and especially Lori Bartczak's work on this project.

We are grateful to the reviewers, including Jim Abernathy, Marcia Avner, Joe Breiteneicher, Sue Hoechstetter, Abby Levine, Jeff Pinzino, Deborah Schachter, and Holly Schadler.

We thank the following organizations for their submissions of examples of foundations involved in public policy, civic activity, or other advocacy activities. Although not all submissions were printed in the book, every example contributed to building a resource that will serve foundations.

A.L. Mailman Family Foundation

Arnold Fund

Association for Small Foundations

Baton Rouge Area Foundation

Battle Creek Community Foundation

The Boston Foundation

The California Wellness Foundation

Charles & Helen Schwab Foundation

Chicago Community Organizing Capacity Building Initiative

Coalition of Community Foundations for Youth

Colina Family Foundation

Community Foundation of Greater Greensboro

Conrad N. Hilton Foundation

Council of Michigan Foundations

The Denver Foundation

East Bay Community Foundation

Foellinger Foundation

Ford Foundation

Funders Concerned About AIDS

Funders' Network for Smart Growth and Livable Communities

The George Gund Foundation

Grand Rapids Community Foundation

Grantmakers for Effective Organizations

Grantmakers for Education

Grantmakers in Health

Greater Kansas City Community Foundation

Greater Milwaukee Foundation

The Health Foundation of Greater Indianapolis

Humboldt Area Foundation

Institute of Politics, University of Pittsburgh

The James Irvine Foundation

The Joyce Foundation

Liberty Hill Foundation

Marin Community Foundation

The Minneapolis Foundation

Ms. Foundation for Women

National Committee for Responsive Philanthropy

New Hampshire Charitable Foundation

New York Foundation

Open Society Institute

Otto Bremer Foundation

Prince Charitable Trusts

The Public Intersection Project, UNC Chapel Hill

Quixote Foundation

Roots of Change Fund

Rose Community Foundation

Skillman Foundation

Steelcase Foundation

Social Venture Partners Seattle

Surdna Foundation

University of North Carolina, Kenan Institute of Private Enterprise

University of Pittsburgh, Institute of Politics

Warner Foundation

The Wallace Alexander Gerbode Foundation

William Penn Foundation

Woods Fund of Chicago

Z. Smith Reynolds Foundation

Editor's Note: I appreciate the time, patience, and work devoted to this book by Vince Hyman, the publishing director at Fieldstone Alliance, as well as Kirsten Nielsen and Becky Andrews. I am also grateful to Marcia Avner for encouraging my involvement in this worthwhile project. An immeasurable amount of appreciation goes to my wife, Colleen Arons, for her support.

Foreword

Hodding Carter III

Viewed primarily as a piggy bank for good works, a foundation has no particular obligation or need to engage in the public policy world. Viewed as an institution that takes seriously the causes its mission statement proclaims, a foundation absolutely must participate in public policy. What appears in the chapters and essays that follow is a case for the affirmative.

This case is one to which I am drawn as a citizen and as the former president of a national foundation that proclaims its intention to—among other things—advance the interests of those least able to provide for themselves. It is one to which my experience in government, as a journalist, and as a participant in numerous nonprofits over the past forty-two years, draws me no less strongly. Foundations are, by the nature of their existence, creatures of public policy—protected by it, regulated by it, and dependent on it for the furtherance of many of the causes and organizations they support. Foundations are, in their sphere, citizens in much the same way as individual Americans, sharing a common space and political heritage. Involvement in the public arena is one of the responsibilities that go with the territory, or so I believe.

Many do not. They argue forcefully that there is no obligation for an individual or a foundation to play a public role. Some believe that to do so can be counterproductive. Others believe it can be politically dangerous, encouraging retaliation. Whatever their rationale, tens of millions of our fellow Americans and thousands of foundations long ago decided that politics and government and policy debates were best left to others.

Those who hold these views are entitled to them. But for me, the case for foundation participation in the nation's civic life is almost self-evident. It rests on practical as well as moral grounds, not least because the multiple causes and purposes in which foundations invest depend so heavily on the public sector. Whether in the arts, education, social welfare, or the environment, foundation giving is a relatively small fraction of the total pie and is unlikely to be much larger in the foreseeable future. Foundation total giving tops $30 billion a year. Federal spending in our fields of interest annually is about $225 billion. State, local, and county governments spend tens of billions more. (Where Knight Foundation is headquartered, Miami/Dade County's school budget alone is $4.2 billion a year.)

More to the point, public policy decisions are having a negative effect in all these fields. Devolution and de-funding march in virtual lockstep. Behind them come slashed services, inadequate facilities, forsworn commitments, and diminished human beings. Illustratively: Knight decides to invest several million dollars on innovative early childhood development programs in a targeted community neighborhood; total public spending on early childhood development in that community simultaneously drops by a factor ten times larger than Knight expenditures. Knight's dollars might as well be snowflakes in a Florida August for all their possible long-term effect.

Assuming that we are not just going through the motions in some feckless mimicry of concern, that we actually care about the outcomes our grant conditions so carefully stress, Knight (and all foundations similarly involved) simply cannot stand aside like passive onlookers at a stranger's funeral. Nor must we. Foundations have ample legal latitude to behave like individual citizens in our communities, putting aside the prohibitions on direct lobbying on legislation and partisan political activity—from Washington to city hall. Even more importantly, we can help our grantees become more effective citizens—to organize, communicate, and coordinate their own advocacy efforts on behalf of the programs we fund. We can do so with our dollars, with our expertise, with our convening capabilities, and with the assistance of our philanthropic partners. Political decisions have produced the grim environment in which so many of our grantees must try to function; political decisions can change it for the better.

There are rarely, if ever, any quick fixes when dealing with complex social organisms. If foundations are to operate effectively in this field, they must decide to do it over considerable time. Our grantees will need our support, direct and indirect, for years to come if they are to have an impact on public sector decision making.

Emmett Carson makes an excellent point in his opening chapter. What is good for the goose is good for the gander when it comes to advocacy. And that is precisely what the democratic process should be all about. It is at the root of the moral case for philanthropy staking out a vigorous position in the world of public affairs. All voices, all points of view, should be heard. A full, unfiltered and unfettered debate is the prerequisite for good policy. Those who are most affected by policy decisions should have at least as much opportunity to influence them as everyone else. But in a political world in which money too frequently trumps all else, those with little or none are at a severe disadvantage. Philanthropy should do much more to level the public policy field on which they must contend. In this field, what we do and say can have multiplier effects of lasting significance.

For those weighing precisely what role foundations should play in the world of public affairs, the real-life examples of the civic engagement of private and community foundations that follow are invaluable. The book's mix of inspiration and practical advice are exactly what the subject demands.

Introduction

David F. Arons

Collectively, foundations in American society are no longer behind-the-scenes benefactors. The foundation world is an increasingly visible and expanding industry. Since 1980, the number of private and community foundations combined grew from around 22,000 to over 64,000 as of 2002.[1] Foundation giving also exploded. From 1995 to 2003 foundation giving more than doubled, increasing from around $12 billion to approximately $30 billion.[2] The foundation world is far from homogenous in terms of its interests. The range of causes championed or supported seems to grow, or at least change, as frequently as new foundations come into existence. Yet, the foundation world shares a common core purpose: to use accumulated wealth to benefit society.

The phenomenal growth in volume and areas of concern are only a couple of the measures of foundations' expansion. Foundations and the associations that support them have become increasingly sophisticated about funding strategies, donor education, financial planning, professional development, and evaluation of their impact on the causes they serve directly or through grantees. In addition, many foundations now seek greater understanding of and recognition for their philanthropy and the positive accomplishments of their grantees through organized public relations activities.

---

[1] Foundation Center, "Foundation Growth and Giving Estimates, 2004," http://fdncenter.org/research/trends_analysis/pdf/fgge04.pdf.

[2] Ibid.

Increasingly, foundations are finding that participation in public decision making is often a critical component in reaching the impact demanded by mission-related goals. Foundation civic engagement brings together the modalities of philanthropy, advocacy, partnering, and communications as means of demonstrating leadership that confers benefits to grantees and the public. Nonprofit and foundation advocacy and civic engagement are increasingly viewed as opportunities to promote affirmative solutions and hopeful agendas and not subscriptions to negative politics as usual.

Foundations' increased growth and exposure have spurred scrutiny by government, media, and nonprofits. Like any maturing industry, foundations face pressure to demonstrate greater accountability, transparency, and performance. The pressure on foundations is perhaps the most intense within the nonprofit sector because charities are continually looking to foundations to help fill in for government cutbacks or to match government funding streams.

Some foundations may be expected to provide leadership in their region and in their cause area. Perhaps this expectation is at times unfair, for community and cause leadership, including advocacy, may be a new role, and only recently have associations devised ways of helping foundations cultivate themselves as leadership institutions. However, many foundations see involvement in broad civic issues and focused public policy efforts as part of their mission-based strategy for success. And indeed, some foundations have adopted the view that participation in public policymaking is not only smart, but a noble mark of active citizenship. The demands for civic, political, economic, and moral leadership are immense and will only continue to grow. Some foundations have hired seasoned public policy leaders, but the vast majority of foundations are small, in pursuit of family interests, and did not necessarily have broad civic or public policy leadership in mind when they were founded.

The confluence of growth, sophistication, and desire for impact call for more foundations individually and collectively to embrace an inherent role in civic life and to affirmatively shape the public policies that directly and indirectly affect those they serve. Participation in the making of public policy is an opportunity to positively affect the "ends" of lawmaking (rights, resources, rules), but also the "means" in terms of how democracy functions (access, accountability, transparency, power). In the twenty-first century, foundation participation in public policy is a mandatory function given the reach of law and policy on almost every foundation interest. Policy participation is also about self-defense, as with any other business or industry. When government is both a partner and a policing force, the old adage "if you are not at the table, then you are *on* the table" rings especially true. In other words, if foundations don't weigh in on the policy issues affecting the communities they serve, the foundation industry, and the nonprofit sector at large, laws may be made by legislators and regulators in reaction to imminent pressures, including scandals and budget crises. But playing defense, while necessary, is not why this book was written. Rather, it was conceived because public policy participation and civic involvement are powerful avenues for empowering communities, realizing philanthropic aspirations, and building the courage required for constant social change.

The 2004 presidential election season saw significant and noticeable examples of foundation participation in civic activity through the sponsorship of nonpartisan voter education and participation projects. Hopefully the civic philanthropy of a few foundations will inspire more grantmaking in the democracy-building arena. Yet, for the most part, the business models of American foundations (as well as grantseeking nonprofits) lack a dedicated public policy component that is driven by a clearly defined rationale and strategy for civic and policy participation. By building public policy and civic leadership into the very fabric of their governance, management, and operations, foundations can adopt a powerful set of tools for realizing mission and for strengthening the environment needed for successful philanthropy and community building.

> **For the most part, the business models of American foundations (as well as public charities) lack a dedicated public policy component that is driven by a clearly defined rationale and strategy for civic and policy participation.**

It is the mission of this book to encourage foundations new to the public policy arena—as well as those reviewing their current approach—to integrate efforts to shape public policy and strengthen civic participation into their core philanthropic and program strategies. While it focuses primarily on private foundations and community foundations, operating foundations and corporate foundations or giving programs might also find useful insights, examples, and lessons to draw on.

This book is not a technical assistance manual. Rather, it aims to motivate and educate. It can't be stated enough that efforts to shape public policy and to strengthen civic life are frequently long-term endeavors requiring courage, sustained passion, leadership renewal, and investment. Success is incremental, but mission clarity, wise use of resources, and resolve will result in the kind of changes that make philanthropy all the more worthwhile.

The chapter authors and contributors include some of the leading thinkers in the foundation world about public policy and philanthropy:

Chapter 1, by Emmett D. Carson, PhD, CEO and president of Silicon Valley Community Foundation, presents a cogent argument for why foundations have a special place at the public policy table.

Chapter 2 is a collection of essays by leaders in philanthropy including William A. Schambra (Bradley Center for Philanthropy and Civic Renewal), Gara LaMarche (Open Society Institute), Jeff Krehely (formerly of the National Committee for Responsive Philanthropy), David T. Abbott (The George Gund Foundation), and Marcia Egbert (The George Gund Foundation). The essays share different perspectives about where public policy fits within foundation mission, programs, and philanthropic objectives.

Chapter 3 shares philosophies and approaches to policy and civic participation from small foundation leaders including Maria Mottola (New York Foundation), Tony Pipa (formerly of Warner Foundation), Patti S. Lieberman (A.L. Mailman Family Foundation, Inc.), and Lenore M. Hanisch (Quixote Foundation).

In Chapter 4, David F. Arons (formerly of Center for Lobbying in the Public Interest), Abby Levine (Alliance for Justice), and Kelly Shipp Simone (Council on Foundations) discuss advocacy language and how to reach common understanding.

Chapter 5 provides a walk-through of the public policy process, explains various types of public policy and civic activities, and presents three short case examples of foundations that used several advocacy strategies to reach a public policy goal.

Chapter 6 presents a step-by-step approach to prepare for public policy involvement.

In Chapter 7, Cynthia M. Gibson, PhD, (Cynthesis Consulting) and Geri Mannion (Carnegie Corporation of New York) share lessons learned about cultivating interest in public policy and developing civic capacity within a private foundation.

Chapter 8, by Stuart Comstock-Gay (formerly of the New Hampshire Charitable Foundation, currently executive director of the National Voting Rights Institute) explains how community foundations may develop capacity, including program fit and donor education for public policy and civic participation.

In Chapter 9, Lloyd H. Mayer, Esq., associate professor of law at the University of Notre Dame Law School and one of the most experienced attorneys in the nation on the laws governing the policy and political activities of tax-exempt organizations, provides a plain-English tutorial about the law as applied to public policy–related grantmaking and advocacy by private and community foundations.

In Chapter 10, by John Sherman and Gayle Peterson (both of The Headwaters Group Philanthropic Services), readers will gain an understanding of the process of evaluation of philanthropic programs and initiatives that involve advocacy and public policy.

This book is a starting point for foundations who want to have a long-term impact on the communities and causes they care about. It encourages one of America's most powerful forces of change—private philanthropy—to realize and assert its rightful place among the policymaking institutions and industries in our society. So let's get started!

A final note: Many terms are used throughout the book. Please see the Glossary in Appendix A for definitions. Note that "nonprofit" generally refers to public charities with a 501(c)(3) designation under the Internal Revenue Code unless otherwise stated.

How to Use This Book

This book is divided into six parts: three major sections and three appendices. Throughout the book you will see many sidebars, which contain tips and other useful information. You don't need to start at the beginning of this book and read to the end to benefit from it. The book has been organized so that you can start at the chapter most useful to you and your organization.

If your question is:	Then read:
What are the advantages of our foundation becoming involved in public policy or civic strengthening activities?	Chapters 1, 2, 3, 7, and 8
If we get involved, what might our role be?	Chapters 1, 2, 3, 6, 7, and 8
How have other foundations been involved in public policy and civic activities? What are some examples?	Chapters 5, 7, 8, and Appendix B
How might our foundation begin to talk about this topic?	Chapter 4
What roles should be filled in the foundation if we become involved in public policy?	Chapters 6, 7, and 8
How does my foundation assess various risks?	Chapters 6, 8, and 9
What are the legal rules we must abide by?	Chapter 9 and Appendix A
How might we evaluate public policy work by grantees?	Chapter 10 and Appendix A
How might we prepare and work together with our board of directors to approve and implement public policy strategy?	Chapters 6, 7, 8, and 9
How can we build internal capacity to both make grants related to public policy and to engage ourselves?	Chapters 6, 7, 8, and 9
What resource organizations are available to help our foundation get started or enhance our advocacy work?	Chapter 9 and Appendix C

The chapters correspond to questions frequently asked by foundations that are either considering public policy work or civic involvement of some kind, or currently include funding public policy activity as part of philanthropic programs, mission-related pursuits, and community development efforts. The table on page 6 is a guide to help you find what you're looking for. If your question does not appear in the table, check the table of contents or contact any of the resource organizations or authors.

Chapter 3 is especially for small foundations, Chapter 7 is especially for private foundations, and Chapter 8 is especially for community foundations. All other chapters are for both private and community foundations but make important distinctions between them as appropriate.

If yours is a

Small foundation…see Chapter 3

Private foundation…see Chapter 7

Community foundation…see Chapter 8

Viewpoints on Foundation, Civic, and Policy Engagement

In Chapter 1 of this section, Emmett D. Carson, PhD, one of the leading voices in the field of philanthropy, presents a case for why foundation involvement in civic and public policymaking is an important and vital role. Chapter 2 shares differing viewpoints from several philanthropic sector leaders about the role of foundations as public policy actors. Chapter 3 includes the views of several leaders of small foundations about the connections public policy has with mission, values, and goals.

SECTION

1

Chapter One

On Foundations and Public Policy:
Why the Words Don't Match the Behavior

Emmett D. Carson, PhD

I n recent years, there has been a sustained and unprecedented effort to encourage foundations of all types to become engaged in public policy. Through national and local conferences, award programs, and educational materials, foundation leaders have ample encouragement and are ready to access a broad range of materials aimed at stimulating their interest in public policy.[3] Despite these considerable efforts, there is widespread belief that, in general, foundations remain steadfast in their unwillingness to engage in public policy as measured by either the actual numbers of foundations or their aggregate dollars directed to engage in public policy.[4]

Unfortunately, there is no readily available data that can either confirm or rebut perceptions about the extent of foundation engagement in public policy. In part, this is due to a problem in defining what constitutes public policy. The term public policy is used here to refer to any efforts by a foundation to support research, convening, advocacy, or lobbying[5]—either directly or through its grantees—to influence public decision making. See Chapter 4 for a discussion of language.

CHAPTER SNAPSHOT

This chapter includes

- A case for why foundations should engage in public policy

- Common impediments to foundations' public policy participation

- Ways to find courage to engage

---

[3] A wide collection of resources is available through the Council on Foundations, Independent Sector, Alliance for Justice, and the Center for Lobbying in the Public Interest.

[4] Karen Paget, "The Big Chill," *The American Prospect* vol. 10, no. 44, May 1, 1999.

[5] *Lobbying* is defined in federal law as any effort to influence specific legislation. While private foundations are prohibited from lobbying (with several important exceptions including self-defense and nonpartisan research), community foundations (as public charities) are not. Private foundations can provide general support to qualifying nonprofit organizations that do lobby as long as they indicate that the grant is not earmarked for lobbying purposes (see Chapter 9).

Another challenge is accurately collecting the necessary data. For example, while the Foundation Center tracks a giving category referred to as public affairs/society benefit, it is too broad a category from which to draw any useful conclusions about foundation support of public policy. Specifically, the category includes areas that are not necessarily related to public policy, such as community improvement and development, philanthropy, and voluntarism. The category excludes subject-specific public policy work, for example, education or health policy, which is embedded in respective subject area categories.[6] As a result of these methodological dilemmas, no data-driven conclusions can be reached about whether foundation support of public policy has increased, decreased, or remained constant.

The purpose of this essay is threefold: to make the case for why foundations should engage in public policy, to discuss impediments that discourage foundations from engaging in public policy, and to suggest what can be done to strengthen the commitment of foundations to engage in public policy. For the reasons stated earlier, this essay is not based on rigorous research but, rather, on one person's informed opinion. Unfortunately, informed opinions are only occasionally more revealing than uninformed opinions and, when it comes to opinions, everyone has them. It is in this spirit that the following observations are offered, recognizing that they are subject to change as new, more factual information becomes available.

The Case for Foundations and Public Policy

In the effort to motivate foundations to become more interested in pursuing public policy efforts, proponents have disproportionately pursued two complementary strategies: 1) to demonstrate that, contrary to popular opinion, foundations are not prohibited from supporting public policy efforts, and 2) to provide case study examples to show both the societal value and the "how to" for foundations to successfully engage in public policy. While these strategies have undoubtedly had some success and would have needed to be undertaken in any scenario, what has been missing is why foundations should engage in public policy. Stated another way, it is not

---

[6] Josefina Atienza and Leslie Marino, *Foundation Giving Trends: Update on Funding Priorities* (New York: The Foundation Center, 2004), 20.

enough to know that you are free to climb to the top of a mountain and that the tools exist to make the climb. If you have not been imbued with passion and desire to climb the mountain, you won't start the trek. While some people may find the desire within themselves to climb the mountain, most will pass by, content to know that the mountain is there, that it could be successfully climbed, but with no desire to climb it.

The proposition that foundations should engage in public policy because it is essential to the development and interchange of ideas integral to maintaining a democratic society, while true, does not motivate many foundations to engage in public policy. The recognition (in the abstract) that public policy work is worthwhile to society rarely sparks a foundation to take on the work—especially if the foundation perceives that there are risks in doing so. Economists call this phenomenon the "free-rider" problem, where individuals acknowledge that a specific activity is beneficial for all (for example, national defense) but no single individual is likely to take the responsibility to provide it because they think that someone else will.

Similarly, it is not enough to say that foundations should engage in public policy because the effort will leverage their grant funds. True, foundation engagement in public policy can mean that relatively small grants can hold the prospect of making significant impact. Unfortunately, this explanation doesn't generate the necessary passion for foundations to engage in public policy.

So, what is the case that might lead foundations to enthusiastically pursue some aspect of public policy grantmaking? The answer to this question lies in asking the boards and staff of foundations to commit themselves to fulfilling the aspirations embodied in their foundation's mission and vision statements. By embracing their mission and vision statements, foundations can find the necessary passion and motivation to want to understand what activity is legal and to learn how to do it. Foundation mission statements represent the voice of their founders (tempered over time by the dreams of contemporary trustees) expressing why and how they would like to change the world, the nation, or their community.

Many foundations' mission statements speak with conviction about lofty aspirations such as eliminating poverty, eradicating disease, and promoting world peace, and to national and local concerns such as improving educational outcomes, providing affordable housing, establishing universal health care, or making arts and culture accessible to all. At their core, such mission statements assert that the foundation has examined some aspect of society, found it lacking, and believes that by championing change they will make the world a better place. The magnitude of societal change that is envisioned in these change-oriented mission statements cannot be achieved through the support of direct human services. Change-oriented mission statements—by necessity—require a foundation to pursue public policy efforts that attempt to fundamentally change how the system operates.

> **The magnitude of societal change envisioned in change-oriented mission statements cannot be achieved through the support of direct human services. Change-oriented mission statements—by necessity—require a foundation to pursue public policy efforts that attempt to fundamentally change how the system operates.**

Only public policy engagement can affect the laws that determine how people will be treated, what services will be provided, what behaviors are acceptable, and the incentives and disincentives to compel compliance. It does not matter how a foundation chooses to engage in public policy, support research to deepen understanding of critical issues, fund grantees involved in public policy, or convene the public on critical topics. Foundations that seek to change some element of society have a different objective than those with "status quo" mission statements.

Status quo mission statements often focus on providing direct human services and do not include a philosophy of social change. Such mission statements are an implicit endorsement that the current socioeconomic system of providing opportunity is essentially fair at allocating scarce resources. Status quo mission statements hold the view that there is no need for a fundamental reordering of any aspect of the existing system. Similar to the kiddie bumpers that are used in bowling, status quo mission statements believe that only a safety net is needed for those who have been unable to achieve success due to their own bad luck, personal failings, or both. To the extent that a foundation moves from support of direct human services to advocating for greater government support of direct human services, it has become a change-oriented foundation.

The genius of the American nonprofit sector is that every foundation is able to determine, through its mission statement, whether it supports a status quo or change-oriented view of what would be most beneficial to society. Foundations that pursue engagement in social change/public policy are neither more nor less admirable than those that have status quo mission statements or a combination of both. Foundations with firm status quo mission statements should not be expected to be active in public policy. However, those foundations that have change-oriented mission statements but are not pursuing any public policy initiatives are not fulfilling the mandate of their founders.

It is important to remember that those foundations that have change-oriented mission statements and choose to become engaged in public policy could end up advocating points of view that would not be supported by many of us. Hot button issues such as gay and lesbian marriage, school choice, right to life/right to choose, universal health care, and equal rights, among other topics, have both strong supporters and vigorous detractors. There is no guarantee what positions foundations that are newly energized to fulfill their change-oriented missions might ultimately advocate.

In fact, it does not take an overly active imagination to believe that foundations, whose founders have benefited from the existing system, might be more likely to advocate public policy strategies that reinforce existing aspects of the system—for example, supporting expanded use of free-market principles to allocate goods and services rather than supporting limitations on the free-market system.

> Democratic society is healthier when the public is exposed to and engaged in debating the kind of society in which we want to live and our mutual obligations to each other. Foundations and nonprofit grantseeking institutions have important roles to play in shaping these discussions.

There is an old saying: Be careful of what you ask for. One person's utopia is another's nightmare. Notwithstanding the inherent risks, whatever one's point of view, democratic society is healthier when the public is exposed to and engaged in debating the kind of society in which we want to live and our mutual obligations to each other. Foundations and nonprofit grantseeking institutions have important roles to play in shaping these discussions, as envisioned by our founding fathers and codified in our legal framework. And, if foundations with change-oriented mission statements accept their calling, they may find the much-needed inspiration to act on their own words and aspirations.

Impediments to Engaging in Public Policy

There is probably a long list of impediments that singularly, or in combination, contribute to why foundations appear unwilling to engage in public policy. Despite all efforts to educate them otherwise, some foundations persist in their belief that support of public policy is either illegal or overly onerous. However, there are at least three other explanations—structural issues, the fear of controversy, and a lack of courage in convictions.

1. Form follows structure

One of the most perplexing conundrums in the nonprofit sector is to reconcile why so many foundations with change-oriented mission statements that say they want to be "catalysts" and "social change agents" are unwilling to engage in public policy. At least part of the challenge is to recognize that the structure of a foundation can either ease or hinder public policy work. As stated earlier, while private foundations may appear to have the freedom to act decisively in support of their change-oriented mission statements, their trustees feel an enormous personal burden and responsibility not to engage in actions that may bring controversy to the family name. After all, while they may personally believe in supporting transformation of some aspect of society, they, and other family members, must continue to live, raise children, conduct business, and worship in the broader community.

The social and economic repercussions from taking difficult positions as suggested by change-oriented mission statements might not outweigh the personal risks to family reputation and honor. Imagine for a moment that each and every grant from your private foundation bears your family name. How committed must you and other family members be to take a position on a controversial topic? What deference or concern would you have for the feelings of extended family members who are not on the board of the family foundation but who are implicated and impacted by its actions?

By contrast, community foundations are required to have community boards that are representative of the community, and so might find it easier than private foundations to avoid issues of individual reputation. Unfortunately, the bogeyman for community foundations is that their public policy efforts will result in harming their fund development efforts. While it is counterintuitive and goes against everything that is commonly believed about the need for community foundations to stay neutral in order not to offend potential donors, the experience of The Minneapolis Foundation has been just the opposite. The Minneapolis Foundation has successfully engaged in controversial public policy efforts and, at the same time, seen its standing in the community improve and its fund development results increase.[7]

While the experience of The Minneapolis Foundation might have been the result of the positive economic market at the time, donors always have a choice of what charitable institution to give to and with which institutions they wish to associate. True, The Minneapolis Foundation has likely alienated some current and potential donors who did not agree with the Foundation's positions on immigration, affordable housing, and the negative impact of massive statewide budget cuts on nonprofit social service agencies. However, the Foundation did attract donors who wanted to be part of its social-change agenda. The Foundation, in effect, created a unique brand identity that distinguishes it in the charitable marketplace.

2. Fear of controversy

The rhetoric of foundations is that they represent the "social risk capital" within democratic societies. The fact is, foundations are extremely risk averse. This aversion to risk is not easily explained. Most endowed foundations are insulated from having to either raise money (the exceptions being community and operating foundations) or from having to worry about market sales of consumer products (a problem for corporate foundations). While the possibility always exists that the public policy actions of an individual foundation could result in adverse legislation for the entire field, there is no evidence that this has ever occurred. In fact, the opposite is true. Congress and the various regulatory agencies have consistently tried to clarify the ways in which private and community foundations, albeit in different ways, can legally participate in the public policy process.

---

[7] Stuart Appelbaum, "The Cost of Sticking Your Neck Out," *Foundation News and Commentary* vol. 46, no. 5, September/October 2005, 42–47.

The often cited and seldom read 1969 Tax Reform law addressed unethical self-dealing practices and placed limits on the ability of private foundations to lobby or support nonprofit organizations that engaged in legislative lobbying. As Thomas A. Troyer notes,

> As the enactment of the 1969 private foundation legislation drifts into the past and those directly involved in the event largely disappear from the scene or fall silent, mythology—far from absent even in 1969—often squeezes out fact. To some of those who think back to it, the legislation seems an aberrant spasm of Congressional anger at foundations, generated by the unfortunate acts of a handful of individuals and organizations, without rational grounding in general realities in the foundation field. The concerns of Congress at which the law struck had roots reaching back for more than two decades, and its core restrictions on the personal use and financial practices of foundations had solid policy justification.[8]

In 1976, Congress passed legislation that clarified how public charities, including community foundations, could "elect" to engage in lobbying without violating their tax status. In 1990, the Treasury Department and Internal Revenue Service adopted regulations that specified how private foundations could "support grantees conducting vigorous lobbying activities."[9] The current regulations expressly allow private foundations to provide general support to nonprofit organizations that engage in lobbying as long as the grants are not earmarked for lobbying. Further, foundations can make grants to public charities for the non-lobbying components of projects. See Chapter 9 for an explanation of how to fund projects that have a lobbying component. Private foundations can actually comment on legislation when requested to do so by a legislative committee. And, perhaps most important, the regulations allow private foundations to discuss broad social problems even if legislation is pending, as long as the foundation does not address the merits of the legislation or provide material that contains a call to action.

---

[8] Thomas A. Troyer, *The 1969 Private Foundation Law: Historical Perspective on Its Origins and Underpinnings* (Washington, DC: Council on Foundations, 2000), 1.

[9] Thomas A. Troyer, "Private Foundations and Influencing Legislation," Center for Lobbying and the Public Interest, May 2000, http://www.clpi.org/privateFoundations.aspx.

The truth is that private and community foundations have ample ways to participate in the public policy process.[10] The sad reality is that foundations do not come anywhere near to availing themselves of the provisions that are allowed by law. While there have been short-sighted proposals that would have curtailed the involvement of grantmaking and grantseeking nonprofit organizations from engaging in the public policy process, these efforts have not been successful. For example, the Istook Amendment proposed prohibiting nonprofit organizations that received federal funds from engaging in advocacy or lobbying.[11] Similarly, the Federal Election Commission recently considered changing the definition of political committees in a way that would have included the legislative advocacy and voter registration activities of nonprofit organizations and foundations. Both of these proposals were met with widespread opposition.

While one might expect foundations, especially private foundations, to be somewhat impervious to external criticism about their grantmaking, the reality is that they are exceptionally thin skinned. Fearful of being accused of wielding power (which they hold), they are overly timid in their use of it, for fear it might be discovered. By not using power, foundations can pretend not to have it and thereby not be held accountable for not using it. Like the university professor who is given tenure for the explicit purpose of pursuing knowledge without fear but, more often than not, becomes the most ardent defender of the established canons within their disciplines, too many endowed foundations with change-oriented mission statements are content to follow the road most traveled.

> The truth is that private and community foundations have ample ways to participate in the public policy process. The sad reality is that foundations do not come anywhere near to availing themselves of the provisions that are allowed by law.

---

[10] Nan Aron, "Advocacy's Efficacy," *Foundation News and Commentary* vol. 45, no. 4, July/August 2004, 36–37.

[11] The Istook Amendment was originally an amendment to a House Appropriations bill. In its first and most potent form, the legislation would have broadened the definition of lobbying to cover more activities than the current IRS code. In addition, nonprofits that spent more than 5 percent of their private funds on activities covered by this expanded definition of political advocacy would not have been able to receive federal grants. Although it passed the House of Representatives, several subsequent versions of the Istook Amendment were defeated thanks to the efforts of the Let America Speak Coalition (co-chaired by OMB Watch, Independent Sector, and Alliance for Justice). A rich descriptive history of the Istook Amendment and other challenges to nonprofit advocacy are in *Seen But Not Heard: Strengthening Nonprofit Advocacy* published by the Aspen Institute.

A favorite tactic of such foundations is to suggest to grantees that they will support a particular grant proposal if only the grantseeker can find another foundation to co-fund the project or idea. Certainly, foundations have better relationships within the foundation community than grantseeking nonprofit organizations. If a foundation is serious about the validity of the project and lacks the resources to fully fund it, it could accept the responsibility of finding and securing the support of another foundation. Of course, by putting the onus on the grantee to find another funder, the foundation all but assures the project's demise or endless delay. Even if a second foundation is interested, that foundation is likely to seek changes to the proposal that the first foundation will claim to be unacceptable, or it will have taken so long to secure the second foundation that first foundation will say that it has either lost interest or no longer has the funds available.

Courage of convictions

As disquieting as it may be, the refusal of some change-oriented foundations to engage in public policy reveals a lack of courage stemming from a belief that they can't actually achieve their change-oriented mission statements. At heart, such foundations say the words but do not really believe that they can be catalysts for the kind of proactive change they claim to want to champion. As a result, such foundations make every effort to avoid change-oriented projects under a myriad of excuses:

- It will never work.
- It is too radical, too different.
- It has never been tried before.
- How will you measure success?

Such statements can often be unconscious strategies to prevent the foundation from funding change-oriented projects. The idea or project won't work if there is no funding and no opportunity to learn from and correct any shortcomings. The project is too radical if measured by the current conventions that have failed to produce the hoped-for changes. The fact that something has never been tried before means that it could be the impetus for change rather than following strategies that have produced failure. Lastly, not everything that is worthwhile can be measured. A negative aspect of the focus on outcome evaluation is that it is sometimes inappropriately used to keep from doing things that cannot be easily counted or measured.[12]

Certainly, there are many instances in reviewing grant proposals where caution is warranted and appropriate. The challenge is for foundations to ask themselves, How often do we take risks consistent with the aspiration of our mission statement? If the answer is never or seldom, they must ask themselves why.

Take a Look in the Mirror

A popular technique to motivate people to stay on their diet plan is to have them look at themselves naked in a full-length mirror. The idea is that once people see a true picture of themselves, they will be forced to reconcile the image they would like to have of themselves with the image that actually exists. To the extent that the image in the mirror does not match the image in one's mind, the necessary internal motivation is created to make a lasting change. While there are those who will be afraid to look in the mirror and those who having looked in the mirror will lower their expectations, many will find the fortitude to make the necessary changes so that their image of themselves more closely matches reality.

Throughout American history, there are numerous examples where progress occurred because individuals or institutions were confronted with the discrepancy between who they claimed to be and how they actually behaved. The civil rights and women's rights movements are but two examples where this strategy has worked to create change on a massive level. This essay asks that each foundation annually examine its mission statement and assess whether it is meeting the moral test of its change-oriented or status quo mission statement. The belief expressed here is that if foundations with change-oriented mission statements discover a disconnect between their words and their behavior, it will create a crisis of identity that will spur them to change.

---

[12] Emmett D. Carson, "On Foundations and Outcome Evaluation," *Nonprofit and Voluntary Sector Quarterly* vol. 29, no. 3, September 2000, 479–481.

Like any diet, good intentions are not enough. Foundations should formally assess what "stretch" projects they have undertaken that are consistent with their aspirations and where they have failed. Failure, in this context, should not be confused with the failure of an individual project, but whether the overall grantmaking portfolio is consistent with the foundation's aspirations to improve some aspect of society. In this context, foundations should be dreamers whose reach exceeds their grasp.

Foundations should bring the same rigor and analysis that they use to assess the risks and returns of their investment portfolios against stated objectives to assess whether their grantmaking goals are consistent with the values expressed in their mission statements. To aid in this process, just as third parties help foundations evaluate whether they are meeting their investment objectives, it might be helpful to have third parties assess whether foundations are meeting their stated aspirations. This is a different measurement process than benchmarking foundations against their peers, which implies that the norm is the goal rather than achieving the mission and related objectives of each individual foundation.

Finally, the burden falls squarely on the shoulders of a foundation's trustees and CEO to determine whether the foundation is fulfilling its mission statement. The board and the CEO are responsible for interpreting the foundation's mission statement, shaping the institutional culture, and establishing grantmaking guidelines. To the extent that a foundation's culture encourages and supports grant proposals that have the potential to change the status quo, staff and grantseeking nonprofit organizations will be responsive. The opposite is also true.

My mother taught me that when the words are different than the behavior, believe the behavior. Ultimately, if foundations are to become more active in public policy, the change cannot be mandated by external pressures, but must start with self-reflection, which comes from self-interest in fulfilling their missions. Only when we create an environment in which foundations routinely look at themselves in the mirror to compare what they say with how they behave—only then can we hope that more foundations will choose to be more active in public policy.

Chapter Two

Philanthropic Leaders' Views on Foundations and Public Policy Participation

I f there is an inherent role for foundations in civic and public policy-making, the next question is, What kind of role should they play? An underlying question is, What constitutes healthy involvement in public policy by foundations? Differing opinions about these questions are presented here.

William Schambra from the Hudson Institute states that foundations can harvest "street wisdom" by helping citizens find their own understanding of the public good rather than building more bureaucracies to study problems and provide "expert" driven solutions.

Gara LaMarche of the Open Society Institute calls for foundations to speak out about public policies that contradict foundation values or that directly affect a foundation's constituency.

Jeff Krehely, formerly of the National Committee for Responsive Philanthropy, shares fascinating research about the methodology used by conservative foundations to support citizen groups and think tanks.

David Abbott and Marcia Egbert of The George Gund Foundation describe their foundation's rationale in supporting the public policy capacity of nonprofits as a means of defending and strengthening philanthropic investment.

CHAPTER SNAPSHOT

In this chapter, multiple authors address the following topics:

- Should foundations serve as quasi–think tanks generating policy ideas and orchestrating advocacy, or play a more facilitative approach?

- How might foundations align public policy work with core values?

- What benefits can be derived from making long-term discretionary grants that may be used for public policy?

- Why might a foundation invest in building the public policy capacity of grantees?

Philanthropy, Public Policy, and the Public Good

William A. Schambra

"A generally agreed-on conceptual definition of the American private foundation is 'untaxed private wealth, privately managed, on behalf of the public good,'" notes Kenneth Prewitt in his essay "The Foundation and the Liberal Society."[13] But that definition is ambiguous. It can mean that what foundations do in the policy arena is by definition, so to speak, in the public good. Or it can mean, more modestly, that foundations should enter the arena of public policy humbly aspiring to operate on behalf of the public good. I would suggest that the major American foundations historically have tended to operate as if the former were true. In the future, they should assume a more modest role as enablers of grassroots citizen involvement in public policy, if they are to aspire to serve, modestly, the public good.

How did modern foundations come to assume that what they did was somehow synonymous with the public good? We can trace this back to their origins in the progressive era, at the beginning of the twentieth century. Progressives believed that industrial peace depended upon the transfer of political power away from everyday citizens and their chaotic, parochial, benighted local organizations, into the hands of centralized, professionally credentialed experts trained in the new sciences of social control.

The first modern foundations—Carnegie, Rockefeller, and Russell Sage—eagerly bought into the idea that the new social sciences offered an indisputably objective and rational way to order public affairs and to deal with the causes, not just the symptoms, of social disorder. As a Rockefeller Foundation mission statement put it in the 1920s, its funding was designed to "increase the body of knowledge, which, in the hands of competent social technicians, may be expected in time to result in substantial social control." Hence, these foundations bankrolled institutions that would ensure the triumph of expertise over popular ignorance: modern research universities like the University of Chicago, the first think tanks like The Brookings Institution, scholarly social journals like *Survey*, and planning and coordinating organizations such as the National Bureau of Economic Research

---

[13] Hudson Institute's Bradley Center for Philanthropy and Civic Renewal, "The Foundation and the Liberal Society," edited transcript of an interview on May 5, 2004, http://pcr.hudson.org/index.cfm?fuseaction=publication_details&id=3349&pubType=PCR_Speeches.

and the Social Science Research Council. Such institutions were to design, demonstrate, and pass on to the state for full funding programs that would get at the heart of social pathologies. As progressive sociologist Edward Alsworth Ross put it, "It is the function of private philanthropy to pioneer, to experiment, to try out new things and new methods," and when they are sufficiently tested, "the community [must] take over the function."[14]

As the late Daniel Patrick Moynihan pointed out in *Maximum Feasible Misunderstanding*,[15] the view of social change as the peculiar province of social science experts only grew more influential for the rest of the twentieth century in a process he called "the professionalization of reform." That process continued progressivism's displacement of the ordinary American citizen from meaningful engagement in reform, for as Moynihan argued, "Professionals *profess*. They profess to know better than others the nature of certain matters, and to know better than their clients what ails them or their affairs." The professionalization of reform meant that, by the 1960s, it was possible for a major national foundation (in this case, the Ford Foundation) to fund a handful of demonstration projects based on a shaky, novel hypothesis that the "root cause" of poverty was denial of access to society's "opportunity structure." The foundation had every reason to expect that the federal government would eagerly adopt and expand the projects throughout the nation in the War on Poverty's Community Action Program. The collision of that abstract theory with the concrete, messy reality of urban politics sobered up the federal government fairly quickly. But it did little to diminish philanthropy's belief that, as a result of its peculiarly close relationship to professionalism and social science expertise, it had a much better understanding of the public good than ordinary citizens, whose views tended to be narrowed and stunted by commercial self-interest or parochial community affiliations.

Consequently, many large contemporary foundations continue to approach the realm of public policy with a pronounced air of detachment and arrogance. They still maintain that they are not interested in addressing immediate needs, but rather in getting to the "root causes" of problems through innovative, experimental programs reflecting cutting-edge professional

---

[14] Edward Alsworth Ross, *The Social Trend* (Freeport, NY: Ayer Publishing, 1970), 135.

[15] Daniel Patrick Moynihan, *Maximum Feasibile Misunderstanding: Community Action in the War on Poverty* (New York: Free Press, 1969).

expertise in the area of concern. When a foundation undertakes a new program, therefore, its first step is to commission a team of university researchers to pinpoint just where the cutting edge is. It then issues a request for proposals, which elicits pledges from various nonprofits—typically those that are large, well funded, and similarly staffed by professionals—to faithfully carry out programs designed according to the foundation's specifications, reflecting the latest and best academic analysis. Even before the formal program evaluations are completed by yet another crew of professionals, the foundation's glossy annual report will celebrate the resounding success of its innovative initiative and will resolve to convey its lessons to public officials, who will no doubt be eager to redesign public policy accordingly.

Although today this approach may not produce the sort of political disturbances that the Ford Foundation provoked with its anti-poverty demonstrations in the 1960s, it remains problematic. The professionalization of reform continues to mean that those who profess to know better about public policy are entitled to impose preferred schemes of social reform on those who know less, which is to say, everyday citizens. Beyond the likelihood of evoking resentment and resistance, the more profound difficulty is that this professionalization erodes the capacity of the American citizen for self-governance.

Ironically, foundations are among the most eager funders of studies documenting the decline of American civic activity—the dramatic withdrawal of citizen attention to and engagement in civic and political affairs and institutions. But foundations seldom consider that they, themselves, may be complicit in that disengagement by funding programs premised on the conviction that sound public policy can only be a product of expert program design and by refusing to fund projects that citizens, themselves, generate and bring to foundations for consideration. An unsolicited proposal drawn up by everyday citizens, reflecting heartfelt but nonprofessional notions of what they need in order to tackle the ills of their own neighborhoods, is likely to be treated with bemused contempt by program staff. It will seem to be just another misguided effort to cadge lowly charity from a foundation that is otherwise quite busy doing "serious" philanthropy by seeking out root causes, not merely meeting immediate needs. The very same staff, however, eagerly attends conferences in Washington, DC, convened to ponder the problems created for the American political system when citizens come to feel they are no longer taken seriously by their leading political and cultural institutions. The mystery of American civic disengagement—why citizens seem to be disenchanted with their professional leadership classes—perplexes philanthropy, even as it conducts its business in such a way that citizens cannot fail to get the impression that their views on public matters are considered naïve, parochial, and irrelevant.

What can philanthropy do, then, to engage in public policy in a healthy way? The first step would be to drop all presumptions of a superior understanding of the public good and to realize that its primary task must be to help citizens work out for themselves an understanding of the public good. In civic renewal philanthropy, programs would not originate at a high level of intellectual abstraction, reflecting only views of university and program staff experts steeped in the latest literature on social policy. Rather, they would originate with the views of citizens at the grassroots, with their understanding of the problems they face and how they would like to go about addressing them. Solutions tailored by citizens who actually live with the problems are more likely to combine the unique combination of elements appropriate for their particular neighborhood at a particular moment. Community ownership will ensure that these approaches are supported and sustained over the long haul, rather than evoking the sort of resistance that often greets programs designed by remote experts and "parachuted" into neighborhoods.

> **What can philanthropy do to engage in public policy in a healthy way? The first step would be to drop all presumptions of a superior understanding of the public good and to realize that its primary task must be to help citizens work out for themselves an understanding of the public good. Solutions tailored by citizens who actually live with the problems are more likely to combine the unique combination of elements appropriate for their particular neighborhood at a particular moment.**

Perhaps most important, the process of formulating and proposing solutions to their own problems cultivates in citizens the skills essential to democratic self-governance—the ability to formulate persuasive public arguments, deliberation, compromise, and moderation of expectations about what the public sector can reasonably accomplish. As Alexis de Tocqueville famously pointed out in his classic *Democracy in America*, only in such small, local, decentralized settings do Americans learn the essentials of the "science of association" so critical to sustaining democratic self-governance in America.

Contemporary policy experts tend to regard references to de Tocqueville's decentralist views as evidence of a romantic, retrograde yearning for the good old days of yesteryear. But the fact is that successful programs of civic education continue to center around the actual deployment of young people into small community settings. There, they soon learn that the wisdom to be absorbed from local grassroots leaders about public life far surpasses the knowledge they thought they had to impart based on their college training. It remains true that an immediate, hands-on encounter with the messy, contentious, half-measured world of everyday self-governing politics is the best training for citizens. They are then able to enter the larger worlds of state and national politics with a mature appreciation for the subtleties, shadings, and complexities of democratic self-governance. For this essential aspect of civic education, books are no substitute.

A foundation driven by a vision of civic renewal philanthropy would abstain from aggressively exporting its own understanding of what the community needs, but at the same time it would hardly sit passively in its own offices and wait for grantees to come to it. The fact is that the most active and effective grassroots civic organizations are typically far too busy dealing with the everyday challenges to spend much time courting foundations. And, of course, every encounter with a foundation in the past—especially any of the large, national ones with proud reputations for innovative, hard-hitting, comprehensive approaches to social problems—has only confirmed the view that it is a waste of time trying to wedge idiosyncratic neighborhood concerns into a foundation's sleek, neatly ordered and measured program silos.

Civic renewal philanthropies must reach out quietly but actively into the communities they wish to assist, harvesting "street wisdom" about which groups genuinely capture a community's own understanding of its problems and which merely reflect back "downtown's" understanding of what the community should want. This requires an enormous act of discipline, for it means the foundation must deliberately bypass large, highly visible, well-funded nonprofits that have built reputations for themselves as the preferred providers of government and foundation-funded programs, that are invariably first in line for grants with the slickest proposals, and whose boards boast well-regarded, persuasive corporate and philanthropic leaders. Civic renewal philanthropy must be prepared instead to seek out groups about which no one in the civic establishment may have heard, and which will surely provoke expressions of puzzlement and concern when a grant for them is announced.

Such groups will more than likely have duct tape on their industrial carpeting and water stains on their ceilings. But their most noticeable feature will be activity. Community residents will cluster there at all hours, understanding that this is the place to come first when they face a problem, even if it doesn't fit into the organization's mission statement. A program officer may find all this bustling and chaotic activity vaguely unsettling—signs of the disorganization, wasted energy, and "mission drift" about which she had been cautioned in her nonprofit management classes. But in fact, this is the unmistakable sign of a community learning to manage its own affairs its own way—the first and indispensable building block of democracy.

This observation begins to suggest how much "unlearning" of customary practices a foundation must do to appreciate and fund civic renewal as civic groups practice it rather than as professional experts preach it. Continuing to reflect its roots in twentieth-century progressivism, philanthropy's very operating code enshrines as unquestionable goods various apolitical, managerial concepts like efficiency, effectiveness, capacity building, and best practices. They uniformly imply that the purpose of grantmaking is to streamline the process by which expert-driven social services are delivered to passive, grateful clients, rather than to help clients mature into "unmanageable" citizens. In this view, effective philanthropy requires that wasteful duplication and redundancy must give way to neatly ordered collaborative consortiums; spontaneous, ad hoc responsiveness to problems must be replaced by benchmarked, multiyear planning; passionate amateur leadership must be superseded by coolly professional nonprofit management; and sustained, active civic presence as a measure of worth must yield to carefully calibrated evaluation of outcomes.

If orthodox philanthropy's goal seems to be to systematically replace democratic self-government's boisterous, unsystematic outpouring of civic passions and energies with smoothly humming managerial processes, it must be the goal of civic renewal philanthropy to accept and welcome those aspects of democracy. It will consider making grants to organizations that have little time to write lengthy reports or file careful budgets; that try to meet whatever need arises next in the neighborhood, rather than adhering narrowly to a tidy program category; that may sit right next door to another similar agency, which the neighborhood nonetheless shuns for reasons that seem petty and irrelevant to funders; that are led by charismatic leaders who may be hopeless managers but are doing wonders for the neighborhood; that may only be around for another five years because the neighborhood is changing; and that may describe what they are doing and why they are doing it in terms of summons from supernatural beings, rather than credentials from secular universities.

All of these are ineluctable facts of everyday life for grassroots nonprofits in the inner city, including the best and most responsive. Moreover, they are facts of life for a neighborhood learning to grapple with its own problems and master the art of democracy. But they are precisely the conditions that prompt foundations to avoid making grants to grassroots groups. How often, for instance, have foundation staff and board airily dismissed a proposal from a grassroots group as "just reinventing the wheel?" But does this not ignore the fact that the art of self-government is passed on only when each neighborhood, each generation, "reinvents the wheel" of its own public life?

How often have foundation staff and board dismissed a proposal from a grassroots group as "just reinventing the wheel?" But does this not ignore the fact that the art of self-government is passed on only when each neighborhood, each generation, "reinvents the wheel" of its own public life?

Foundations would more adequately harness private wealth to the public good if they learned to abstain from dictating their own understanding of the public good—no matter how well grounded in elegant theory or meticulous research—and instead quietly help the public to work out its own understanding of the good in its own way. This seems to be a far more modest project than seeking out the "root causes" of social problems. At the same time, though, there is high ambition in a project that might help Americans learn once again how to govern themselves. It would require philanthropy to stop merely funding studies of American disengagement from civic life and, instead, start behaving as an institution that genuinely wishes to cultivate civic reengagement. That would mean acceptance of a degree of messiness, disorder, and uncertainty that seems quite remote from the spotless, tasteful corridors of establishment philanthropy.

But that simply means acceptance of American democracy as it *is*, rather than as some foundation wishes it to be.

When Foundations Should Lead— and When They Should Get Out of the Way

Gara LaMarche

I believe foundations must lead with more than their dollars. They and their key executives and board members must also lead with their voices. Many leading foundations have spoken out forcefully about Congressional review of the rules about payout rate and other issues that primarily affect foundations themselves. But some foundations are reticent to speak out about social justice or war and peace issues, even as they fund important work in those areas, for fear they may be seen as competing with or drowning out the voices of their grantees.

This concern deserves respect. Humility by foundations is still too rare, and social movements should be led by those who are most directly affected. That's why, for example, Open Society Institute (OSI), Mott, Casey, and other foundations supported the Campaign for Jobs and Income Support, and before it the State Welfare Redesign Grants Pool, which strengthened the participation of low-income people and their advocates in state debates about the overhaul of welfare laws, resulting in improved child care, transportation, and job training measures in a number of states. That's why so much of OSI's funding for civil liberties advocacy after September 11 was directed to the Tides Fund to enable Arab-American and Islamic community groups to stand up for their own rights in the wake of the PATRIOT Act.

But in the interdependent ecosystem of advocacy and social change, elite voices play an important part, too, and they always have. Think of former Ambassador to France Felix Rohatyn's recent criticisms of the death penalty, or New York Episcopal Bishop Paul Moore's advocacy for the poor during New York's 1970s fiscal crisis, or former Secretary of State George Shultz's questioning of the so-called war on drugs. When George Soros spoke out against the discrimination against immigrants in the 1996 welfare bill, the frontline advocates we supported through the Emma Lazarus Fund did not feel overshadowed; they stood up and cheered, for it was a time when far too few voices of the powerful were being raised.

Another example was in December 2001, when Attorney General Ashcroft, in his testimony before Congress on the PATRIOT Act, questioned the patriotism of those who opposed the administration's actions. We at OSI were stunned at the return of such McCarthyite intimidation tactics. We waited a day or two for prominent voices, such as senators or former government officials, university presidents, or religious leaders, to condemn the outrageous equation of dissent with disloyalty. Nothing came. We decided to take out a full-page ad in the *New York Times* and asked a variety of prominent people to subscribe to a simple statement, not condemning any specific administration policy—such as increased surveillance, military tribunals, mass questioning of Arab-Americans, detention on Guantanamo, and so on—even though each of these, in my opinion, is deserving of condemnation. We simply said that whatever one thinks about the merits of these policies, the country is stronger for vigorous debate and questioning. In those fearful days, we couldn't get a single signer. Many of the prominent people we asked, including former Republican leaders, agreed entirely with the statement. But they found one reason or another for not lending their names, and the more candid told us that the administration would find a way to punish them for any public criticism along these lines. So we took out the ad ourselves and signed the names of our trustees and principal officers. I say this not in self-congratulation—in fact, it took little courage for those of us in such a privileged position to stick our necks out a little. But that is exactly my point. It would be nice to have more company in such matters, not because we are lonely, but because when the powerful speak out in solidarity with those who are marginalized it provides cover and validation for them.

> I recently read an interview with the retiring president of a major foundation, someone I admire a great deal. He looks forward to stepping down, he said, so he can speak out more on social and global problems. Why on earth wait?

I recently read an interview with the retiring president of a major foundation, someone I admire a great deal. He looks forward to stepping down, he said, so he can speak out more on social and global problems. Why on earth wait? It's not only at the most senior level that more people must look for their voice. It's throughout the foundation world at every level. Some of you know that when I accepted the Ylvisaker Award for OSI at the Council on Foundations meeting, I challenged foundations—particularly those on the Texas host committee—to do more about the racism of the criminal justice system. When blacks constitute 13 percent of drug users and 74 percent of drug incarcerations, everyone should stand up and take notice. Perhaps we have not come as far toward a color-blind society as many would like to think. After I spoke, many dozens of people came up to me in the next day or two to thank me for speaking out, including virtually every person of color in attendance. If every one of those people who said they wished they could address the issues that OSI is trying to attend to, or wished their institutions were more receptive to social justice issues, resolved to work together to change those institutions, the status quo would change. None of us can escape personal responsibility.

There is also a time when foundations should get out of the way. What do I mean when I say foundations should sometimes "get out of the way?" How is that consistent with my belief that we should set public policy goals in key areas of our mission and raise our voices when we see injustice or unmet social problems?

I mean that for all the support foundations can give with their money and their voice, and for all the importance of elites in the ecosystem of change I referred to earlier, meaningful progress and effective solutions rarely emerge from the top and trickle down. Funding is more about an eye for movement and a boost for the efforts of others, than about the "creation" of movements themselves. In describing George Soros's work to support civil society in Eastern Europe and other parts of the world, Aryeh Neier has called this process "seiz[ing] the revolutionary moment."[16] In recent years, as foundations have been under pressure from consultants, their boards, and colleagues in philanthropy to become more "strategic," some have involved themselves too much in directing the fields they support and the organizations that comprise them. It is one thing to have a vision of social change and a framework for making judgments about what initiatives and interventions will foster it and how they all work together; this is some-

---

[16] Judith Miller, "A Giver's Agenda: A Special Report; With Big Money and Brash Ideas, A Billionaire Redefines Charity," *New York Times*, December 17, 1996.

thing foundations working in public policy must do in order to be effective. It is quite another to direct the field by designing rigid models that organizations must follow in order to receive grants or to run foundation-created programs that compete with others in the same field.

Finally, getting out of the way should mean, in most cases, identifying key groups that share a foundation's goals in an area of interest—it could be civil rights, or health, or education—and trusting them, in a supportive relationship, to set their own course and make their own decisions about programmatic priorities. That is best done with general support that gives organizations the flexibility they need and multi-year grants that provide room to plan and give some relief from the endless cycle of fundraising and the paperwork that most foundations seem to generate. That is what anyone running an organization wants, though many who cross over from tin-cup rattler to banker often forget it. And as noted in the earlier part of my talk, that kind of approach has been instrumental in the effectiveness of conservative philanthropy.

Paul Ylvisaker, who I mentioned earlier, was the director of the Public Affairs Program at the Ford Foundation from 1955 to 1967—a critical period in American life when the Ford Foundation was instrumental, along with some smaller foundations like the Taconic Fund, in providing support to the nascent civil rights movement. I'd like to close with remarks he made about foundations almost forty years ago: "What we represent," Ylvisaker said, "is the resilient margin of the industrial order, the most stretchable part of the world's status quo. The program question for us is whether we are stretching our resources and ourselves as far and fast as the situation demands. Not our own immediate situation, which is but a cozy corner in the walled castle of industrial affluence, but the universal circumstance, which is the growing discrepancy between those inside 'the system' and those without."[17] These are still good questions today.

---

[17] Paul Ylvisaker, "What Is New in American Philanthropy," in *Conscience and Community: The Legacy of Paul Ylvisaker*, ed. Virginia M. Esposito (New York: Peter Lang Publishing, 1999), 273.

Effective Grantmaking for Policy Change: Lessons from the Right

Jeff Krehely

In 1997, the National Committee for Responsive Philanthropy (NCRP) produced *Moving a Public Policy Agenda: The Strategic Philanthropy of Conservative Foundations,* the first study to document how conservative philanthropy was impacting and driving right-wing public policies. Since *Moving a Public Policy Agenda* was released, the nation has seen a change in administrations and Republican lawmakers have expanded their power, essentially controlling all three branches of the federal government. This imbalance in power has allowed President George W. Bush to govern without having to compromise much on his domestic or foreign agendas.

In light of these significant political changes and the very public and successful role that conservative charities have played in advancing a policy agenda, NCRP and its members thought it was critical to revisit past research on right-wing philanthropy. One goal was to increase the number of foundations studied to better understand the philanthropic sector's role in pushing the United States in a conservative direction socially, economically, and politically.

In March 2004, NCRP released the new study *Axis of Ideology: Conservative Foundations and Public Policy.* The study expanded on the original twelve foundations previously studied in order to gain a more complete perspective on the field of conservative philanthropy. In total, 79 conservative foundations were identified, and their grantmaking to 331 public policy organizations from 1999 to 2001 was examined using information gathered from IRS Form 990-PF, which private foundations must file annually with the Internal Revenue Service.

The study found that from 1999 to 2001 more than 254 million dollars were awarded to conservative public policy organizations working in broad issues areas including

- General policy (including think tanks)
- Education

- Legal
- University scholarship and research
- Social
- Business
- Religious
- Military/defense
- Media
- Nonprofit infrastructure
- Civil rights
- Environment
- Other/miscellaneous

While the issue areas received millions of dollars in funding, the average grant size was just $52,788, indicating that although the total amount of funding that supports a conservative public policy agenda is great, the actual organizations receive relatively small grants. In most cases, however, the reason that the grantees have been so effective has less to do with the dollar value of their grants and more with the type of funding they receive. Traditionally, conservative foundations have given far more in general operating support than their mainstream and progressive counterparts. This study found that overall, 37 percent of conservative grantmaking dollars were given for operating support, while the Foundation Center reported that in 2001, the 1,000 largest foundations in the United States gave only 13.6 percent of their grants in the form of general operating support.

Traditionally, conservative foundations have given far more in general operating support than their mainstream and progressive counterparts. Overall, 37 percent of conservative grantmaking dollars were given for operating support, while the 1,000 largest foundations in the United States gave only 13.6 percent of their grants in the form of general operating support.

From 1999 to 2001, conservative grantees received $94,296,085 in general operating support, which is almost $17 million more than the amount received for program support over the same period (total program support equaled $77,548,005). This flexible funding has allowed grantees to build strong institutions, do innovative work, and respond in a timely manner to policy issues without having to wait for a project-specific grant. It also benefits conservative funders because general operating support grant dollars may be dedicated solely to lobbying without threatening the charitable status of the foundation.

General policy organizations working at both the national and state levels on a variety of issues received the bulk of the funding at 46 percent of all grant dollars awarded. This reflects the fact that the large national conservative organizations such as the Heritage Foundation are receiving most of the funding, and, more importantly, many of these conservative policy organizations are working in a variety of areas and do not specialize in just one issue. The other areas that also had high levels of funding were education (organizations working on school choice and reforming higher education) and legal organizations, both receiving 10 percent of conservative grant dollars.

Within the top twenty-five grant recipients, many of the organizations receiving the bulk of the funding were national policy organizations, such as the American Enterprise Institute and the Heritage Foundation, that were previously identified in the 1997 report, but there were also more socially conservative organizations present, including Focus on the Family and the Independent Women's Forum. This finding signifies the increasing sentiment in the United States to gravitate toward the "traditional" values that have opposed the gay and women's civil rights movements, among other socially progressive causes.

The success of the right did not start without some planning and coordination. In fact, the origin of today's conservative movement can be found in a memo written in 1971 by Lewis Powell, before his nomination to the Supreme Court. Powell described what he saw as the liberal attack on the American free-enterprise system and the need for all sectors, both public and private, to retaliate. He called upon the American business community to fight these dissenting voices and to fund an organized, coordinated, long-range plan against the left that would be amply financed and implemented through united action and national organizations.

While this memo was drafted more than three decades ago, it is clear that many conservative foundations and right-wing organizations have followed this plan of attack and, with it, have achieved success. This success can be attributed, in part, to the role conservative foundations and philanthropists have played in promoting a right-wing agenda. In particular, the following grantmaking strategies have led to this success:

- **Flexible Funding:** Conservative foundations are more likely to provide their grantees with general operating support, allowing them to use the money as they see fit, often not requiring extensive evaluations of how the funds have been used. This flexibility allows organizations to respond in a timely manner to current issues and events, allowing the organizations to remain at the forefront of the policy process without having to wait months for a program-specific grant.

- **Long-Term Funding:** Conservative foundations are more likely to create new organizations and fund them for the long term, sometimes for decades, not just years, allowing the organizations to focus on their program work rather than having to worry about where next year's budget will come from. They realize that permanent, systemic policy change takes years, if not decades, to implement.

- **Focus:** Conservative foundations generally concentrate on funding a small group of grantees, including groups that are working toward a common goal.

- **Public Policy Expertise:** Conservative foundations and their grantees understand that policymaking is not an activity that happens only in Washington, DC, and perhaps at state capitals. Investing in organizations that help set the policy agenda, inform and mobilize the public, lobby lawmakers, broadcast conservative ideas, challenge existing regulations and laws in the courts, and monitor policy implementation is a priority for conservative funders, as is making sure that this full spectrum of activity is happening in cities, counties, and states, as well as in Washington, DC.

- **Alignment:** There is considerable alignment and cohesion on the right. Based on interview findings, conservative funders and nonprofits are all naturally committed to the broader goals of the political right; deliberate coordination is not necessary. Many foundation board members come from the business sector and naturally support the free market and minimal government and regulatory ethos that grantees are working for. Not surprisingly, there is general agreement about priorities and goals among foundation board and staff members, grantee board and staff members, and foundations and grantees.

Although it is true that mainstream and progressive foundations have far more assets than the right, conservative foundations have been far more successful at supporting policy changes because they have acted strategically with their limited funds. Many mainstream foundations, rather than giving general operating support to advocacy organizations, give project-specific support to groups that provide direct services, which, as valuable as they are, often do not address the root causes of society's problems that create the need for such services in the first place. Other foundations are afraid to fund advocacy, fearing IRS retribution in the form of an audit or loss of tax-exempt status, mainly due to a lack of understanding of the laws that regulate the philanthropic community.

Although it is true that mainstream and progressive foundations have far more assets than the right, conservative foundations have been far more successful at supporting policy changes because they have acted strategically with their limited funds.

An even bigger hurdle that prevents large mainstream foundations from supporting a progressive social or policy change agenda is the fact that their boards of directors are dominated by individuals who work in the for-profit sector and have little social, economic, racial, or gender diversity. These individuals generally do not reflect the people and communities that eventually receive the services that many foundations support, yet they traditionally set the programmatic goals for foundations and approve all grants.

Incidentally, the strategies listed above can also lead to effective grantmaking for nonpolitical purposes. Other emerging research at NCRP, for example, shows that nonprofit organizations place value on long-term and flexible foundation funding for much of the work that they do. If a nonprofit has a mostly unrestricted revenue stream, it has more freedom to respond to changing community or constituent needs, whether the nonprofit is primarily an advocacy organization or a direct service provider. Likewise, reliable long-term support allows nonprofits to devote more time and creativity to fulfilling their missions. Fundraising and development are costly activities, often for reasons unrelated to whether a nonprofit is managed efficiently or not (for example, the complicated and varied hoops that grant applicants are forced to jump through).

In the years since George W. Bush became president, the United States has invaded Afghanistan and Iraq; the civil rights and liberties of a wide range of immigrants have been compromised; women's reproductive rights, both domestically and internationally, have been eroded; gay and lesbian Americans are facing the largest attack in years against their civil rights; the federal tax system has become radically more regressive, with benefits going to the very wealthiest Americas; and the federal and state governments are facing record budget deficits that will have long-term economic ramifications.

Conservative nonprofit organizations, foundations, corporations, and various individuals have had a hand in nearly all of these situations, events, and outcomes. The right wing is undoubtedly winning the cultural, social, economic, and political wars in this country. The political center and left may need to stop asking, "How can we push back the right?" and instead start wondering if it is not already too late.

Unless progressive people with wealth decide to support a political agenda in this country in a radically new way, it is unlikely that the current crop of progressive and mainstream foundations have the institutional will to change significantly the way that they make grants, as well as the kinds of people who govern them. Instead, similar to the conservative philanthropic movement that got started a few decades ago, this new approach on the left needs to be led by individuals who have not been captured by the power and baffling politics of institutional philanthropy. With the rapid growth of the philanthropic sector—which is predicted to continue at an even faster clip in the coming years—the opportunity is ripe for the emergence of such leadership.

The first task at hand for this new group of philanthropists would be to articulate a set of core values for progressives, leaving behind the current tendency to see only as far as their own self-interest or identity will allow them. Basic principles of fairness and equity undergird all progressive causes: environmentalism, LGBT rights, public education reform, reproductive choice, tax reform, racial equality, and so on. That these basic principles—articulated in a new, cohesive, and coherent way—would resonate with the majority of Americans is the progressive community's biggest asset, but progressives have yet to exploit it.

Funding "Upstream" for Success

David T. Abbott and Marcia Egbert

A social worker discussing her growing politicization told a local radio interviewer, "We felt like we were saving people from drowning in a river when finally someone said 'Hey, why doesn't someone go upstream and see who's throwing them in?'"

A similar realization has spread among those in the funding community, where year after year, dollar after dollar is spent ameliorating conditions that don't seem to change.

But what if investments were made to change the policies that aggravate the conditions? What if the funding community looked for the root causes of problems our foundations address, and funded research and advocacy to address these issues? In other words, what if funders sent a few people upstream?

Upstream is where public policy is debated, influenced, and formulated. Government has an enormous role in determining the broader landscape in which nonprofits operate. A homeless shelter director ought to care about the availability of state housing funds. A local job-training program ought to be concerned about federal workforce development policy. And all non-profit leaders should care about whether our national tax and fiscal policy creates a climate for increasing or shrinking available public resources.

Why The Gund Foundation funds advocacy

Funding advocacy and funding direct service are flip sides of the same coin. Foundations cannot hope to improve conditions for large numbers of people or make a lasting impact on an issue without affecting the policy environment providers operate in and drawing as much public investment to an issue as possible. At the same time, we cannot ignore the immediate pressing needs in our own backyard. Direct service and policy grantmaking go hand in hand. They can be used together effectively to address the issues and concerns to which foundations are committed.

While private philanthropy annually contributes an extraordinary amount of money to causes promoting the common good, its combined resources pale compared to the resources of the public sector. Appropriate, targeted investments in advocating for policy change can leverage public dollars far beyond any funds for direct service a foundation might be able to provide. That means we can help a lot more people than we would otherwise. Consider this example: for years The George Gund Foundation has supported local low-income housing programs with grants that totaled in the neighborhood of a million dollars per year. Over the last decade, we simultaneously invested in an advocacy campaign to create a state housing trust fund. Now, the Ohio Housing Trust Fund provides nearly $60 million annually to support similar programs that help thousands more families annually.

Funding advocacy and funding direct service are flip sides of the same coin. For years The George Gund Foundation has supported local low-income housing programs with grants that totaled in the neighborhood of a million dollars per year. Over the last decade, we simultaneously invested in an advocacy campaign to create a state housing trust fund. Now, the Ohio Housing Trust Fund provides $60 million annually to support similar programs.

Perhaps one of the most potent rationales for funding public policy and advocacy is to promote the nonprofit sector's role as the voice for the powerless, a surrogate for those who typically are excluded from public policy discourse. When foundations underwrite such work, we bring the views represented by millions of Americans with little or no direct access to the halls of power into the marketplace of ideas.

Public policy not only impacts the constituents and clients nonprofits serve, it also impacts every facet of nonprofit operations. Statutory and regulatory policies set the framework in which nonprofits conduct their business. For nonprofits to sit on sidelines while the environment in which they operate is formulated by policymakers does a disservice to their clients.

Finally, funding advocacy should be done because it *can* be done. Contrary to the belief of many in philanthropy, funding public policy advocacy is legal and actually supported through provisions in the federal tax code. Of course there are parameters, but they are quite easily understood and they are there to be employed for the benefit of nonprofit organizations and, ultimately, their constituents.

How The Gund Foundation supports advocacy

There are many ways funders can support the advocacy capacity of nonprofit organizations. Some are strategies foundations may have been employing for years and not thought of them as impacting the policy arena, and others are undoubtedly new to many foundations. Here is a representative sampling of the types of approaches we support at The Gund Foundation:

- Lobbying (might as well lead the list with the one that seems to make folks the most uncomfortable; we are clear to *never* earmark funds for this purpose and to follow carefully the IRS "safe harbors" for private foundation funded advocacy)

- Research (applied, not theoretical)

- Policy and fiscal analysis (the most important aspect of this work is that it be done in real time as it relates to policy and political processes)

- Communications (we have learned our lessons about the inadequacy of funding top-shelf research and analysis without providing support for ways for key policymakers to know about it)

- Community organizing and coalition building

- Litigation (this one sometimes makes folks' palms sweat as much as lobbying, but there are those occasions where nothing short of legal confrontation will move the needle on an issue)

This is neither an exhaustive nor a required list. The point is that these are approaches that contrast to direct service grants and are ones we have found to be effective in furthering our particular mission. The list may look quite different in another foundation.

The unique role of philanthropy

The philanthropy sector should embrace the unique role it plays in engaging the public policy arena. We are a comparatively nimble sector. While we clearly strive to operate at the highest levels of transparency and accountability, we are free of many of the bureaucratic restraints that slow a government's ability to respond to social concerns. That allows us to engage in our communities in ways that inevitably shape the debate, formulation, and impact of public policy. What are some of these roles? Here are a sample half-dozen:

- Catalyst
- Research patron
- Experimenter
- Convener
- Legitimizer
- Mediator

It is a great luxury to be in a field that can both support and withstand risk-taking. Engagement in the policymaking process may carry with it some inherent risks, but nowhere in philanthropy is the opportunity for great reward more evident than in working to prod, coax, cajole, or force systemic change. As our president, Geoffrey Gund, noted in his letter in our 1999 annual report, "… in recent years we have gradually focused more of our funding on the sometimes elusive front of pubic policy and advocacy activities that could lead to lasting solutions to the deeply entrenched, seemingly intractable problems that so clearly separate the haves from the have-nots in this country." We can think of no more noble bet to place.

— — —

Conclusion

Several common threads run through the essays presented in this chapter. All authors assert that there is, indeed, a role for foundations in the public policymaking process, and that segments of the foundation world have found healthy ways to get involved. Differences in approach to foundations' roles range from serving as a behind-the-scenes facilitator of civic engagement to out-front, bully pulpit advocacy. The styles might serve as a continuum for foundations to consider as they discover for themselves how they want to operate in the policy arena. All of the essays recognized the need for foundations to allow for the nonprofits they fund to determine the strategies that best work to advance causes within the current policy environment. Also identified was the connection between core foundation values and public policy work as a key ingredient of success.

These insights and lessons will begin to help in specific capacity building and strategy development steps presented in later chapters. Foundation values and philosophy are indeed part of the basis for why foundations engage in advocacy and attempt to shape the policy environment. The next chapter adds another key dimension to why foundations are getting into public policy-making: it is simply good business. In Chapter 3 several small foundations share their stories of how public policy participation is connected to their core operating philosophy and is one important part of their business strategy. The chapter also provides a look at public policy from the perspective of one of the fastest growing segments of the foundation world: small foundations.

Chapter Three

Small Foundations, Public Policy, and Strategic Impact

Small foundations make up a large and growing segment of the foundation world. According to the Association of Small Foundations, there are approximately 60,000 small foundations (defined as those with few or no staff and an average asset size of $18 million).[18] Small foundations have great potential to be successful in the public policy arena because they generally have fewer decision makers who need to be "bought in" before investing in public policy approaches to reaching philanthropic goals. In addition, the relatively inexpensive nature of public policy work compared to funding direct service programs that require greater infrastructure may create efficiency for small foundations. These are structural attributes. However, the real reason small foundations should consider integrating public policy into philanthropy is the potential outcomes. The foundation essays in this chapter serve as models of this integration. The first essay, by the New York Foundation (one of the largest members of the small foundation community, with $70 million in assets), is presented to share how a small foundation's original desire to be involved in public policy and community change have helped it build a lasting legacy of significance. The second essay, about the Warner Foundation, shares how the foundation married public policy and funding direct service to be effective in reaching certain goals. The third essay, from

[18] Association of Small Foundations' web site, http://www.smallfoundations.org.

the A.L. Mailman Family Foundation, shares thinking about how a small foundation might give alongside large nationally focused foundations to advance its mission. The final essay in this chapter, by the Quixote Foundation in Seattle, Washington, shares how the foundation leverages relatively few dollars by funding organizations involved in public policy efforts that have "momentum" and that are connected to the passions of the founding family members. Note: with the exception of the New York Foundation, the other foundations are closer to the average asset size.

The New York Foundation Converts Guiding Principles to Policy Engagement

Maria Mottola

Though the New York Foundation was founded in 1909, its values have been remarkably consistent over time. Funding work that advocates for policy change has always been a comfortable fit. Early on, our trustees recognized the need to be clear (and pragmatic) about the role a modest-sized foundation could play in the life of a diverse and complex city. A 1947 report on the foundation's first forty years of grantmaking—spanning years that included two world wars and the Great Depression—reads in a way that feels very contemporary and begins to lay out the values that guide our work even today. The trustees made what I consider an eloquent pitch for funding advocacy for social change: "Philanthropic foundations cannot begin to solve single-handedly the numerous social problems that face us. They can, however, provide much of the seed money with which these problems can be made the concern and responsibility of the public at large."

Our foundation has always limited the bulk of its giving to New York City. In 1909 and today, trustees of the foundation had a deep concern for the needs of the city where they lived. "New York is not only a large community, but its problems represent a cross section of the nation's. Its requirements can be studied firsthand," reported trustees in 1947. Early on, trustees valued personal observation and were concerned about effecting change locally as well as more broadly. Today, we still make frequent site visits and set up opportunities each year for grantees and trustees to meet.

For example, Jackson Heights and Flushing Queens were chosen for the 2006 grantee/trustee site visit: both neighborhoods that reflect how larger issues of immigration, employment, housing, and civic participation were being felt on a local level.

The New York Foundation has always valued flexibility. The trustees wrote in 1947, "It might have been possible to devote a major portion of the funds to building up a single project, or at best a highly concentrated program in one field, with an impressive physical structure and public reputation…Too often such structures become monuments, static concepts in which the zest for experiment and progress is lost. Rather, the Foundation has made its influence felt in scores of varied activities." Today, the Foundation still does not limit its grantmaking to specific projects or issue areas. We make both general purpose and project grants, responding to needs as they are presented to us by those who carry out the work.

Just as the funded projects vary, so too do the issues. It is fascinating to track key policy issues as they changed (or didn't) over time. Public health, education, civic affairs, prison reform, and "intergroup relations" were all early issues tackled by foundation grantees. Later, fair housing and employment, preserving public hospitals, legal defense, and civil rights emerged as critical concerns. Today immigrants' rights, affordable housing, public school reform, and jobs are some of the issues our grantees focus their work on.

> Our staff and trustees are always aware of how larger issues play out on the local stage. We place a high value on the involvement of people in shaping solutions to problems in their communities, believing that organizations that engage people in meaningful ways offer the clearest path to social change.

A desire to experiment has been an important component. The New York Foundation has always been known as an early supporter of untested new projects and organizations. "On the frontiers of public service, there are experiments and opportunities which need funds but cannot obtain them from routine philanthropy or government. These experiments may fail. They are not yet understood or perhaps even approved by established institutions." Each year, approximately half our grants are to new organizations where our foundation's grant provides core support. Trustees then and now valued the foundation's responsibility to take risks, to be far-seeing, and to support work in its earliest stages.

These guiding principles helped set a framework for the Foundation to take the lead on funding advocacy and policy change, even in its earliest grants. "The Foundation, quite properly, has devoted a majority of its funds to attacking root causes…the guiding principle has not been simply to 'relieve' distress but to correct the conditions which cause it." Because we concentrate on our city's neighborhoods, our staff and trustees are always aware of how larger issues play out on the local stage. We place a high value on the involvement of people in shaping solutions to problems in their communities, believing that organizations that engage people in meaningful ways offer the clearest path to social change. By being flexible, we are able to respond to larger issues as they emerge, funding work in real time as it becomes critical to the constituents served by our grantees. And finally, because we are willing to take a chance on ideas that are yet untested, we can be agile, supporting efforts before there is any guarantee of success.

Using Public Policy Grants to Increase Effectiveness: A Small Foundation's Story

Tony Pipa

In 1998, the Warner Foundation began making grants focused on stimulating long-term improvements in economic opportunity for disadvantaged individuals and communities and improvements in race relations throughout North Carolina. From 1998 through 2003, during which time I served variously as board member and executive director, the Foundation—founded by a married couple, Michael Warner and Betty Craven, out of the sale proceeds of a successful software company—made annual distributions approaching $1.5 million, with an average grant of $37,000.

Flexibility and pragmatism as grantmaking principles

As a relatively small funder covering a geographically large state, one interested in producing transformative change in highly dispersed communities affected by persistent poverty, the Warner Foundation placed a high premium on leverage—looking for opportunities where its grants might have considerable breadth or depth of impact in proportion to its limited funds. This led the Foundation to be quite flexible in the uses of its funds and created a willingness to operate at multiple levels, working with very small community-led organizations that directly served individuals as well as larger, more established organizations whose statewide scope and advocacy on policy positions offered the chance to affect large numbers of people at once.

The Foundation approached its public policy work from a pragmatic rather than political perspective. Rather than push a specific agenda, the motivating factor for entering the policy arena was generally to expand a strategy that had been proven effective (no matter the political bias or viewpoint of those who created it) or introduce a policy idea that might significantly improve the constraints or environment for low-income people to improve their situation. The founding donors always attempted to tie the Foundation's grants directly to how and what individual lives might be changed, no matter if those grants were direct service or meant to affect public policy. This combination of elements has also led to a desire to accomplish multiple goals with the same grant, sometimes trying to affect individuals and policy at the same time.

For instance, one of the foundation's first policy grants supported an effort to train low-income beneficiaries to testify and participate in the creation of local policies to govern the distribution of Temporary Assistance for Needy Families (TANF) benefits (North Carolina legislators had created the opportunity for some counties to devise their own systems—separate and apart from the statewide structure—as welfare reform occurred). At the time of the grant, many of the preliminary steps of policymaking had already taken place, so we suspected that this effort might not alter the final rules significantly. But we also recognized that if the training were successful, the program participants would likely start to advocate for themselves in situations that extended beyond the extant policy debate about welfare reform. As we later witnessed, some of the participating parents did, indeed, become very active at their local schools.

Foundation involvement at different stages in the policy process

Trying to maximize its effectiveness by filling such niches also led the Warner Foundation to be involved at different stages in the process of policy development, albeit not on the same issue. The Foundation funded opposite ends of the spectrum—from research that attempted to establish the need for a new policy discussion, to the successful implementation of policy recently passed. For example, the Foundation funded a public report by the North Carolina Center for Public Policy Research that collated and presented data regarding differences in outcomes among the races on a host of important quality-of-life indicators, complete with recommendations on what steps state government could take to reduce the gaps (in the process the foundation also received an excellent set of benchmarks from which to measure its own effectiveness on certain issues over the long term). At the opposite end, the Foundation created a new staff attorney position for the Community Reinvestment Association of North Carolina (CRA*NC) so that the organization could litigate on the behalf of low-income residents who were losing their homes due to hidden costs in mortgage loans, simultaneously setting a precedent for a newly passed predatory lending law, one of the toughest in the nation.

Civic engagement for civil rights

Some of the most effective funding that the Warner Foundation did in the public arena did not involve attempting to set or change actual policy. While funding in remote and under-resourced areas of the state, the Foundation realized that it was a small player compared to the influence and funding provided by various government agencies. Thus it looked for ways to build successful partnerships and add value to public service leadership. For example, on a site visit to a community in western North Carolina where the new Latino immigrant community was experiencing discrimination and racial slurs, it became clear that the county manager—who was in attendance—was a prime mover behind the proposed effort to address the issue. By helping get the project underway and build its track record, the Foundation was giving the county manager time and opportunity to use the credibility and influence of her office to ensure the project's success and identify local resources that would continue to sustain the effort.

Building relationships is hard work that pays off

Building such relationships and finding such funding opportunities can present a challenge, especially for a small family foundation, since it can mean building familiarity with a wide variety of issues and building relationships with a potentially large set of public officials. If a foundation is not interested in staffing up, it can overcome that challenge by focusing strongly on one particular issue, thereby deepening its knowledge and analysis and building relationships with others who are its champions. By doing so, a foundation likely commits to measuring its effectiveness by measuring how successful it has been in helping set policy on that particular issue. Other small family foundations have chosen to be very geographically focused, constraining themselves to familiarity with the local issues where they are based. This often provides significant opportunity for board members to utilize their wide-ranging networks of personal and professional relationships in learning more about issues and in formulating strategy.

Foundations that are tied to measuring effectiveness through outcome measures often avoid getting involved in attempting to affect public policy because they struggle to identify appropriate and satisfying measures of progress, especially throughout the sometimes long time frame that new policy development requires. This poses an additional challenge for small foundations, since they often do not want to diminish their already limited grantmaking funds. As demonstrated earlier, the Warner Foundation overcame this problem by making grants that combined both policy and direct service objectives. In the case where this did not neatly occur, however, we found it particularly important to be clear about the assumptions we held regarding how a specific policy effort would improve the lives of our intended constituency and how the grant we were making would further that particular agenda. In this sense, the Foundation could attach a sense of importance to an issue and prioritize to what extent it wanted to continue to be part of the process if progress slowed or unforeseen barriers surfaced.

Making grants related to public policy has been an important tool. One $40,000 grant to the North Carolina Low-Income Housing Coalition, for example, seeded and sustained a legislative effort to strengthen the loans utilized by manufactured and mobile home owners, adding consumer protections to those loans and improving the possibility of building equity through such a purchase.

The Warner Foundation found that making grants related to public policy has been an important tool in maximizing our effectiveness. One $40,000 grant to the North Carolina Low-Income Housing Coalition, for example, seeded and sustained a legislative effort to strengthen the loans utilized by manufactured and mobile home owners, adding consumer protections to those loans and improving the possibility of building equity through such a purchase. This undertaking could ultimately affect thousands of low-income residents in the state, helping them build some measure of wealth. The grant also provided a nice complement to the many grants the foundation had made to local community development corporations to support first-time homebuyers in some of the state's most rural and poverty-stricken areas.

In summary, by working at multiple levels, the Warner Foundation not only maximized its understanding of the difficulties facing low-income residents and their struggle to build wealth, but it maximized both the breadth and depth of its impact on the issue.

At A.L. Mailman Family Foundation, Advocacy Is an Essential Piece of Business

Patti S. Lieberman

At the A.L. Mailman Family Foundation, we see advocacy as an essential piece of our business. Our mission is to enable every child to develop to his or her potential and to support families and communities to better nurture their children. We cannot effectively promote this mission without also advocating for changes in public policies that impact children and families. We are a small foundation, yet we fund nationally. We must, therefore, be strategic in how we leverage our dollars and in our funding choices. When we think about advocacy, we think about it on two levels: first, how we advocate for the *issues* we care about—including communicating our mission, determining whom to fund, looking for ways to influence public will, and informing policymakers—and, second, what we enable our grantees to do.

We select grantees whose activities support our mission, and we publicize those grants on our web site.

As a national funder, we get a bigger bang for our buck by funding national intermediaries such as National Center for Children in Poverty, Zero to Three, and National League of Cities. We do project-oriented funding rather than general support. For these organizations, we fund legislative briefings, publications, resource development and dissemination, targeted research, and public engagement and communication efforts—all activities that serve to inform and influence an ever-widening circle of stakeholders and policymakers.

The evaluation of advocacy differs from evaluation of other projects. We have learned to look beyond what is tangible and easily measured to take into account a broader definition of success. Assessing the outcome of advocacy work is complicated and needs to be looked at over time. Sometimes advocacy work can result in specific new dollars or policy changes. Sometimes producing a legislative brief can result in demand for more information. Sometimes advocacy involves relationship building and results in attracting new funders or getting the media to take up the charge. But sometimes successful advocacy may simply be sponsoring key, yet varied stakeholders to work together—including government representatives (who are funders too). Advocacy is by nature collective; it depends on bringing together coalitions, adding voices to a chorus, changing attitudes or perspectives. This work takes time.

Some of our most successful funding occurs when we bring government representatives, nonprofits, and funders together to work on an issue as a team. This kind of advocacy does not involve supporting a specific piece of legislation, but it is advocacy in that we are working to change and improve a public system. Having the understanding, the buy-in, and the reality-check from government agencies is essential to developing public systems that are informed by the work of the nonprofit and the philanthropic sectors, yet balanced by the perspective of the public sector. This informed, collective voice is essential to changing systems to benefit children and families.

At Quixote Foundation, Public Policy Is Core

Lenore M. Hanisch

Arthur Stuart Hanisch established the Quixote Foundation in 1997 to support progressive philanthropic interests ranging from environmental conservation to documentary filmmaking. Public policy work centered on his personal involvements rather than formal initiatives. The notion of taking on causes others are unlikely to champion was close to Stuart's heart and continues to motivate the board since he passed away in 2002. Core passions include justice and fairness, democracy, environmental stewardship, and women's issues. As the Foundation matures, the board has begun to align its grants with these core passions and to engage more deliberately in public policy.

Sustainable change requires three elements: action, education, and policy. Public policy work not only prevents problems from getting worse, but also protects the progress made through action and education.

This evolution reflects our belief that sustainable change requires three elements: action, education, and policy. Public policy work not only prevents problems from getting worse, but also protects the progress made through action and education.

For example, direct action, such as restoring the water quality of a river, is terrific. Water won't stay clean if people use toxic fertilizers on their riverfront lawns, though, so education about alternatives is needed in the mix. Eco-friendly landscape practices will help, but won't preserve water quality if upstream factories are dumping chemicals or soil runoff from logged areas is raising the river's temperature. If you don't change the related policies, you're not protecting the water—you're just bailing it.

Sometimes all three elements of change are represented within one grant. At other times, the Quixote Foundation balances its grantmaking by funding diverse projects. We recently supported action by a reproductive health care provider, brought in education via an organization that trains young women for political involvement, and made a related grant to a group active in the selection of judicial nominees who decide reproductive rights policy.

Regardless of amount, grants have a disproportionate effect when they're thoughtfully placed and well timed. We look for a direct connection between decision makers and the policy work we help support. A nonprofit group's request to release research on voter-verified paper ballots to the news media might be interesting, but of questionable impact on decision makers. The same study would be a much stronger candidate for funding if it were reported directly to a legislative committee drafting national standards for election integrity. Grant recipients can be small or large, well-funded or struggling, long-established or new to the field, as long as our support is used in a way we believe is strategic.

We also look specifically for policy issues that have substantial momentum. The Quixote Foundation's priorities evolve with current events, and lively activism and public attention add leverage to the money we give. A recent, modest grant to support several collaborating nonprofit groups has had phenomenal ripple effects because it was timed at the moment when the issue became widely known to the public and legislators alike.

Small family foundations have to apply their support surgically in order to multiply the impact of each dollar. We have the chance to fill a gap left by corporate and other funders who steer away from controversy, need to defend their giving budgets in terms of marketing and public relations goals, or are subject to pressure for instant results. Grants for direct action often provide immediate feedback. Well-designed education programs can yield tangible results quickly. The outcomes of policy grants are more slowly revealed, but the strategy of providing three-part support genuinely enhances our overall efforts—a built-in opportunity to make family foundations effective.

– – –

Conclusion

The small foundations represented in this chapter may be more sophisticated in terms of their approach to public policy and may have more assets than most in their class. However, they are among the thousands of small-to medium-sized foundations in the United States that have to make tough choices about where and what they invest in. All of these foundations place a high value on the power of public policy and civic engagement as avenues for reaching mission-related goals. Their choice of approaches in grant-making differ from local to national and in their posture toward grantees from major facilitator in community-based projects to minority investor in national policy campaigns. The idea behind this chapter is to illustrate that once public policy becomes viewed by a small foundation as a critical factor in the achievement of its mission, there are a variety of sound and effective ways to be involved. Perhaps the fastest growing segment of the foundation world is small family foundations. We hope that such foundations take away lessons not only about the placement of advocacy among philanthropic and social change tools, but also the following:

- Speaking up as an institution about policy and civic issues that affect mission-related concerns can be part of philanthropy.

- Helping others to be involved in the noble exercise of democracy through permissible advocacy activities can literally expand the impact of foundation giving and defend the advances philanthropy makes through grant-supported programs.

- Small foundations are exceptionally well placed to fund and facilitate civic and public policy participation because many local and state policy efforts do not require huge sums to get started. Rather, the number one need of grantees who engage in public policy is the commitment of funders over a longer period of time than is needed for most discrete service projects.

Foundations in Public Policy and Civic Activity:
Language, Process, Strategy, and Examples

This section begins by unraveling the many terms used to label and describe public policy and civic-related activities (Chapter 4). It then proceeds to organize and explain the public policymaking process in brief (Chapter 5). Various public policy and civic activities are identified and brought to life by three foundations, presented in mini case examples that share strategies, lessons learned, and results. The goal of this section is to acquaint foundation staff and trustees with an organized way to identify possible capacity building activities, strategies, and timing for public policy engagement.

Note: The information, including lessons, examples, and "how-to" steps in the following chapters are not intended to be legal advice. Foundations need to seek knowledgeable legal counsel when considering funding or participating in public policy activities. Chapter 9 provides a thorough explanation of what foundations can and cannot do under the law in the public policy and civic arenas.

SECTION

2

Chapter Four

Advocacy Language

David F. Arons, Abby Levine, and Kelly Shipp Simone

The use or misuse of language when talking about public policy and civic participation can serve as a barrier to foundation and nonprofit communication about public policy and, more generally, civic activity. When someone hears "advocacy" or "public policy," the first word that often jumps to mind is "lobbying." Lobbying is one—but only one—important part of public policy work. Influencing public policy and civic participation includes a wide range of activities, all of which are means of supporting and reaching foundation goals and having social impact.[19] Figure 1, Policy Pyramid (page 62), illustrates one way to categorize and define these methods. The increasing size of the boxes from top to bottom represents the approximate amount of legal latitude foundations are permitted. Foundations are prohibited from engaging in partisan political activities and must conduct philanthropy and implement programs in a nonpartisan manner.

Note: The law governing foundation public policy and civic participation is discussed in Chapter 9.

CHAPTER SNAPSHOT

This chapter discusses the following:

- Differences between lobbying and advocacy

- How most nonprofits refer to and discuss public policy activities

- The importance of specificity in using public policy, advocacy, and political words within foundations

Note: Unless otherwise stated, the term "nonprofit" refers to public charities (including community foundations) under section 501(c)(3) of the Internal Revenue Code.

---

[19] Alliance for Justice, *Investing in Change: A Funder's Guide to Supporting Advocacy* (Washington, DC: Alliance for Justice, 2004), 5.

Figure 1. Policy Pyramid _____

Specific **voter participation
and education activities**
during an election season

Lobbying
*Efforts to influence
specific legislation*

Public policy advocacy *
*Identifying and promoting change
in how influential institutions govern
and otherwise affect communities*

Civic engagement
*Participating in and leading community
activities intended to improve democracy,
solve problems, and create opportunities*

* Adapted from *The Lobbying and Advocacy Handbook for Nonprofit Organizations: Shaping Public
Policy at the State and Local Level,* by Marcia Avner (Saint Paul, MN: Fieldstone Alliance, 2002).

Civic engagement and public policy advocacy include a wide range of activities designed to shape decisions and uses of resources that affect people,
causes, and communities including public events, writing letters to the
editor, asking parents to immunize their children, advertising campaigns
to stop children from smoking, researching the developmental damage in
young children who ingest lead paint chips, promoting ballot initiatives
to preserve green space, introducing a legislator to a health clinic in her

district, educating organizations about how to contact their legislators, and encouraging neighbors to vote. Civic activity can encompass any activity that influences social, political, or economic systems.[20] Civic engagement at its broadest means involvement in community life. Sometimes engagement involves public policy advocacy which is comprised of actions designed to shape how we are governed. Public policy advocacy doesn't always have to be directed at government. Sometimes businesses in an industry are the target of organized advocacy by consumer groups, shareholders, or workers. For example, nonprofits have organized and pursued education campaigns to urge consumers to only buy coffee brands that use fair trade practices.

Lobbying Versus Advocacy

If you have ever wondered what term to use when discussing advocacy or work in the policy arena, know that many others have also been confused. Words including lobbying, advocacy, education, organizing, and mobilization all have their own localized meanings. Colloquially, the word lobbying might convey backroom deal making that deep-pocketed business lobbyists engage in. The 2006 lobbying scandal by Jack Abramoff may have furthered a negative image of professional lobbyists. Yet, many in the nonprofit sector embrace and strengthen the noble role lobbying can play in making sure that public policy improves causes and communities. Lobbying by nonprofits is indeed one of the best ways to enhance democracy and ensure that more people have a voice in public decision making. The Center for Lobbying in the Public Interest provides numerous examples of the benefit to people and communities from public interest lobbying.

As mentioned, lobbying is one of the most stigmatized words in American society. Despite popular misperceptions, lobbying—as defined by the Internal Revenue Code—is attempting to influence specific legislation.[21] It is important to recognize, however, that nonprofit lobbying does not mean an organization is acting in a partisan manner. Nonprofits under section 501(c)(3) of the tax code may not be partisan. One might argue that even if lobbying is not partisan, it still must be political. This is where it is

[20] Alliance for Justice, *Investing in Change: A Funder's Guide to Supporting Advocacy* (Washington, DC: Alliance for Justice, 2004), 1.

[21] See the glossary in Appendix A and Chapter 9 for more on the definition of lobbying.

important to be precise. Politics is all around us. It is how alliances are built, power is used, and decisions are made in a democracy. BUT, it doesn't necessarily mean an organization is partisan (aligned with a party or politician), or makes decisions behind the public's back.

Contrary to common public perception of lobbyists, public interest lobbying (nonprofit lobbying) often involves organizations working together, quite publicly, to inform policymakers about the impact of laws (or proposed laws) and to make recommendations about how to change them. As an example, public interest lobbying can mean advocating for more disclosure requirements by all institutions and for information to be publicly accessible. It is because of Congress's need for more information from the charitable world that in 1976 it reaffirmed that lobbying is a permitted activity by any charitable organization, including community foundations. Although private foundations are generally restricted from legislative lobbying, there are important exceptions to the lobbying restrictions private foundations may take advantage of (see Chapter 9 for these). Beyond lobbying, other public policy shaping strategies are available to all foundations. See Chapter 5 for illustrations of various public policy shaping and civic strengthening strategies.

> In 1976, Congress reaffirmed that lobbying is a permitted activity by any charitable organization, including community foundations. Private foundations are restricted from legislative lobbying, with several important exceptions. Private foundations can support nonprofits that engage in a wide range of public policy activities, including lobbying.

Advocacy is a widely used, broad term that may or may not include legislative lobbying depending on the activity. It is fair to say that when someone is lobbying, he or she is advocating—speaking up on behalf of someone or some cause. However, when a person is advocating, he or she is not necessarily lobbying. Advocacy is also a term used to describe the work of giving voice on behalf of a victim of crime or someone seeking public benefits. Since advocacy carries these two meanings, the phrase "public policy advocacy" is often heard to describe efforts to change or shape laws and regulations to distinguish that activity from client advocacy. This phrase is also frequently used to describe lobbying or influencing legislation, but it is important to be precise when planning specific actions because only "lobbying" is defined by the tax code that governs foundation and nonprofit activities. The desire to persuade is an attribute that lobbying and advocacy have in common.

Research has demonstrated that many nonprofits say they are "educating" policymakers even when the nature of their communication on policy matters goes beyond sharing information to include persuasion and outright requests for a legislator's support on a bill. Some nonprofits believe that using the word educate is safer and less political. One danger is that code words can reduce the level of clarity and understanding among board members, and staff. A second danger is that watering down the word lobbying by saying "educate" might ultimately dilute the actions themselves.

According to research by Tufts University, OMB Watch, and the Center for Lobbying in the Public Interest, language makes a difference in how organizations report the frequency of public policy related activities. In their study of over 1,700 charities across the United States, one-third of respondents were asked how frequently they "lobby," one-third were asked how frequently they "advocate," and one-third were asked how often they "educate" policymakers. The questions kept all other words the same—which allows us to look at how nonprofits react to the terms lobby, advocate, and educate. Twenty-nine percent of respondents said they "never lobby" while only 15 percent said they "never advocate" and 12 percent said they "never educate" respectively. Moreover, 61 percent of respondents that reported no lobbying expenses on their IRS Form 990 reported on the survey that they do lobby to some degree, but the survey definition was broader than the IRS definition.[22] This finding illustrated that for the very same activity—influencing legislators' decisions about specific legislation—respondents felt more comfortable with words that are less stigmatized than the word lobbying.

> Many nonprofits, including foundations, are genuinely trying to be so careful about their own policy work that they avoid anything that might label them as partisan entity . . . Instead of being afraid or confused by language, the philanthropic world should focus on the activities behind the labels and not let words alone deter interest, investment, or participation.

Why is this? There are probably many partially correct answers. One reason is that some charities that receive government funding for programs have been admonished not to use the words lobbying or advocacy when they approach government because of regulations prohibiting the use of government funding for lobbying and the perception that government dollars free up private funding for lobbying. Another reason is that there is still a lot of confusion in the philanthropic world about the differences between legislative lobbying and partisan po-

---

[22] Gary D. Bass, David F. Arons, Kay Guinane, and Matthew Carter, *Seen But Not Heard: Strengthening Nonprofit Advocacy* (Washington, DC: Aspen Institute, 2007).

litical activities during an election season. A third reason is that many non-profits, including foundations, are genuinely trying to be so careful about their own policy work that they avoid anything that might label them as partisan entities.

- - -

Conclusion

Here is the bottom line on language. Instead of being afraid or confused by language, the philanthropic world should focus on the activities behind the labels and not let words alone deter interest, investment, or participation. That said, foundation managers and board members should develop a shared understanding of what key terms generally mean so they can make informed decisions about how to get involved. The Glossary in Appendix A will help you get started.

Foundations considering grant proposals from nonprofits, individuals, or government agencies that want to engage in the policymaking process should be unafraid to ask questions of potential grantees to understand what they mean by these terms. In a legal context, private foundation restrictions on the use of grant funds for lobbying demand that they have a clear understanding of what potential grantees or partners want to do in the policy arena. Again, see Chapter 9 for more detail on the legal rules for foundation grant letters and the Toolkit in Appendix A for sample foundation grant letters.

Community foundations also should know what potential grantees want to do in the policy arena, since the lobbying activities of grantees can count toward their lobbying expenditure limits under certain circumstances. Beyond

the legal reasons for having an understanding of terminology, it is important to be able to fully understand what tactics and strategies are being used
to shape public policy especially in evaluating a grantee's work or your own
institution's policy activities. All public institutions should be aware of how
the public perceives civic and policy activity. Indeed, perception can be
reality. By harnessing the terminology of public policy, foundations can be
empowered as a participant in the policy process through proficiency with
key terms and the powerful actions behind them. Chapter 5 takes a more
in-depth look at the public policy process.

Chapter Five

Public Policy and Civic Engagement: Foundations in Action

David F. Arons

P ublic policy is all around us. It directly or indirectly influences almost every person, program, or problem that foundations and other organizations want to help, create, or solve. Laws and regulations, as implementing tools of public policy, govern many facets of foundation life. Grantmaking, tax incentives for donors, staff and board compensation, and rules about involvement in legislation and elections are just a few ways that laws enable and restrict foundations' activities. Public policy also shapes the demands placed on organizations and causes that rely on foundations as a source of funding, leadership, and programs. For almost any cause, laws and regulations, or the lack thereof, influence the volume of need and the scope of opportunity to perform in the public interest.

So where do public policies come from? According to Deborah Stone, author of *Policy Paradox*, "Policy is a rational attempt to attain objectives."[23] Most objectives for which public policy is derived involve one or more of the following justifications or values: security, liberty, equity, efficiency, and community.[24] In the philanthropic world, these values are often implicit or explicit in mission and value statements.

What is public policy participation? Public policy participation is the utilization of tactics and strategies to gain access to

[23] Deborah Stone, *Policy Paradox: The Art of Political Decision Making* (New York: W.W. Norton & Company, 1997), 37.

[24] Ibid.

public decision making and to influence government, media, individuals, and other institutions that make decisions affecting the public. It is also a commitment to a long-term process whereby the public, institutions, and decision makers come together to deliberate and decide the rules of society. Foundations are key actors in this process. As discussed by Emmett D. Carson in Chapter 1, mission can and should be the primary driver for foundation engagement in the public policy process. Indeed, mission is the appropriate lynchpin for connecting a foundation to the policymaking process because actions based on mission will likely motivate foundation trustees, staff, and grantees to make public policy issues a priority. Once an organization decides to shape public policy outcomes, the next questions that often arise include: How should we get involved? Can we get involved legally? What are other foundations doing? So here is the good news:

If your foundation wants to get involved in public policy, it is not alone.

Often the decision *whether* to become involved in public policy is deterred by confusion over *how* to be involved (see Chapter 6) and by concerns over whether involvement is legal or appropriate. (See Chapter 9, The Legal Rules for Policy and Civic Impact, by Lloyd H. Mayer). In order to make informed decisions as a foundation about involvement in the public policy process, it is helpful have some illustrations of how other foundations are involved, to be aware of some of the typical barriers as well as motivating factors that lead organizations into the public policy arena, and to identify some of the roles foundation staff and board members can take on.

TIP

Influence the Private Sector Too

Many tactics described here can be used to influence private sector practices, including the decisions of corporations that affect the public. Shareholder organizing, consumer boycotts, and class action suits are among such tactics. Domini Social Investments (http://www.domini.com/shareholder-advocacy/index.htm) is one place to learn about shareholder advocacy and proxy voting.

There are many ways to shape or influence public policy as well as strengthen the democratic process. Developing and implementing effective public policy strategies is analogous to composing a symphony. Various instruments are available and range in terms of their complexity, limitations, power, and expense. Each brings a different tone, range, and value to bear on the overall score. Just as a composer gains experience manipulating these orchestral forces to achieve the impact he or she wants, an organization be-comes more successful in achieving its public policy goals as it understands and employs policy shaping strategies with partners, including grantees.

In this chapter, we describe two major categories of strategies and tactics that often overlap: 1) public policy shaping activities and 2) civic strength-ening activities.

Public policy shaping activities are designed to influence the content and implementation of laws, rules, and regulations. *Civic strengthening activities* are designed to improve community life and the democratic process itself through increased civic participation, improving public leadership, greater transparency in institutional decision making, and other means. There are at least eleven different tactics that foundations are using to shape public policy consistent with their mission and six different categories of civic strengthening work. (There are probably more that we did not identify.) Figure 2, Public Policy and Civic Strengthening Strategies (pages 72–73), lays out these activities.

Putting Strategies to Use

Certainly all of the activities defined here are not necessarily appropriate for your foundation or for every effort to shape public policy or for civic work. However, it is important to know of the range of strategies that might be available to your foundation or to your grantees and partners. The sub-ject of the next chapter is deciding which strategies to use and how. Many if not most efforts to shape policy use several strategies simultaneously and continue to modify them for each phase of the policy process and the chal-lenges presented along the way. The case studies that follow are an attempt to bring these activities to life.

Figure 2. Public Policy and Civic Strengthening Strategies _____

Public Policy Shaping Activities

1. **Convening stakeholders around policy**
   Holding meetings, roundtables, forums, conferences.

2. **Building partnerships and coalitions**
   Linking and building teams of people and organizations to work on policy issues.

3. **Public policy capacity building**
   Enhancing the will and capabilities of people and organizations to participate in the public policy process.

4. **Public interest research and dissemination**
   Sponsoring or conducting nonpartisan research about public policy issues.

5. **Public and consumer education**
   Conveying information to the public or segments thereof about specific policies or more generally about government performance.

6. **Media education and influencing**
   Producing news and shaping news coverage of policy issues before the public and policymakers.

7. **Administrative and regulatory advocacy**
   Educating and influencing the rule making, agency adjudications, informal policymaking, analysis, and implementation by government agencies.

8. **Judicial advocacy including litigation**
   Bringing legal claims before the courts to rule on a dispute about a matter affecting injured parties, but the outcome has broad implications for a specific cause or community. Another example of judicial advocacy is when foundations demonstrate support for a party's position in a lawsuit by filing an amicus or friend of the court brief.

9. **Organizing and mobilizing**
   Bringing people and organizations together to create power and take action toward shared goals. Nonprofits may organize and mobilize people to affect public policy goals and to raise awareness of a social problem or demonstrate solidarity.

10. **Lobbying and supporting other nonprofits that lobby**
    Attempting to influence specific legislation (prohibited with certain important exceptions by private foundations; permitted by community foundations within expenditures limits).

11. **Demonstrating and other direct action techniques**
    Includes a range of activities that are usually conducted as an event—picketing, mass marches, and sit-ins.

Civic Strengthening Activities

1. **Voter registration**
   Signing up individuals to be eligible to vote. Must be nonpartisan and can target historically low voter turnout areas.

2. **Voter turnout—get out the vote (GOTV)**
   Encouraging voter participation through physical activities like door knocking, providing rides to the polls, phone calling, even child care while parents vote.

3. **Voter and candidate education**
   Conducting nonpartisan efforts to educate voters about policy issues facing causes and communities. Tactics may include flyers, ads, radio messages, public meetings, and paid and earned media.

4. **Research on civic activity**
   Organizing an inquiry about citizen participation in the democratic process or other systems of government; research on voluntarism; participation in public decision making; and advocacy by nonprofits and individuals.

5. **Civic education**
   Developing school and community-based educational programs to teach the importance of understanding how democracy works; also why and how people participate through advocacy, voluntarism, and service learning.

6. **Civic infrastructure support**
   Increasing the capacity of individuals, systems, and organizations that help make democracy operate including the government's election processes and projects designed to motivate citizen participation in their communities during the election season. Nonprofit efforts include activities to aid nonprofit-sponsored candidate forums and get-out-the-vote or other nonpartisan voter participation and education activities.

Notes: All election-related activity conducted by private and community foundations must be strictly nonpartisan. See Chapter 9 for the rules governing foundation funding of advocacy and permissible voter participation activities.

Convening, partnerships, coalition building, capacity building, research and dissemination, media education, judicial advocacy, organizing and mobilizing, lobbying, and demonstrating are all tactics that can be used and are used as vehicles for strengthening civic engagement as well as for shaping public policies. By engaging in these activities, people and organizations are strengthening civic behavior.

Mini Case Studies— Examples of Using Public Policy Strategies Together

Following are three stories. The first is from a private foundation, The Joyce Foundation, which funded a full-scale public policy effort regarding welfare reform that resulted in increased collaboration among state government officials, better welfare payment rules in Illinois, and increased knowledge about barriers to work faced by women. The second story, by Woods Fund of Chicago, describes a funded collaboration of organizations that took on policy issues around immigration and resulted in a strong, diverse group of organizations capable of influencing public policy across the political spectrum. The third story is by Rose Community Foundation, a community foundation that spearheaded a policy shaping campaign that resulted in city-wide teacher compensation reform. In each story, multiple strategies were used. Notice that the progress made did not happen overnight but rather was achieved through patience and determination.

Editor's Note: Foundations should consult knowledgeable legal counsel prior to the outset of public policy engagement. The following examples are not held out to be examples of the legal rules in action. They serve as examples of activities used by foundations in the public policy context. See Chapter 9 for an explanation of the legal rules for foundation conduct in the public policy and civic arenas.

Foundation involvement in welfare reform

Mary O'Connell

In 1996, Congress passed sweeping welfare reform, and the states began reshaping policies to move people off welfare and into the workforce. The 1996 law essentially upended the nation's safety net. It ended the federal guarantee of assistance for poor families, set work requirements and a five-year limit on benefits, and turned over to the states unprecedented power to reshape their welfare plans, without much guidance or assistance for doing so.

As a Midwest grantmaker, The Joyce Foundation knew that states like Wisconsin, Michigan, and Minnesota have been pioneers in developing new welfare policies, and that reform would have major implications for the lives and economic prospects of tens of thousands of Midwest families. Foundation staff also recognized that welfare reform was a major policy opportunity for addressing employment issues facing the low-wage labor market, which had been a Joyce Foundation grantmaking area beginning in 1995. Staff members consulted with leading researchers and policy advocates, both nationally and in the region, to develop an approach to welfare reform that included three strategies: 1) policy development and advocacy; 2) research; and 3) communications.

1. Policy development and advocacy: Beginning in 1996, The Joyce Foundation helped create and fund a network of state welfare officials called the Midwest Welfare Peer Assistance Network (WELPAN), who met regularly to share ideas and problems of implementing welfare reform at the state level. Joyce also funded national groups including the Brookings Institution, the Center on Budget and Policy Priorities, and the Center for Law and Social Policy, which provided solid research and analysis of national welfare trends and policy options. The Foundation also supported a network of state-based advocacy groups (organized regionally as Midwest Partners) that monitored state implementation, tracked the findings of welfare researchers and their own observation of family experiences, and provided critical policy input, both on post-1996 state policies and on the reauthorization debate.

2. Research: The Joyce Foundation funded over $8 million in research at leading universities and other institutions to evaluate the impact of the reforms on families in seven Midwest states (Illinois, Indiana, Iowa, Michigan, Minnesota, Ohio, and Wisconsin). The Foundation board supported the research agenda and made clear that the studies were not an end in themselves, but a set of evaluations meant to shed light on a major social experiment and suggest ways to improve its outcomes.

3. Communications: To ensure that the research findings informed the continuing evolution of welfare policy, The Joyce Foundation included funding for communications in all of its research grants. It also published and distributed to policymakers a series of state-level research summaries and an overall synthesis of research findings in an accessible guide,

Welfare to Work: What Have We Learned? Findings from Research on Welfare Reform in the Midwest. The report was published in April 2002, as Congress was preparing to reauthorize the 1996 legislation. It earned coverage from the *New York Times*, major regional papers, and some broadcast (principally radio) coverage, followed by a second wave of editorials, op-eds, and columns. Joyce Foundation grantees disseminated the report to policymakers, including members of the House and Senate; provided a briefing for staffers on Capitol Hill; delivered the report to White House welfare staff; posted findings on key policy web sites; and made presentations at several venues, including to Midwest state legislators at a Women in Government conference.[25]

Impact on policy

At the state level, Joyce Foundation grantmaking helped shape welfare policies in several ways. In the wake of the 1996 law, state policymakers had to shift the function of their departments from processing welfare applications and sending out checks to providing people in trouble whatever assistance they needed to get jobs and support their families. WELPAN, an idea developed by Joyce Foundation staff and University of Wisconsin researcher Tom Corbett, brought together top Midwest state welfare officials to think through this shift and strategies for meeting the new goals.

Generally, state administrative officers have few opportunities and little funding for such collaboration. Through regular meetings beginning in 1996 and continuing today, Midwest welfare officials have shared ideas and successes and identified emerging problems (for example, the bureaucratic rules that required people to reapply frequently for food stamps during working hours, which made it hard for working families to keep the food subsidy). Midwest states were especially important innovators on welfare policy, and it is arguable that WELPAN contributed to the quality and sophistication of welfare policies in the region. In 1996 some observers feared that states would compete with each other to cut benefits and trim welfare rolls at whatever cost to poor families; instead, Midwest states pioneered approaches that supported work and helped families make the transition into the workforce.

---

[25] This is a useful example of the type of nonpartisan analysis and research that private foundations may financially support. See Chapter 9 for more details about funding nonpartisan analysis and research.

Advocacy groups (both national and state) that were supported by The Joyce Foundation also influenced state welfare policies. The Chicago-based National Center on Poverty Law (now called the Sargent Shriver Center) persuaded Illinois officials to continue to pay welfare benefits out of state funds to people who worked at least thirty hours per week, so that they would be supported in making the transition to work without using up their federally mandated five-year time limit on welfare benefits. This innovation was unique to Illinois.

Another example of policy impact is the contribution of researchers at the University of Michigan, led by Professor Sheldon Danziger, in identifying the obstacles (health problems, domestic abuse, transportation difficulties, and so on) faced by women attempting to make the transition from welfare to work. The Michigan researchers showed that the more barriers a woman faced, the less likely she was able to successfully negotiate the transition to work. This finding led states to recognize the diversity of the issues faced by the welfare population and the need for more flexible policies and more intensive services to help those hard to employ.

> **It does seem clear that The Joyce Foundation study helped shape the understanding of welfare reform by both the public and key policymakers and contributed to the debate over reauthorization.**

At the federal level, the policy impact is less clear. Federal welfare policy remained in legislative limbo from April 2002 until February 2006, when the Temporary Assistance for Needy Families (TANF) program was finally reauthorized, without fanfare, as part of the federal budget reconciliation bill. It is thus difficult to state what impact, if any, Joyce Foundation grantmaking had on national welfare policy.

It does seem clear that The Joyce Foundation study helped shape the understanding of welfare reform by both the public and key policymakers and contributed to the debate over reauthorization. Editorials, congressional speeches, and other summaries of the effects of the 1996 reforms closely parallel the key messages in The Joyce Foundation study, to wit:

- Welfare rolls declined,
- Most people who left welfare went to work,
- But they took mostly part-time, low-wage jobs,
- And they remain poor.

Policies should support work (through child care and other forms of assistance that help people stay employed) and seek ways to enable new workers to escape poverty by moving up the job ladder.

Lessons

Several elements of the Foundation's approach to welfare reform offer potential lessons for future policy work:

- *Range of approaches:* Underlying the whole project was a clear and comprehensive grantmaking strategy. Welfare reform was such a major policy and social change that a broad range of tools was essential for addressing it. The 1996 welfare law included no mandates and little funding for research to evaluate its results. Joyce and other foundations stepped into the breach. The Joyce Foundation set a goal of having a high-quality evaluation in each of its seven states, with a focus on welfare-to-work policies and a geographic focus on major urban areas. In addition to the research, the Foundation supported policy development, advocacy, and communications, and it worked with policymakers, advocates, and researchers to bring the best information and ideas to the policy arena to improve the lives of Midwest families.

- *Regional focus:* Midwest states share some common economic and demographic characteristics and a sense of regional identity. They were leaders on welfare reform, both before and after 1996. Hence the regional convening of policymakers (through WELPAN) and advocates (through Midwest Partners) made sense. Similarly, the regional focus of *Welfare to Work: What Have We Learned?* was important because it drew attention to the effects of welfare reform in the part of the country that had seen some of the most significant policy innovations.

- *Communications:* The research funded by The Joyce Foundation provided a potentially significant contribution to the understanding of the impacts of welfare reform. But the results, represented in two dozen major studies from universities and research organizations, came out at different times and in different forms. To a policymaker, they were overwhelming in their detail and complexity. The creation of *Welfare to Work*, with its very accessible design and clear synthesis of the findings (backed up by much more detailed information on the web site), put the information in the hands of policymakers in a way they could understand and use.

On the other hand, the nearly four-year delay in reauthorizing welfare reform and the fact that there was very little public input into the final product remind us that politics and timing remain critical elements of policymaking, ones over which researchers and public interest groups have little control.

Woods Fund of Chicago funds campaign to aid immigrants

Jeffrey T. Pinzino

In funding public policy advocacy, it's always satisfying to share stories of massive grassroots efforts led by grantees that resulted in major new public policies being written, preferably within the one- or two-year grant period most foundations work with. These *do* happen from time to time, but are the exception rather than the rule. How then, do foundations recognize effectiveness in policy advocacy when it doesn't lead to a dramatic, short-term victory?

Organizing stakeholders into a coalition

Woods Fund of Chicago has been a funder of the Grassroots Collaborative since its inception in 2000. The Collaborative was started by several community groups responding to a challenge from the Woods Fund that encouraged collaboration between organizations for greater policy impact. After a year of deliberate discussions, the Collaborative formed with some of Chicago's most prominent organizing and advocacy groups, including Chicago Association of Community Organizations for Reform Now (ACORN), Chicago Coalition for the Homeless, Illinois Coalition on Immigrant and Refugee Rights, SEIU Local 880, The Illinois Hunger Coalition, American Friends Service Committee, Interfaith Leadership Project, and Metro Seniors in Action.

Community action by Grassroots Collaborative pays off

Grassroots Collaborative has played a major role in several successful policy advocacy campaigns over the course of its existence. The Collaborative helped to pass a living wage ordinance in Chicago. It was instrumental in a campaign that increased tenfold the number of families with children eligible for free health insurance. It was significantly involved in getting a raise for homecare workers, yielding over $300 million dollars to many of the lowest paid workers in the state.

> **Grassroots Collaborative has played a major role in passing a living wage ordinance, increasing the upper limit range on free health insurance for children, helping to secure a raise for homecare workers, and mobilizing thousands of low-income and immigrant constituents.**

Organizing and Mobilizing: The Collaborative was one of the local organizers of the Immigrant Workers Freedom Ride. At public events, member organizations of the Collaborative have mobilized thousands of low-income and immigrant constituents on immigration and civil rights issues. It is an exceptional group, unique in the Chicago landscape for its inclusiveness and reach.

Public Education: The Collaborative was also heavily involved in a campaign aimed at making Illinois drivers' licenses available to undocumented immigrants. The intent was to help decriminalize immigrant workers, many of whom had been working and driving in Chicago for years. When the campaign first began, many detractors said that it was too close to September 11th to be taken seriously, that Republican legislators wouldn't support it, and that there would be a public backlash. The Collaborative decided to focus its organizing efforts on the issue anyway.

Forging Unusual Alliances: The Collaborative presented the immigrant drivers' license issue as a matter of highway safety. The auto insurance industry lobby signed on in support, and one by one, Republican legislators were signing on as well. The Collaborative brought four thousand immigrants to the state capitol in support of the proposed legislation, the largest gathering of immigrants in Springfield to date. Major new partners, including the Metropolitan Alliance of Congregations and Centro Sin Fronteras, joined the Collaborative to help move the issue. The message was effective enough to get editorials written in favor of the legislation at every major newspaper in Illinois.

Key Outcomes: Ultimately, the legislation failed to pass by one vote. Although the measure was voted down, the members of the Collaborative established themselves as a player in public policy advocacy in Illinois. They proved they could mobilize large numbers of people and bring together a diverse group of powerful organizations under one banner. They proved their detractors wrong by putting immigrant issues back on the political map in Illinois. They showed they could work both sides of the aisle politically, forge creative alliances, and win public support for their efforts. Their work positions them strongly both for the continuation of this campaign and for taking on other issues currently being explored by members.

General operation support catalyzes strong advocacy

Woods Fund was one of the few Chicago foundations providing general operating support to the Grassroots Collaborative throughout the campaign. Woods Fund also supported six of the Collaborative members involved in the campaign, either with grants for general operating support or grants to support public policy advocacy. (See Chapter 9 for an explanation of how private foundations can fund public policy activities through general operating support or special project grants.)

Taking the long view, an investment in policy advocacy is an investment in groups to build power over time.

The key lesson for the Woods Fund of Chicago was the realization that the payoff for supporting policy advocacy is not always changing policy. Risk is part of the nature of the work, and no group will win every policy they take on. Taking the long view, an investment in policy advocacy is an investment in groups to build power over time, and by that criterion, the campaign made tremendous progress. The Collaborative put immigration issues back on the map in Illinois, and other immigrant rights policy initiatives have had an easier time because the drivers' license campaign paved the way. As a result of the campaign, Grassroots Collaboration will be a stronger force for statewide policy change on this and future issues. Woods Fund considers this to be a wise investment.

Rose Community Foundation funds an effort to transform teacher compensation

Phil Nash

In November 2005, a decisive majority of Denver voters approved funding for a groundbreaking teacher compensation program called ProComp (short for Professional Compensation for Teachers) that rewards teachers in the Denver Public Schools (DPS) on the basis of student achievement, knowledge and skills, professional evaluation, and incentives for taking positions in hard-to-staff schools. The successful ballot initiative provides approximately $25 million annually to fund the higher cost of teacher salaries anticipated under this innovative compensation system.[26] This is a description of Rose Community Foundation's six-year involvement in the project.

In its education program area, Rose Community Foundation funds efforts to improve the quality of classroom teaching—the most critical factor in student achievement outside of home and family environment. Yet traditional methods of teacher compensation do little to promote or reward quality teaching, including linking pay to student achievement. Rose Community Foundation combined the tactics of research, policy development, an educational campaign to teachers, and, finally, support for an advocacy campaign to urge the voting public to implement the ProComp system in order to dramatically alter education practice to the benefit of students—and to achieve the Community Foundation's education program goals.

1. *Research phase*: In 1999 Rose Community Foundation approved a grant of just over $90,000 to help Denver Public Schools and the Denver Classroom Teachers Association develop a plan to pilot "pay for performance" (PFP). A labor agreement between the union and the school district envisioned a two-year pilot in sixteen elementary, middle, and high schools overseen by the PFP Design Team (two leaders of the teachers union and two DPS administrators). The PFP Pilot was researched by an external entity, which eventually became the Boston-based Community Training and Assistance Center (CTAC). Rose Community Foundation made a grant of $1 million to cover a significant share of the research costs. The

---

[26] Note that although ballot initiatives and referenda occur as part of the electoral process, efforts by nonprofits to urge voters to vote for or against a ballot initiative or referendum are considered direct lobbying because, in effect, the voting public becomes the legislature. See Chapter 9 for the rules governing nonprofit efforts to influence the outcomes of ballot initiatives and referenda.

pilot's original purpose was to test three different approaches to paying teachers and their impact on student achievement. During the planning stage, Rose Community Foundation, CTAC, and the PFP Design Team came to the conclusion that an effective pilot could not be implemented in only two years. As a result, Rose Community Foundation made a second $1 million grant, contingent on the teachers union and DPS expanding the pilot to four years. The Foundation also recruited other funders to join the project. In all, approximately $7 million in philanthropic dollars supported the four-year project. In addition, DPS's contribution of public dollars was estimated at more than $7 million.

2. *Policy development phase:* As the Pay for Performance Pilot moved toward completion, the Joint Task Force on Teacher Compensation (a group of Denver Classroom Teachers Association leaders and DPS administrators) was studying compensation models to develop a new compensation system to recommend to the district and the teachers union. It became clear that teacher performance *alone* could not be the foundation of a compensation system. The system that was ultimately proposed included four components: student growth, expansion of knowledge and skills, professional evaluation, and incentives for teaching in hard-to-staff schools and hard-to-fill positions. Communication efforts directed at teachers included newsletters and a web site, however, as the union vote on the proposed system approached, a survey of teachers showed that many were undecided and indeed uneducated about the issue.

3. *Education campaign to teachers:* In the weeks leading up to the union vote, Rose Community Foundation and The Broad Foundation funded a political consulting firm to conduct a full-scale educational campaign encouraging teachers to vote favorably for the new compensation system The foundation had not anticipated a need to conduct a campaign, but it became apparent that the entire project was at risk because simply making information available was not enough. In fact, information about ProComp had not penetrated many of the school buildings. Rose Community Foundation decided that financing an educational effort aimed at the teachers in the buildings where they taught was a justifiable

investment in producing a favorable vote on a policy that would benefit over 70,000 DPS students. The lesson we learned is that simply making information available was not an effective tactic: asking people to make significant changes in how they are paid requires a face-to-face, hands-on approach to information delivery. The teachers needed opportunities to be educated about the proposed pay system that would directly affect their work and their paycheck. Given the short time frame, the "can do/must win" strategic and tactical approach of a political campaign was needed.

4. *Advocacy campaign to Denver voters.* Once the teachers and the DPS board were in agreement on ProComp, the final step to implementation was to obtain the necessary funding for the anticipated higher salaries that teachers would earn under this system. There was no excess or flexibility within the district's budget, so new funds would have to be raised through a mill-levy campaign. Rose Community Foundation made a $250,000 grant to fund what became a $1.1 million campaign to pass the mill levy in November 2005. Fortunately, Denver's very popular mayor agreed to campaign for ProComp, and many highly visible leaders got involved. The campaign proved to be more than a request for a mill-levy increase; it became a vote of confidence in DPS.

Results: System approved, pending public support

The mill-levy election to fund ProComp passed with a substantial margin of victory. The new system makes it possible for teachers to increase their salaries at a much faster pace and to break through the ceiling of the existing compensation system, based on a set of factors that include performance and choices within the control of the teachers themselves. Teachers are signing up in much higher numbers than anticipated. The new teacher compensation system allows current teachers to opt into the system over a period of seven years. All newly hired teachers will be part of the ProComp system.

In the meantime, the fact that the school district and the teachers union have agreed on a revolutionary teacher compensation proposal based on something other than years of service and level of education was newsworthy enough to be covered on the front page of the *New York Times* on Sunday, May 9, 2004. The path to this milestone in the annals of public education was more than four years in the making, and it still has a long way to go.

Key lessons for other funders

The senior program officer for education cites several key lessons from this process:

- Long-term philanthropic engagement in policy can make a difference. In this case, the foundation's senior program officer remained a champion of the project through three superintendents and two interim superintendents over a four-year period, often helping to smooth over the recurrent and predictable rifts between the union and the district.

- In public policy work, funders will encounter major rifts and barriers between groups. Good, objective research followed by policy development can reduce these rifts. In this case, barriers between unions and district administrators can be broken down and goodwill developed if both are engaged in a shared learning process. Both the research phase and the policy phase provided this opportunity.

- Personal contact can be key to helping people understand policy changes that need to be made. The campaign needed to get to the teachers face-to-face in their school buildings to communicate directly the impact and benefits of the proposed policy changes.

- Communications about policy should be succinct, credible, and personal. Here, communications to teachers union voters were brief and offered by credible sources (this campaign hired union organizers as consultants as well as Denver Public Schools teachers).

- Economic factors play a critical role in building consensus for reform. When opponents become contentious over budgetary priorities in completely different areas of debate, the resulting ill will can taint the existing areas of common ground.

— — —

Conclusion

Private and community foundations are involved in a wide variety of public policy and civic participation activities designed to advance their philanthropic goals. A key purpose of this chapter was to present evidence that the foundation world is successfully serving mission-related goals by leveraging private philanthropic dollars to create significant public revenue streams that fund well-researched policy change. Most importantly, the causes served by foundation philanthropy are benefiting from foundation policy activity.

Public policy embodies the rules and values that govern and hold our society accountable. Foundations can be vital actors in shaping public policy. They can help grantees and those they serve fully participate in our democracy. Seldom do institutions work alone in the policy arena. Success, failure, setback, and progress are standard phases of most efforts to shape laws and rules. In this chapter, you learned that you are not alone in this work. Second, there are many types of strategies and tactics that may work in different situations (and often in combination) to generate sufficient support for policy change. A key lesson is that when one tactic stops working, try another and another until you find what works. Also, employ complementary strategies such as research and communications. Ultimately, you will develop and master your own advocacy toolbox. The three foundations profiled in this chapter shared experience in using multiple tools during the same policy effort. Strategies emphasized included research, convening, agenda-building, organizing, lobbying, communications, collaboration, policy development, funding, and others. Each foundation used a different mixture of strategies to reach its goal. Yet all share commonalities: stamina for their issue over a period of years, passion to make lives better through public policy change, understanding that education of policymakers was requisite to building support, and viewing successful collaboration among stakeholders as a critical vehicle for success.

If the forms of policy shaping activities and civic strengthening activities still seem like a hodgepodge of unrelated concepts, Chapter 6 will help pull the pieces together so that you can help your foundation build capacity and strategy for public policy success. In Chapter 6 you will have the opportunity to walk through a step-by-step process for building a public policy program and strategy in your foundation. In addition, there are numerous short examples of foundations engaged in each type of policy shaping or civic strengthening activity in Appendix B. Again, remember that before emulating the policy work of other foundations, consult knowledgeable legal counsel.

Chapter Six

A Step-by-Step Approach to Building Capacity and Public Policy Strategy for Foundations

David F. Arons, Abby Levine, and Kelly Shipp Simone

Editor's Note: Nothing in this chapter should be construed as legal advice. When preparing for public policy participation, it is important to consult knowledgeable legal counsel familiar with the law in the area of foundations and advocacy.

Now that you have read about how other foundations have used various types of public policy tactics and strategies (Chapter 5 and Appendix B), it is time to move ahead and prepare your foundation to succeed in the public policy arena. You will need two things: 1) an understanding of how to put together public policy strategies that are derived from mission-related goals and 2) an organizational plan for participating in public policy or civic activity. This chapter provides a step-by-step approach to learning these concepts and skills, but by no means is it "the" definitive approach. For some this chapter may be too prescriptive. However, for other foundations, particularly foundations that are new to public policy and advocacy, a beginning recipe might be called for. Either way, the following steps should be tailored to your individual foundation's experience. (If you have questions on how, contact the authors in this book via the publisher.)

CHAPTER SNAPSHOT

This chapter is designed for foundations that are new to public policy, civic engagement, and advocacy, and for foundation support organizations that help foundations with policy work. Included are the following topics:

- How to recognize the public policy implications for philanthropic work

- How to determine the opportunities for foundation involvement

- How to establish principles to guide policy involvement

- Roles for foundation staff and leaders

- Factors influencing nonprofits' attitudes and behavior related to public policy participation

- Determining political risk and the wise use of power

- How to allocate resources for public policy work

- Choosing tactics and strategies based on careful preparation

The following twelve steps are intended to help your foundation begin to get its feet wet in the public policy arena. They are:

Step 1: Choose an Advocacy Mindset

Step 2: Recognize the Public Policy Dimensions to Foundation Work

Step 3: Develop Public Policy Awareness

Step 4: Assess the Foundation's Personality Type

Step 5: Assemble the Public Policy Team

Step 6: Establish Principles for Public Policy and Civic Participation

Step 7: Use Collaborations, Partnerships, and Other Resources

Step 8: Prioritize Issues

Step 9: Build a Strategy

Step 10: Determine Political Risk

Step 11: Allocate Resources

Step 12: Execute and Chronicle Strategy

Step 1: Choose an Advocacy Mindset

What does a foundation that supports public policy look like? It looks like you, because people make foundations work. There is no archetype; the range of activities and even underlying motivations are too broad. However, we can identify some of the behaviors of foundations that avoid advocacy.

Foundations can impede their grantees from engaging in public policy by including overly restrictive language in grant agreements that prohibit grantees from using grant funds for any type of public policy work. (See the Toolkit in Appendix A at the end of the book for sample foundation grant letters that do not overly restrict grantee advocacy.) These reticent funders—called "paranoid grantmakers" by Bill Roberts and Lee Wasserman—share several traits.[27] They

- Don't allow grantees to mention the words "lobby" or "legislator" or "law" in their proposals

---

[27] The traits noted by Bill Roberts and Lee Wasserman are from a presentation before the Environmental Grantmakers Association on September 24, 2003.

- Don't admit to funding advocacy or campaigns to pass laws
- Never participate in meetings where lobbying is discussed
- Believe all public policy shaping activities must stop in an election year

To the contrary, foundations have a unique opportunity to be an uplifting force in the nonprofit sector. They can inspire and enable people and organizations to meaningfully shape our society. An advocacy mindset is truly an attribute of active, concerned leadership. An advocacy leader is willing to champion its own core beliefs as well as the concerns of others it believes in.

> **The art of effective public policy work is not about drawing lines in the sand or using coercive tactics to achieve outcomes at any cost. Public policy and civic leadership motivates groups to work together to find common ground, mitigate differences and downsides, and look for realistic but forward-thinking solutions.**

Inherent to any leadership activity is risk. Enemies can and will be made. But the art of effective public policy work is not about drawing lines in the sand or using coercive tactics to achieve outcomes at any cost. Public policy and civic leadership motivates groups to work together to find common ground, mitigate differences and downsides, and look for realistic but forward-thinking solutions. It also is an opportunity to nurture ideas and solutions from citizens and community-based organizations and to empower those often unheard to become vocal champions for their causes. Similar to the work of running a foundation, public policy participation is in part about staying true to mission and the community in which the foundation operates. There is an inherent accountability in taking on policy work because foundations are powerful and can influence policies that affect an entire population, not just those served by their grantees. Foundations can confer great benefits to communities and causes through public policy participation. Take this role on with optimism. Don't be a paranoid grantmaker. Find advisors and board members who are comfortable with these activities so your foundation's full potential can be unleashed.

Action: As a leadership group, discuss the meaning of advocacy as it applies to your organization. Decide whether you are currently blocking useful mission-based advocacy or fostering it, and whether you are open to change.

Step 2: Recognize the Public Policy Dimensions to Foundation Work

Choose any area of philanthropic interest and there is likely a set of public policy issues that relate in some way. This is not surprising given that many foundation programs are designed to supplement or fill gaps in need left by the government, businesses, and nonprofits. Even programs to strengthen citizen participation in democracy aim to maximize opportunities for participation under the law or to remedy problems caused by flaws in policy or the lack of laws themselves.

The first step for foundations beginning to think about the relationship of public policy to foundation- or donor-supported activities is to answer the following question:

How do laws and policies affect the goals of each project or program as well as our foundation's mission and values?

Let's take an example.

The (fictitious) Jane Doe Foundation is a family foundation that makes grants to nonprofits serving youth to create tutoring opportunities for children in school. The Foundation set a goal to support the development of state-of-the-art tutoring programs in its community. To find out about the impact of laws and policies on their goal, the foundation might query grantees about school districts' policies regarding tutoring in terms of when it is offered, public resources for tutoring, and the nature of the tutoring. The foundation might want to ask: Are current government policies advancing the goal set by the Jane Doe Foundation with regard to excellence in tutoring? What barriers do government laws or regulations present to reaching the goal? How would laws or policies need to change to remove the barriers to Jane Doe grantees being better able to supply state-of-the-art tutoring programs?

Over the past few years, many foundations have come to realize that shrinking government investment in social programs, education, environmental initiatives, and community development programs undermine philanthropic investments in nonprofit programs. Government's potential to hurt as well as help nonprofit endeavors makes it important for all foundations to understand the role of laws and policies in the success of their philanthropy. The Jane Doe Foundation might also examine how other nonprofits and businesses are involved and invested in tutoring school-based children. The opportunities and barriers to more tutoring services might also be influenced by these institutions. A potential public policy solution will likely have an impact on these stakeholders. If there is a solution available without requiring a change in law or regulation then it may be well worth the time to pursue shared goals through convening, deal making, and resource sharing.

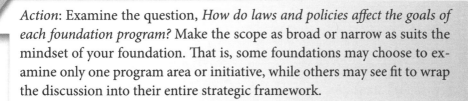

Action: Examine the question, *How do laws and policies affect the goals of each foundation program?* Make the scope as broad or narrow as suits the mindset of your foundation. That is, some foundations may choose to examine only one program area or initiative, while others may see fit to wrap the discussion into their entire strategic framework.

Step 3: Develop Public Policy Awareness

After you do the basic homework about how laws and government policies affect your foundation's goals, it is time to examine what new policy proposals are either pending in the legislative process or could be shaped for consideration by government. The same is true for administrative rules and procedures implemented by government agencies. It is important to know whether an executive branch agency is considering changing rules that would ultimately help or harm your grantees as they seek to reach goals shared by your foundation. Often either a grantee will know the impact of public policies on grant-supported work, or an association to which it belongs will know about pending changes. For example, if a foundation supports the Boys and Girls Club locally, it is likely that the Boys and Girls Club's national or state government relations office would be able to help find out the status of legislation or regulations.

Note that developing a basic sense of how public policy is affecting foundation program areas does not require a veteran lobbyist. Rather, it may involve asking grantees and other partners for input. It may require assigning someone who is capable of interviewing grantees and other nonprofits that work on public policy issues, conducting Internet and library research, and talking to policymakers and other experts.

Even if you do not foresee your foundation delving into the details of tracking specific bills or administrative rules, it is important to learn the basics of how public policy is made and changed and the potential opportunities for foundation involvement.

Policy proposals mature into law through consistent pressure from affected individuals, interest groups, business and nonprofit sector trade groups, media, think tanks, and from government itself. Some policy ideas become law or a new administrative practice because of insiders who know legislators or other policymakers, or the nuances of every process. Just as corporations employ lobbyists to help them protect a tax break, there is a role for the use of insiders by nonprofits, including capitol-based associations of foundations working together to protect and advance laws affecting the philanthropic sector. But overall, former House Speaker Tip O'Neill's statement that "all politics is local" still applies today. Political power is formed at the grassroots local level. Knowing that voters care about an issue is the power that influences lawmakers—even when strong interests might be on the other side. Foundations are not the same as voters, but they do represent power because of their wealth, credibility, leadership, knowledge, and moral authority. They also work with grantee nonprofits that represent voters. How foundations tap these inherent assets for use in the public policy process is central to the formulation of any strategy on public issues.

This is also the step where you should begin to learn about the rules governing lobbying activity. Understanding the rules not only helps foundations and grantees stay within the boundaries, but also helps foundations understand their potential role in the policy process. Chapter 9 is a good place to start.

It can be important to avoid narrow policy silos when working with the public and grantees to determine opportunities for improving public policy or addressing public concerns. For example, if a foundation portfolio or a nonprofit's focus is on improving public education, it would be wise to also consider how employment, health, and housing issues are affecting the

Media Power

Elected and appointed officials read and watch the news everyday to understand what is being said about them and what issues are on the public's radar screen. Foundations entering the public arena as funders of organizations that advocate policy or as participants themselves should think carefully about how to communicate with and respond to the media. Key resources for foundations media work include:

Communications Consortium Media Center—a public interest media center dedicated to helping nonprofit organizations use media and new technologies as tools for policy change. http://www.ccmc.org

The Communications Network—an association of foundations that provides training and resources in public relations and strategic communications. http://www.comnetwork.org/aboutus.htm

The Spin Project of the Communications Leadership Institute—helps nonprofits communicate effectively about their causes. http://spinproject.org/

readiness of children to learn. Many public policy issues—such as housing, environmental issues, education, and job growth—often have overlapping and intersecting aspects, including a common constituency, shared values, or shared funding base. These overlaps provide a golden opportunity to help grantees representing different social needs to coalesce as appropriate and develop flexible and varied approaches that can serve many causes.

How the policymaking process works

The process of making and shaping public policy can seem like a spider-web. If you don't know what you're doing, you can get stuck wasting time, reputation, and money. At the outset, it is helpful to have at least a beginning sense of the major phases of public policy development. Discussions of policymaking tend to emphasize the partnering, persuasion, negotiating, and direct action with government—especially legislators—to secure policy outcomes. This neglects the equally important role of working to improve and evaluate the *implementation* of public policies. Legislation is sometimes needed to change policy, but often changing regulations, executive orders, or other administrative practices can yield the intended results. *Moreover, administrative or regulatory advocacy is not a restricted activity for any type of foundation in the way lobbying by private foundations is restricted.*[28]

So, what are the major phases of public policy development and what are the points at which foundations can get involved as institutions?

The good news is that foundations can and do get involved in most phases of public policy development. Foundations frequently have broad and in-depth knowledge of community needs and the problems of particular segments of the population. As a result, foundations are especially needed as players in the early stages of policy development, what might be called the **investigative** phase, which includes

1. Identifying public problems or opportunities

2. Determining who is affected and involved in the issue

3. Gathering information about what options and solutions exist

4. Bringing key players together for deliberation and discussion

While many foundations are accustomed to being called on during this investigative phase, they are increasingly involved in the second phase, sometimes called the **action for change** phase. This phase includes

5. Planning for public policy and civic action

6.   Building the capacity of groups that will engage in advocacy

7. Organizing and mobilizing activities to influence government decision makers or other stakeholders to agree to a policy change or new way of doing civic business

The third phase might be called **implementation**. This part of the public policy development process includes

8. Working with agencies and other groups to put the agreed-upon change into place

9. Evaluating results

---

[28] In general these activities are not restricted under federal law. Some states may require reporting such activities as lobbying but do not restrict the amount of activity that may be conducted. Check your state's law by asking your attorney general's office or state nonprofit association, and consult with knowledgeable legal counsel.

Public policy is developed to address problems and create opportunities—sometimes for purely political reasons. As noted above, the process for making and shaping public policy begins when a problem or opportunity arises. Foundations and other nonprofits determine who is involved or affected to truly learn the scope of the issue. Unless it is a recurring issue, most organizations spend time gathering information and doing further research about the nature and possible options for addressing the issue. Once the facts are better understood, foundations, grantee organizations, government officials, and others are better able to collectively discuss options. Sometimes, deliberation and discussion can result in a solution if key decision makers are at the table, consensus builds quickly, and the procedures for solving the issue do not require complex legislative, fiscal, regulatory, or political decisions to be made. But, rarely do all the political stars align to create such a smooth path to resolution. Compromise is part of the process, so long as the compromises made are not to core values or principles.

> ### The Policy Process
>
> Three resources for learning about the public policy process and how foundations can have an impact include
>
> - *Public Policy Grantmaking Toolkit* by Northern California Grantmakers, http://www.ncg.org/toolkit/home.html
> - *Funding Health Advocacy* by Grantmakers in Health, http://www.gih.org/usr_doc/IssueBrief21_Funding_Advocacy.pdf
> - *Foundations & Public Policymaking* by the University of Southern California, http://www.usc.edu/schools/sppd/philanthropy

Foundations, grantees, and allies then begin the action for change phase; they plan for more deliberate and formal activities designed to shape policy. At the same moment, partners in public policy determine what capacity is needed by those organizations that will carry out various strategies and tactics of policy participation. For example, a foundation might determine that the grantees most likely to lobby for a legislative proposal need to know more about the legal dos and don'ts of lobbying. Stakeholder foundations might fund training events for grantees to build their knowledge so they can know what is legal lobbying. Next organizations begin direct action—working to influence government decision makers. When it is time to activate and influence government decision makers, private foundations that understand the laws and particularly how to use the legal exceptions to restricted lobbying will know what they can and cannot do in the way of advocacy. (See Chapter 9 for the legal rules.)

Figure 3. Opportunities for Foundation Involvement in Public Policy Development _____

Phases of Public Policy Development	Possible Foundation Roles
Investigative Phase	
Identify public problem (or opportunity)	• Foundation helps identify or speak out about the problem (or opportunity) or provides space and encouragement for others to speak out about it. • Foundation expresses concern or interest to top decision makers in public and private sectors.
Determine who is affected and involved in the issue	• Foundation organizes a gathering of concerned persons and organizations to explore the issue(s). • Foundation staff participates in meetings of other groups, agencies, and coalitions. • Foundation commissions research to determine the scope of the problem and who is affected.
Gather information about what options and solutions exist	• Foundation sponsors or commissions further research to explore the policy options and outcomes.
Bring key players together for deliberation and discussion	• Foundation staff formulates its own institutional goals as related to the public issue. Foundation staff works with key grantees and stakeholders to understand opinions and positions and to forge alliances, partnerships, and consensus positions where appropriate.
Action for Change Phase	
Plan for public policy and civic action	• Foundation works together with allies and other partners to identify what resources are needed to pursue policy options. • Foundation makes planning grants to organizations to develop ideas and strategies for policy options and approaches. • Foundation staff learns the basics of the policymaking process for that specific issue, whether it is legislation, regulations, or guidelines. • Foundation staff works with partners and allies to map out a strategy. Note that since private foundations are restricted from engaging in any grassroots lobbying and most direct lobbying (several exceptions exist including self-defense lobbying; responding to requests for technical advice and assistance; and preparing nonpartisan analysis, study, or research) they may not be permitted to participate in planning efforts around specific legislation. They may participate in planning around broad policy topics, for example, the need for a fair health care policy.
Build the capacity of groups that will engage in advocacy	• Foundation makes grants (or supports through contributions of staff time) to organizations, partnerships of organizations, and coalitions to establish strategic and tactical resources. • Foundation connects grantee organizations to advocacy support organizations that provide training in how to shape policy and public opinion, organize, lobby, and understand the laws governing participation (listed in Appendix C).

Organize and mobilize activities to influence government and media (and possibly business and nonprofit) decision makers	• Foundation engages in policy change and/or civic activities as an institution up to the limits of the federal tax laws and in adherence with the principle of nonpartisanship. • Community foundation lobbies or conducts administrative, judicial, or media advocacy as appropriate with partner organizations. • Private foundations engage in activities under the lobbying exceptions or other non-lobbying activity allowed under the law. (See Chapter 9 for descriptions of what is and is not lobbying).

Implementation Phase

Work with agencies and other groups to put the agreed-upon change into place	• Foundations convene stakeholders to make recommendations about how government should implement the law through regulations or other rulemaking. Note that often as the legislative or policymaking phase shifts to policy implementation, some advocacy groups will step back and new groups more focused on carrying out programs under the law will step in. A foundation in close communication with grantee organizations involved in leading policy and civic efforts should ask for updates on which organizations are emerging and stepping back in each phase. • Foundations can advocate for and against administrative rules and regulations, given that such activity generally is not considered lobbying. Again, see Chapter 9 for the exceptions to the lobbying restrictions for private foundations. • Foundations can build key partnerships between and among nonprofits, government agencies, and for-profits to identify promising practices and apply them in policy implementation.
Evaluate and track results	• Foundations can fund ongoing evaluation of programs and projects delivering services governed by the laws. Conversely, foundations might want to evaluate what would have happened if certain policy proposals that were defeated in the policymaking stage had been enacted. • Foundations can also conduct their own evaluations or hire consultants to do them (see Chapter 10 on evaluation). • Foundations are also uniquely positioned to help nonprofits and all stakeholders reflect on how they carried out policy shaping tactics and implementation activities. • Foundations are among the best storytellers about what happened as a result of public policy. Sharing the stories of policymaking and the results with media and the public is a valuable service foundations can take on.

It's never over!

Be aware that issues that seem resolved may come back in the same or different form.	• Few public policies are completely static once they are enacted. There is constant rethinking and reevaluation, especially if public funding is at stake. Proponents of any policy are always trying to prove the worth of their program, and opponents are always trying to demonstrate why it should be different. Advocates must also be vigilant in the administrative rulemaking and adjudication process to ensure due process and that the laws are carried out as the law proscribes. Foundations as stakeholders have a vital role to play in the life span of public policy.

Once the government has approved a sought-after policy, the implementation phase becomes exceptionally important because the benefits of the legislative change may come to fruition. Foundations can and should want to be at the table with agencies and other nonprofits to provide input on how policy will work in practice. Evaluating and tracking results are often overlooked but are necessary for understanding lessons learned and for planning future policy initiatives. (See Chapter 10.)

TIP

Warn Advocacy Groups Before You Shift Focus

Nonprofits that specialize in public policy advocacy often become frustrated with foundations that change priorities and cease funding in a certain policy arena. Informing and working with nonprofit advocacy groups early on as the decision to change focus is made can not only aid the conclusion of the grantor-grantee relationship, but hopefully retain a collaborative relationship on other levels. Another option is to provide a bridge grant to help previously supported grantees transition to new sources of support without losing the momentum on their policy issues.

Finally, it is important to know that the policy process is never over, as policy and those making public decisions are rarely static for long. Foundations have ample opportunity to be part of advancing policy to benefit the causes they serve. New issues come up and old issues come back, and nonprofits must be ready to participate as a regular activity.

Figure 3, Opportunities for Foundation Involvement in Public Policy Development (pages 98–99), illustrates generic steps along the path of policy development and shows where grantmakers can play key roles.

Note: Public policy work can be proactive (promoting an idea) and reactive (opposing actions or ideas). During the course of most public policy initiatives participants engage in proactive and reactive tactics and approaches. For example, policymakers often want counterproposals when they decide to alter government programs delivered by nonprofits. Foundations can play a key role by enabling nonprofits to deliver counterproposals and by helping to bring nonprofits and government together to discuss issues.

You should now have a general sense of the flow of public policy development from identifying needs to forming policy solutions, and how policy solutions come to be approved into laws, regulations, and programs. You should also have a beginning sense of places in the process where foundations might get involved.

If what you have read thus far seems simplistic, it is. Each phase of the public policy process has its own steps and nuances that you will learn on the job from grantees, from web- and print-based materials, and from the experienced policy advocates you will work with and come to rely on for information.

Before moving ahead to assemble a strategy for addressing specific issues through the public policy process, it may be especially important for your foundation to assess the kind of relationships it generally has or wants to have with grantee organizations that are deeply involved with the day-to-day policymaking process.

Step 4: Assess the Foundation's Personality Type

There is no doubt that public policy work can and will challenge a foundation's character, thinking, and operating systems. Because of the inevitable waves in the sea of public policy, it's helpful to know now what kind of boat you have and how it wants to steer. Depending on the issues, mission, and institutional traditions, your foundation will likely adopt one of four general postures or "personalities" toward public policy and civic grantmaking. Awareness of these will help the foundation determine the kinds of resources, skills, governance, and staff work required to be successful and consistent as a foundation.

Proactive/Facilitative: These foundations seek out public policy or civic issues they want to put their money and power into. They are also quick to get involved if the right issue is put before them. Their style of organizing, convening, and grantmaking aims to encourage and enable others to take on leadership positions and be out in front rather than the foundation being out front. These foundations empower nonprofits and other groups to conduct policy activities in their own way, to take their own positions, and to operate with their own style. An advantage of this posture is that the money and partnership received from a foundation is empowering because it transmits the credibility and financial power required to build a powerful advocacy force. A disadvantage to the foundation is the potential frustration should groups that receive foundation investment deploy policy strategies, messages, or postures the foundation disagrees with. Certainly key responsibilities of being a facilitator are patience and acceptance.

Proactive/Prescriptive: These foundations are involved in public policy issues in the same way many large nonprofits are. They spot issues, do their own analysis, and formulate their own positions and strategies for engagement. By doing more of their own public policy work, these foundations may believe they have more influence, or at least greater control over how policy formation and advocacy are carried out. Their thinking on policy matters carries over into their choices of grantees and the nature of their grantees' and partners' advocacy. The advantages here are obvious: more control, possibly leading to solutions or changes orchestrated by the foundation, and more visibility. But more accountability comes with it. These foundations are deeply part of the action—playing multiple roles of funder, sponsor, spokesperson, and partner, and thus incur more public scrutiny, but may see more reward for their own direct policy work. Foundations in this camp must also be careful not to become overreliant on a small group of partners and consultants.

Reactive/Facilitative: These foundations wait for public policy and civic issues to be presented to them as an opportunity for investment or participation. These foundations rely on citizens, nonprofits, or other foundations to frame what is at stake on a given issue. Then these foundations play enabling roles including grantmaking, providing space, or other means of helping build the capacity of those who will be involved. An advantage of this approach is that groups focusing on policy change will appreciate unqualified support. Moreover, foundations in this category may be comfortable as the broker or mediator among differing factions about a shared concern. This flexibility requires that the foundation trust grantees and understand that change in public policy often faces setbacks and that change takes time.

Reactive/Prescriptive: Foundations in this group may not be at the edge of the horizon line as spotters of policy issues, but once engaged they have their own ideas on how issues should be addressed and hence might want a certain amount of control over the strategies employed by grantees. Again, control may be a positive for some foundations, but for others it can be overwhelming. A foundation should be prepared if it wants to not only make the grant but share in the work. Grantees, nonprofits, and other foundations that work closely with the reactive/prescriptive foundation need to spend critical time early on in the policy effort to tap its potential aggressiveness.

Note that foundations may fit into more than one of these four personalities depending on the issues, circumstances, and leadership involved.

Action: The power of foundations to use money and influence to shape how institutions approach public policy issues is real. Foundations should think about their influence on the missions and programs of the grantees and other community groups. Assistance should include thinking about the impact of receiving foundation funding or other support on the grantee's programs, reputation, and other relationships. Use the descriptions above along with Figure 4, Where Does Your Foundation Fit? Consider the mix of proactive/reactive and prescriptive/facilitative that suits your foundation.

Figure 4. Where Does Your Foundation Fit? _____

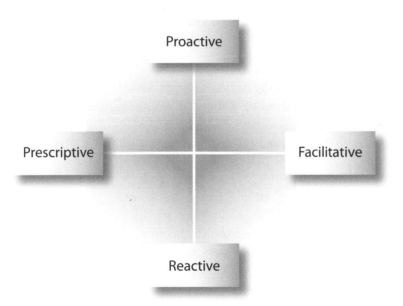

Following is one example of a "proactive and facilitative" approach to grant-making by the William Penn Foundation in Pennsylvania. This approach involved collaboration among multiple partners on a relatively large scale. Examples of other approaches may be found in Appendix B, which contains short examples of foundations involved in public policy and civic activities.

William Penn Foundation's Large Investment in Comprehensive Policy Strategy Yields Positive Results for Child Care

In 1997, the William Penn Foundation (WPF) made a $7.1 million grant to the United Way of Southeastern Pennsylvania, toward Child Care Matters (CCM). CCM is a collaborative effort to demonstrate how to improve the early childhood educational system and to move policy toward increased support for quality child care that is available and affordable to families in need. William Penn Foundation extended the grant in 2000. The initiative's public policy goals included the following objectives: restoration of income eligibility for state subsidies, the establishment of state health and safety funds to ensure compliance with child care programs' licensing standards, and creation of a Pennsylvania Office of Child Care. During the three-year period, state expenditures on child care rose dramatically (8 percent, 15 percent, 21 percent). The William Penn Foundation used funding and collaboration to help the United Way be the major driver of the campaign. The Foundation gave the United Way a planning grant to build the collaboration and partnerships.

Key organizations in the collaboration included Delaware Valley Association for the Education of Young Children (DVAEYC), Delaware Valley Council for Early Care and Learning, Philadelphia Citizens for Children and Youth (PCCY), and Philadelphia Early Childhood Collaborative.

Following is a brief interview with Helen Davis Picher of the William Penn Foundation about the initiative:

> ***How did WPF use its power to encourage collaboration?*** Financial power certainly was one tool to bring groups together, but WPF's knowledge of the issues, overview perspective on what was needed to strengthen early childhood education, and ability to encourage leaders to work together were key. Heavy-duty monitoring was another tool

for watching the collaboration form and progress. WPF did not assign roles to participating organizations in the Child Care Matters collaboration. They worked together to determine which organizations were best positioned to take on certain leadership roles. Philadelphia Citizens for Children and Youth emerged as the lead group on the public policy piece. They had a strong staff person for this kind of work.

How were CCM's policy goals chosen? WPF didn't steer the goal setting. The participating groups in the collaboration set the goals. WPF had a behind-the-scenes role in the public policy part of CCM. This was one of the earliest public policy grants we ever made.

In addition to the stated legislative outcomes, including greater appropriations for child care, what were some of the process goals achieved? For example, do these organizations now work together as a result of their experience in CCM? The organizations in the collaboration have a strong policy presence and there has been a continuing effort to work together although CCM is over. The Early to Learn (E2L) initiative of the United Way includes the groups that were together in CCM but doesn't only address policy; they work on nonpolicy areas as well. E2L's focus is primarily on providing technical assistance for quality improvement and integrating child-serving systems. Its public policy component is part of a demonstration project and not direct advocacy.

Is it fair to say that improved collaboration among these groups is one of the results of WPF's sponsorship of CCM? Yes. There is improved collaboration.

Did WPF hear pros or cons from the press and policymakers during CCM about the foundation's role in the effort? The press was handled by the United Way. WPF was not identified by the press as a policy player. We heard from policymakers, but only that they were glad that we were promoting quality child care.

How did CCM help to mature WPF's approach to public policy–related grantmaking? It was an enormous leap for us and for the board. After the first three-year period was over, we renewed funding for the initiative with the bulk of the funding going toward the public policy piece for another three years because by that point the board realized that some of the most important achievements from the initiative were coming from the policy work.

Early on, was there any resistance from the board that staff had to address? We had to convince some board members and had to explain to them that what we were doing was advocacy and education but not impermissible lobbying. We had to act to address the policy aspects of child care, including the quality and funding, because welfare reform was going to have such a large impact.

Did certain board members see the urgency of being involved more than others, and, if so, how did you deal with that difference? We have a generally diverse board so they knew about the situation facing kids.

What lessons did you learn from the policy participation piece that could be shared with other foundations?
- The importance of bringing groups together, identifying a lead group with financial capacity (including the ability to handle the money), and having accountability structures in place.
- Look for organizations with leadership on the substance of the issues and willingness to work with others—the human relations piece.
- Providing core support (in the form of general purpose grants) provides organizations the flexibility to develop policy and non-policy strategies collectively and to change them going forward as appropriate. Giving core support is a newer strategy for us and one that the board now understands as a grantmaking strategy that can lead to specific results.

Does WPF have its own vision or model of what a healthy public education system looks like before it ventures into public policy grantmaking in this area? Does it need to have a complete idea before it gets involved? It is helpful to have some guiding principles before going in. We don't have to have all the answers but we need to have somewhat of a broad vision, knowledge of the field, what certain elements will always be needed—like good governance in any system and trust in the groups we fund.

Action: Consider your foundation's personality type in a general sense and specifically for various projects. Reflect on the question of whether modifying your foundation's place on the proactive/reactive and facilitative/prescriptive continuums might positively affect the grantor-grantee relationship and resulting work.

Step 5: Assemble the Public Policy Team

You've done your homework. You've identified how public policy affects mission and philanthropic goals. You've studied the basics of how public policy is made and the legal rules. And, you've reflected on your foundation's operating style. Now it is time to assemble a team of people within the foundation to take on the next steps.

The main jobs of the public policy team include

- Establishing principles or a guiding framework for engaging in the public policy process as a grantor and as an institutional participant.
- Educating and motivating team members and others within the foundation (especially trustees) on the importance, legality, opportunities, and risks of any public policy shaping or civic strengthening effort.
- Recommending a course of action to the foundation's trustees, including positions on key issues.
- Funding trusted organizations to help develop policy positions consistent with foundation mission and goals.
- Providing oversight of the implementation of foundation public policy efforts.
- Participating in select public policy activities as part of the foundation's strategy.
- Evaluating and chronicling public policy efforts.

Some of these jobs are discussed as separate steps later in this chapter.

Choosing team members

Your public policy team might be exclusively employees of the foundation. It also might include or be led by trustees as a committee of the board. It could also include other stakeholders in the foundation, including grantees, other nonprofits, or business leaders.

Some foundations recruit government officials to be part of their public policy committee or advisory group to provide an insider's perspective as well as access and political clout. Here, the foundation should consider the government official's position in advance to avoid likely conflicts of interest and to ensure that the insider's perspective does not come to dominate the selection of issues, strategy, and solutions. The job of an elected official is, in part, to compromise with other legislators and interest groups. It is important for the public policy team and the coalition you are working with to decide independently of a legislator's influence when to compromise and when not to.

There are a wide variety of possible roles on a foundation's public policy team.

Roles of trustees

The public policy role of a trustee stems from his or her responsibility as a fiduciary and policy maker for the foundation. As always, the duties of obedience, loyalty, and care apply. Board members do not act alone in these roles. They rely on staff, grantees, and community members to identify public policy issues and the choices facing the foundation, its grantees, donors, and constituents at large.

There are several steps a board of directors or individual trustees may take to establish a role in public policy:

- Seek information to assess the foundation's current level of participation in public policy both through grantmaking and through the foundation's own action.

- Determine the foundation's potential role in policy by reviewing the foundation's governing documents, mission, and legal rules to help align organizational values with public policy and civic objectives.

How to Assess the Foundation's Potential Role in Policy

- Review the foundation's governing documents (such as articles of incorporation, trust instrument, by-laws) to verify that no restrictions exist

- Review the legal rules governing the foundation's ability to engage in public policy

- Determine how policy work can assist the foundation in achieving its mission by enhancing the objectives of philanthropic programs

- Assess the know-how of staff and trustees for immediate public policy action

- With the help of staff, grantees, and board members with policy experience, develop a process for how the foundation will involve itself in policy. Will the foundation set a policy for determining which issues to be involved with? Will it take each potential opportunity on a case-by-case basis?

- Board members can communicate a public policy role through funding guidelines and decisions. For example, if the foundation has made the choice to emphasize grants to nonprofits that engage in public policy, the board should revisit its grant guidelines to ensure that the nature of the work for which funding may be used is clear. If the board envisions the foundation as a convener on community issues, the board may need to revisit its fiscal priorities to ensure funds are allocated for events and meetings that allow for such a role.

A trustee's role does not have to stop at setting the grant guidelines, approving grant proposals, making legal determinations, or articulating board opinions in a broad sense about what the foundation should do. Trustees can also become involved in implementation of policy strategy.

Consider what skills and assets board members have to contribute to the policy efforts. Do they have connections to policymakers or community leaders, expertise in particular issues to share, particular skills such as communicating with diverse groups? Board members or trustees may put these assets to use in the implementation of public policy work in key ways. Following are a number of roles board members might play in motivating, framing, developing, and implementing public policy participation.

- *Instigator/Motivator*: A board member who raises issues and concerns and pushes the board and staff to ask tough questions about the foundation's involvement in policy and community issues.

- *Door Opener*: A board member who uses his or her own relationships and contacts to facilitate the foundation's public policy agenda.

- *Spokesperson*: A board member who volunteers to stand in front of the media or policymakers on behalf of the foundation. For example, many organizations have a board member provide testimony before a legislative committee.

- *Mentor*: A board member who uses previous public policy experience to educate foundation staff and other board members new to policy.

- *Program Developer*: A board member who works with the board and staff to assess the public policy implications for foundation work and to develop appropriate roles and strategies for the foundation in the public policy and civic arenas.

Roles of foundation staff

Foundation staff can play an essential role in public policy work. First, staff personnel are often the primary points of contact between the foundation and its grantees and donors. As such, staff can communicate to potential grantees and the community the foundation's messages regarding policy work that the foundation is willing to support or participate in. This may include speaking with potential grantees and the community at large, communicating the foundation's policy work through speeches, and authoring articles in newsletters or other publications. By serving as an active voice for the foundation's policy work, staff can ensure that a clear message is sent regarding the foundation's policy goals and activities.

Staff members may be directly involved in policy work by participating in meetings and forums, mobilizing others, or meeting with policymakers to discuss the foundation's work or general policy issues.[29] Staff are also in a

---

[29] Private foundation staff must be aware of restrictions on direct lobbying when planning ways to communicate with policymakers about issues. See Chapter 9.

position to identify opportunities for and barriers to involvement in policy. Staff members may be the first to recognize a need for policy change in the issue area in which they work. For example, a program officer or donor advisor may note the lack of communication among grantees working on the same issues and, in response, develop mechanisms to enhance information sharing among interested organizations. Foundation staff may also play one or more of the roles that board members also provide; however, staff do not have the ultimate legal accountability that board members have. Following are several roles staff might play in the development and implementation of public policy–related grantmaking and program activity.

- *Instigator/Motivator*: Like board members, staff can raise important questions, propose ideas, and encourage civic involvement by their foundation.

- *Grantmaker:* Program officers and other staff make the frontline decisions about whether and how foundation funds and other resources are used for shaping public policy and strengthening civic engagement.

- *Capacity-builder:* Program officers and donor advisors are well positioned to motivate and educate peers regarding public policy and civic opportunities.

- *Collaborator:* Foundation staff who manage a set of issues often have a unique bird's-eye view on a field such as children's health, arts, or housing. They also have the ability to bring together community leaders and organizations in a specific field to discuss and possibly work together on shared policy concerns.

- *Teacher/Facilitator:* Foundation staff often have knowledge and skills about the policymaking process that can be shared with grantees, building their capacity for effective policy participation during the length of the grant period.

- *Donor Advisor:* Community foundation staff can educate donors about the potential for their contribution to go to organizations that advocate policy change—how their contributed dollars can leverage more money from government that can be used for vital services.

- *Researcher:* Foundations today are amazing repositories of information about programs and projects affecting the quality of life. By compiling and sharing evaluative data about the effectiveness of nonprofit programs, policymakers and the nonprofit sector will be better informed. Many foundations also do their own research on policy issues. Because of foundations' credibility with policymakers, their research can be especially persuasive.

- *Scout:* Foundations are in constant danger of becoming too reliant on established nonprofits to elevate ideas and frame the debate. Foundation staff who find ways to scout issues themselves by talking with people in their communities have opportunities to discover new policy ideas and new ways to look at ongoing policy issues and community concerns.

Public policy team leader

Foundation staff who run the day-to-day operations (or the trustees in small foundations without staff) also play the crucial roles of convener, secretariat, and often chairperson for the public policy team. These jobs are important because no public policy initiative is successful unless there is a person or small group dedicated to driving and monitoring the process. The job responsibilities of a public policy team chairperson are

- Organizing meetings and conference calls
- Setting the agenda for key meetings
- Coordinating relationships with partner organizations and individuals
- Ensuring those involved in implementing public policy activities are focused and working in a timely and effective manner

Leading the group to make collective decisions

The list of roles foundation staff and trustees might play is certainly not complete, but hopefully it will help identify the types of skills you want to have on the foundation's public policy team or committee. The composition of the committee becomes especially important as it takes on the task of establishing a framework or principles to govern decision making, resource allocation, and participation. Note that research shows that nonprofits (not foundations) participate more if the chief responsibility for public policy advocacy is entrusted to someone who is not the executive director.[30] Interviews and focus groups with nonprofits revealed that executive directors, who have so many responsibilities, may not devote sufficient time to advocacy for the organization to have a sustained presence at the policymaking tables of government. If the same is true for foundations, then it might be more effective to appoint a trustee or senior staff person as the coordinator or chairperson of the public policy team. An alternative structure is for a trustee or grantee to serve as the chairperson and a staff person to serve as the day-to-day coordinator of the work.

Action: Select the policy team members.

Step 6: Establish Principles for Public Policy and Civic Participation

Public policy principles are the rules of engagement for foundation activity in the policymaking and civic arenas. They are criteria that govern goal setting, decision making, and implementation with regard to public policy–related grantmaking and program activity. Principles are established either at the full board of trustee level or by a committee of the board (a public policy team or committee). Principles may also be established between an original donor and an advisor in a community foundation to guide how incoming funding requests are evaluated. On a day-to-day basis, principles can help program officers, donor advisors, and managers of public policy efforts align strategy and tactics with core mission-related goals and foundation values. They also can mandate that certain considerations be taken into account when strategy is formulated. Figure 5, Sample Public Policy Principles (page 114), shows some hypothetical examples of principles, their connection to mission and values, and why they might exist.

[30] Strengthening Nonprofit Advocacy Project (SNAP), OMB Watch, Tufts University, Center for Lobbying in the Public Interest (2002), http://www.ombwatch.org/snap.

Figure 5. Sample Public Policy Principles

Jane Doe Foundation (fictional foundation) Public Policy Principles	Rationale to align public policy activities with the foundation's mission and values
Mission statement: The mission of the Jane Doe Foundation is to raise the educational achievement of girls attending public schools. Our philanthropic goal is to make high-quality tutoring widely available to girls in schools throughout St. Paul.	
Principle (as a means of reaching the higher educational achievement by girls in the mission statement): The Jane Doe Foundation's public policy involvement will aim to strengthen the availability and quality of tutoring for girls in schools. (An assumption is made that availability and quality are necessary factors for higher achievement, as the mission calls for.)	**Rationale:** By establishing this principle, those who will plan public policy activities at the Jane Doe Foundation know that every strategy, tactic, or activity they undertake to shape public policy must connect to strengthening the availability and quality of tutoring for girls in schools and thereby raise achievement of girls in public schools.
Values statement: The Jane Doe Foundation values state that youth have a fundamental right to quality education.	
Principles: 1) The Jane Doe Foundation will oppose efforts that undermine the right to education and support efforts that advance the idea that education is a fundamental right. (Again, an assumption is made that higher educational achievement by girls cannot be reached unless all have the opportunity for equal education.) 2) The Foundation also stands for access to quality education. Therefore, the Foundation will engage in philanthropy and advocacy to achieve this goal.	**Rationales:** 1) Foundation public policy planners will have to assess how their specific efforts in the policy arena are consistent with this principle. 2) This second principle creates a mandate to devote some programmatic and public policy efforts toward access to quality education.
Principle: All proposals from prospective grantees and Foundation program plans that call for involvement in the public policy process must be approved by the Public Policy Committee.	**Rationale:** This principle establishes clear authority for decision making. Also, by having a group of people in charge of making the final decision, it takes pressure off of any one person to approve or oppose a certain proposal or program.
Principle: The legality of all grantee proposals and Foundation program activities that relate to public policy will be explained in writing to the Public Policy Committee in consideration for approval.	**Rationale:** This principle sets out another procedure to help avoid risk. (Note that it is helpful to be able to consult an attorney knowledgeable about foundation advocacy activities.)
Principle: The empowerment of youth and especially girls in schools to participate in public policy activities carried out by grantees and the foundation is an important consideration in the approval of proposals and use of foundation resources.	**Rationale:** This principle encourages program officers who receive public policy–related proposals and grantees to make efforts to include the main constituency of the Foundation in planned public policy activities.
Principle: The Jane Doe Foundation recognizes that participation in democratic processes including public policymaking is a right and a responsibility.	**Rationale:** This recognition sends a clear signal to all who work and volunteer for the Foundation that civic participation is vital to how the Foundation will function.

Caution: Public policy principles should not be drafted so specifically that they have to be reshaped for every new situation that arises. Conversely, they should also not be so general that any decision can be rationally related to a principle. They should be designed in a manner that aids in setting specific criteria for determining what kinds of proposals and potential activities are consistent with foundation beliefs and how it wants to conduct philanthropy. In essence, public policy principles should help influence the establishment of grant guidelines.

Knowing your foundation's boundaries for public policy work as well as the authority, decision-making structure, and process will enable you to be absolutely clear in dealings with prospective grantees and partner organizations.

Action: Discuss and set principles.

Step 7: Use Collaborations, Partnerships, and Other Resources

Influencing public policy is not, by nature, an isolated act. In fact, policy work particularly lends itself to working with others—through collaborations, partnerships, and resource and information sharing. Whether a foundation seeks to access "how-to" information or subject matter expertise, leverage resources, or increase visibility, a foundation interested in public policy can seek resources from established service providers, join coalitions working on a particular policy issue, establish formal or informal networks, or enter into many other creative arrangements to reach the foundation's goals.

Collaborations come in many forms, ranging from formal organizations with their own corporate status, formal membership, and paid staff to informal volunteer-driven groups that may come together to address one particular issue. The composition of collaborative groups may also vary greatly. For some policy issues, a collaboration of funders may be most effective. Others funders might find that a working group of foundations and other organizations, including government, produces the knowledge, labor, creativity, and power needed.

Sampling of Potential Partners

- Local, state, or federal government agencies or officials
- Other funders
- Community or issue leaders
- Grantees
- Service providers

Grantmakers and grantseekers can also be collaborators in the policy process. As described in examples in Chapter 5 and Appendix B, foundations collaborate with nonprofits when they make grants to directly or indirectly support public policy participation and civic action. Indeed, some foundations find that they can maximize resources by serving as a broker or sponsor of a coalition of grantee nonprofits.

There are many resources available for developing effective collaborations and partnerships. (See the set of practical books on collaboration published by Fieldstone Alliance.) Sometimes collaborations for public policy work produce particular challenges and opportunities. Challenges for collaborations for policy work include defining common goals and similar, or complementary, strategies and styles for reaching those goals. As discussed throughout this book, funders have different perspectives on their roles in policy work. While some may be actively involved in taking a side and speaking publicly about it, others may take the position that the role of a funder is to be a neutral convener or educator. Developing shared goals or ways to mediate the differences can be challenging. Despite the challenges with working with others, strategic partnerships and collaborations have certain tangible benefits that are well worth weighing against the challenges of setting goals and sharing resources. Working with others can

- *Provide political cover*. Political cover helps deflect criticism and potential negative impact of actions when working on policy issues. As a foundation participating in a collaboration, your role may be to provide political cover, or the group may provide political cover for the foundation. For example, as a funder you may be interested in the issue of funding for education, but you do not want to take a position for or against a related, but separate, teacher pay issue. If the collaboration collectively decides to not address the separate teacher pay issue, the foundation may be less vulnerable to pressure from government to weigh in as a trade-off for government support for education funding.

Alternatively, a foundation could participate in a regional or national association of grantmakers to ensure issues impacting the philanthropic sector are addressed. The foundation has an impact on the actions of the larger organization's agenda while at the same time limiting its individual exposure to actual or perceived political risks. For example, the Council on Foundations works to maintain a legal system that encourages formal philanthropy and charitable giving by individuals. An individual foundation could help shape the Council's position on the issue of what administrative expenses should count as private foundations' qualifying distributions while still choosing not to directly advocate on the issue as an individual foundation. Working with others in these ways would enhance the dialogue on issues while limiting a foundation's exposure to criticism on the issue.

The foundation may also serve as the provider of political cover. For example, a private foundation may serve as the voice of a coalition criticizing the state board of education's requirement of abstinence-only sex education for public school students in order to provide political cover for its coalition partners that fear the act of challenging the state's position may harm their future stream of state funding. By becoming a powerful voice early on in a policy debate, a foundation can give other groups space to advocate.

- *Maximize networks.* Policy change is not often brought about through the isolated acts of one individual or organization. Bringing stakeholders together inherently expands the networks and resources available to bring to bear on an issue.

- *Leverage resources.* Because limited resources are available to address policy issues, working with others formally or informally allows organizations not only to limit the duplication of efforts, but to use resources efficiently by capitalizing on different partners' strengths and resources. Imagine a community addressing the issue of continued pollution. One local environmental nonprofit

> **Sampling of Organizational Resources for Funders**
>
> - *General:* Council on Foundations, Independent Sector, Association of Small Foundations
>
> - *Legal:* Alliance for Justice, Center for Lobbying in the Public Interest
>
> - *How to Participate:* Center for Lobbying in the Public Interest
>
> - *Issue Based:* Associations of Foundations, Affinity Groups of the Council on Foundations
>
> - *Geographic Based:* Regional Associations of Grantmakers
>
> (See Appendix C for contact information)

may be very successful at organizing grassroots support for policy change while another partner may have expertise developing effective media relations. Perhaps the grantmaker has a good relationship with policymakers and can share the coalition's research with them. By coordinating the activities, the groups can leverage their individual resources and skills for maximum impact.

Assessing how to effectively use networks, partnerships, and collaborations

When should a foundation lead an effort and when should it follow? When should it serve solely as a funder and when should it also be an active participant? A foundation's role in collaboratives, partnerships, or other joint efforts frequently will vary according to the topic, the type of collaboration, the assets and skills of the foundation, the importance of the issue to the foundation, and many other factors. Some of the questions to address before proceeding include

- Is there an existing network or group that is addressing this issue, or is there a need to establish a new mechanism for collective action?
- What are the assets that the foundation has to contribute? Some assets to consider include:
  - *Subject area expertise* that the foundation may have developed from its own research or staff
  - *Time,* including staff time to lend to support the group
  - *Funds* to grant directly to the group or to use to help leverage other resources
  - *Connections* to policymakers, media, and other organizations or influential individuals
  - *Organizational capacity* to serve in roles such as the fiscal sponsor or facilitator
  - *Physical resources* such as meeting space or other office resources
- What is the foundation's level of interest in the subject? Is the issue at the core of the mission of the foundation or important to the community the foundation serves?
- What types of risk or political capital is the foundation willing to use on this issue? Is the foundation concerned about the impact of the issue on

its image as a neutral player or the potential impact on future fundraising in a community? Is this an issue where the foundation is interested in putting its connections and resources to use?

- What are the foundation's goals for its involvement in the collaboration? Is the goal to achieve a specific result or to bring together interested parties to achieve the best solution to a problem?

By considering these questions, funders can enter into relationships that are more likely to effectively reach the foundation's goals—whatever those goals may be.

Using foundation power wisely

Particularly when working with others on a policy issue, an important final consideration is how the foundation can use its position in the community effectively. Being a grantmaker often comes with inherent power, including the power to bring individuals and others to the discussion table. The foundation can also provide a gateway for grantees and others to access policymakers, the media, and other influential individuals. For example, the Robert Wood Johnson Foundation's Connect project involves foundation staff linking grantee community health organizations to members of Congress.[31] The Foundation's access to legislators and ability to organize meetings with them are ways in which it uses its power and influence to provide access and opportunities for its grantees.

> ### Research Shows Funding Consistency Critical
>
> Consistency in funding is important to public policy success. Nonprofits throughout the country report that a lack of consistency in funding by foundations for multiyear efforts to shape policy makes it difficult for nonprofits to build and sustain sufficient power long enough to succeed at making important public policy changes.*
>
> * Gary D. Bass, David F. Arons, Kay Guinane, and Matthew Carter, *Seen But Not Heard: Strengthening Nonprofit Advocacy* (Washington, DC: Aspen Institute, 2007).

Funders also exercise power when establishing and implementing their grantmaking priorities. For example, making grants available for special projects and for direct services may have a different impact than making discretionary grants that allow for a variety of strategies to address an issue. In essence, the way a foundation chooses to allocate its grant dollars may impact the ways in which the community responds to issues. For example, The California Wellness Foundation found that "core operating support grants have provided clinics and consortia the ability to become more strategic about how they

---

[31] For more information about Robert Wood Johnson Foundation's Connect project, visit http//www.rwjf.org/publications/connect/index.jhtml.

tackle the challenges they face and craft their own solutions to enhance their effectiveness." [32]

Foundations do not have to work in isolation to accomplish their policy goals. They have assets to bring to bear on an issue and can simultaneously benefit from the assets of other organizations. By recognizing and effectively using those assets and power, foundations can enhance their work in achieving desired policy outcomes.

Finally, it is helpful for foundations to have an understanding of those factors that are internal to grantee nonprofits (e.g. inside the organization) and external (e.g. the funding environment) that influence nonprofits' participation in the public policy process. Knowing more about what influences grantee nonprofits *before* sponsoring their involvement in the public policy process will help foundations ask better questions about capacity, organizational preparedness, and other factors that might affect their work.

Understanding nonprofits' participation in public policy

Grantmaking to nonprofits that engage in public policy advocacy or become involved in civic issues more broadly is probably the most common foundation policy-related activity. As more foundations consider such policy activities, it is important for foundations to have a sense of some of the factors that motivate and deter nonprofits' policy participation.

According to the Strengthening Nonprofit Advocacy Project (SNAP) survey of over 1,700 charities around the country, 46 percent of responding charities said they never influence government but, at the same time, reported that they do either lobby or testify before government. [33] This finding suggests that many organizations do not consider their work as influencing government decision making even as they identify themselves as an organization that advocates on specific legislation. Why this disconnect? One explanation is

---

[32] Ruth Holton, "Reflections on the Safety Net: A Case for Core Support," September 2003, http://www.tcwf.org/pdf_docs/reflections/sept2003.pdf.

[33] The Strengthening Nonprofit Advocacy Project (SNAP) investigated the frequency and nature of several forms of 501(c)(3) public charity participation in the public policymaking process and examined factors that influence their decisions whether to participate. The survey research included responses from over 1,700 501(c)(3) organizations and excluded hospitals, universities, and religious organizations. The study was conducted by Tufts University, OMB Watch, and the Center for Lobbying in the Public Interest (CLPI). Findings may be viewed at http//www.ombwatch.org/snap and in Gary D. Bass, David F. Arons, Kay Guinane, and Matthew Carter, *Seen But Not Heard: Strengthening Nonprofit Advocacy* (Washington, DC: Aspen Institute, 2007).

that nonprofits do not want to be known publicly as "lobbying" organizations. This behavior relates back to the stigma behind such terms as lobbying but also relates to their self-image as an organization. Some nonprofits downplay their role in public policy because they want to be known for providing effective services, not for pleading with the government. Unfortunately, too many nonprofits do not see their public policy role as a positive and equal activity with charitable service—one that helps to hold government accountable as a partner with the nonprofit sector and that works with government to use taxpayer dollars wisely in providing services to the public.

Barriers to nonprofit public policy participation

The SNAP research asked charities to rank several commonly reported barriers to public policy participation as they applied to their own organization. Figure 6, Barriers to Participation, shows how respondents ranked each aspect.[34]

Figure 6. Barriers to Participation _____

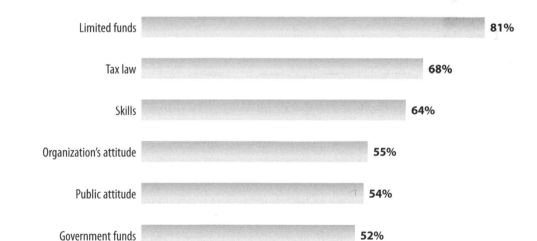

Limited funds	81%
Tax law	68%
Skills	64%
Organization's attitude	55%
Public attitude	54%
Government funds	52%
Attorneys or accountants	51%

Percentage of respondents who name this factor as a barrier

[34] Ibid.

Foundations can play an immediate and lasting role in helping nonprofits to overcome the number one barrier to public policy participation: money. They can also aid with the second and third highest barriers by helping nonprofits connect to advocacy law educational organizations, including the Alliance for Justice and the Center for Lobbying in the Public Interest. Foundations may also provide grants so that grantees can acquire the training they need. These resource organizations have developed tools designed to help nonprofits develop staff and board skills and to overcome many of the barriers to participation.

Well worth mentioning is how the influence of government funding affects nonprofits' public policy behavior. The SNAP data show that as the percentage of a nonprofit's funding from government increases, so does its fear of government retribution for criticizing government as part of a public policy effort. Simply put, nonprofits don't want to bite the hand that feeds. Foundations can help out by encouraging nonprofits to conduct their public policy work (and specifically, lobbying work) within coalitions and associations that can provide political cover.

The influence of foundations

There are at least four comments commonly made by nonprofits about foundations' influence on public policy participation. The first is that foundations don't care that much about advocacy and public policy work. Second, foundations often use language in their grant letters that unnecessarily restricts them from engaging in public policy. (See Appendix A for sample grant letter language.) Third, foundations wait until there is a crisis before they fund nonprofits to engage in policy advocacy. For example, some nonprofits report that foundations wait until there are massive government budget cuts before funding advocacy groups to fight to restore program funding. Fourth, foundations change their program interests too frequently and are not consistent in their support for public policy initiatives, which take more time than direct service programs to show results (as mentioned earlier in this book). These comments are based on the focus groups and interviews from the Strengthening Nonprofit Advocacy Project.[35]

---

[35] The SNAP project included focus groups with executive directors and board members of charitable organizations that were grouped by level and sophistication of their advocacy on policy matters.

Motivating forces for public policy participation

Drawing again on the SNAP data on nonprofits, organizational mission is reported as the top reason most nonprofits get involved in public policy. This is good news; if a nonprofit sees that its goals can be reached by influencing policymaking, then its frequency of participation may be increased. Of course, this assumes that one or more barriers do not counteract or undermine the connection between mission or values and policy or civic engagement. One of the many ways in which foundations can build the capacity of nonprofits for successful public policy is to help identify ways in which their mission and values may be realized by participating in policymaking, and also by strengthening citizen participation on public issues. This kind of capacity building also offers foundations a low-risk way of expanding the human, civic, and financial resources aimed at achieving their goals. Figure 7, Incentives to Participation, shows the factors that motivate nonprofits.

Figure 7. Incentives to Participation _____

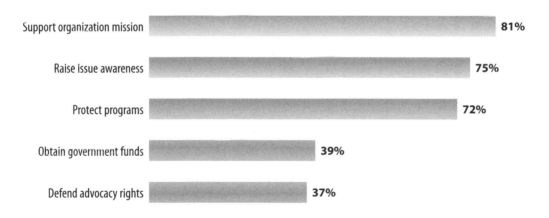

Percentage of respondents who name this factor as an incentive

In general, foundations should know that there are combinations of incentives and barriers that affect charities' willingness to get involved in public policy, and that foundations themselves can play both a motivational as well as deterring role. As your foundation thinks through how it wants to be involved in a certain policy issue, invite opinion from nonprofit leaders about what motivates their participation and what challenges their commitment to sustained public policy initiatives. Few organizations do public policy shaping work alone. Developing a nuanced understanding of how other organizations approach policy is another way that foundations may prepare for policy activity. Knowledge of what motivates and deters public policy participation among nonprofits will aid a foundation in prioritizing what issues it commits to. After all, a foundation would want to be able to invest with some certainty that the grantee is committed and ready to act.

Actions: Address the questions posed in this step. Determine what networks and coalitions are available to your foundation and which groups are addressing issues allied with your mission. Find out what prevents and facilitates grantees' policy actions. Talk with your constituents and allies in order to develop a nuanced picture of the current policy environment and ways you might participate.

Step 8: Prioritize Issues

Most foundations and nonprofits have many interests that all relate to a core mission or overarching purpose. Several likely products of the first seven steps include

- A list of important public policy issues
- A greater understanding of the potential for foundation involvement in the policymaking and civic processes
- Ideas about the possible roles the foundation and individuals within the foundation can play
- New awareness about factors that influence grantees' policy participation

The next step is to prioritize the issues the foundation is going to work on. Following are several factors a foundation might want to consider:

- *The needs of people served as a result of foundation philanthropy.* Is this a policy matter born out of a crisis? For example, advocating for government funding for victims of hurricane Katrina became a number one priority for many organizations. Possible closures of human service organizations due to state fiscal crises is another type of crisis. It is easy for nonprofits to argue that there is always a crisis. When setting priorities it is important to weigh the importance of policy efforts that aim to make long-term change versus provide short-term relief.

- *Political climate.* How fertile is the political and policymaking environment for the change the foundation seeks? How do the issues that are important to your foundation relate to the chief concerns of those in decision-making positions in government? How partisan in nature are the issues your foundation believes to be at the top of the priority list? Unless a legislature is dominated by one party, it can be difficult to enact a legislative proposal without securing bipartisan champions. If the issue you are working on is in the executive branch, then be aware that even if a career government agency official supports your cause, final decisions on policy are often made by appointed officials who will consider the politics surrounding the issue.

- *The capacity of partner organizations (including grantees) to be effective advocates.* Even if the issue your foundation has chosen to be a top priority is also a relatively high concern among elected and appointed policymakers, are other stakeholder groups prepared for effective advocacy? If the answer is no, then the priority level of the issue for the foundation might be lowered until advocates are ready. Note: Several organizations that provide training are listed as resources in Appendix C.

- *Trustee support for the issue.* In the public policy realm the stakes are high and reputations are on the line as people and institutions become vocal for changes that affect large numbers of people and communities. Trustees are ultimately responsible for what happens in the life of a foundation. Choosing issues that have a high degree of support among the trustees will increase the likelihood that the foundation will devote adequate resources and commit to the issue over the long term. Unless enacted in reaction to a major crisis, most policy issues take several years to ripen in terms of support by decision makers. For foundations to be successful, they must show stamina for the often uncomfortably long period of time it takes to make policy change. The stamina required must be appreciated and demonstrated at the trustee level.

- *Likelihood of success in a defined period of time.* The time it takes for policy change can seem long for many institutions. Even knowing that stamina is required, the foundation should factor in whether success can be achieved, in some form, in a reasonable period of time. What is reasonable might depend on the foundation's assessment of how long the window of political opportunity is open. It also might depend on competing priorities within the foundation. Success also includes small victories along a path to change. For example, building a diverse coalition to work with is a success in itself.

Action: Determine your foundation's priorities for public policy change in light of the considerations discussed.

Step 9: Build a Strategy

Few public policy strategies are developed fully by one person. A public policy strategy is almost always a product of a core group of individuals representing organizations working in coalition. A strategy may involve several forms of public policy or civic strengthening activities, or only one form (for example, legislative or research, outlined in Chapter 5). Whether the strategy calls for the use of one or many forms of policy or civic participation, various tactics are employed simultaneously and sequenced to build sufficient power, status, education, motivation, urgency, and mobilization required to trigger change.

How does one know whether a legislative strategy, or a media advocacy strategy, or a research strategy, or some combination of any of the eleven forms of participation described in Chapter 5, is needed? Once strategies are chosen, how are individual tactics selected? The answer to this questions is more art than science. Knowing which tactics to use, when to use them, and how to deploy them is gained from experience working in the public policy process at each level of government. Policy advocates differ. Federal level lobbyists do not always have experiences that immediately translate to the state or local level and vice versa. Some advocates are far more experienced than others in navigating executive branch agencies, but may not know the first thing about building media support for a public interest issue. The inevitable gaps in policy experience are another reason why an effective public policy team includes members that have experiences with different forms of policy and civic participation or at least those with relationships with advocates they may draw upon for advice.

Analysis is key

More often than not, it is grantee nonprofits that will carry out public policy activities. It is prudent for foundations considering public policy grant applications to evaluate whether the grant applicant has considered the following questions: What do we want to change? Why? How will altering public policy help our cause? What methods of policy or civic engagement seem to be appropriate as action for change strategies? Why these strategies? Many nonprofits with experience in public policy have particular strengthens in one or two types of policy shaping activity, including legislative branch or local organizing. Recognizing that influencing public policy often takes years and potentially several strategies, foundations can have more realistic expectations if grantees provide a reasonable explanation of how they plan to effect policy change.

Fundamental questions in building a strategy

There are several core questions that are helpful to answer in advance to determine what strategies and subsequently what tactics to use as part of a strategy:

- What governmental procedures are necessary to make the desired changes in laws, rules, or policy?
- What kind of organizing, positioning of the message, and building power are necessary to effect policy change?

- What is needed to motivate decision makers in the policymaking process or other community building processes to make the change?

- What opportunities for change presently exist? Are there issues or public priorities championed by others that could be coordinated with your policy goals? This question substantively relates to understanding the political environment and assessing whether the foundation's top policy issue is also a matter of concern to policymakers and to the community.

Figure 8, Strategy Choice Process, is designed to help connect the goal of your policy change effort with targeted decision makers and consequently the types of strategies and tactics your foundation or grantee nonprofits might use to influence them.

Once one or more strategies are selected, it is time to choose and choreograph tactics. Again, you will come to rely on advocates who have experience with each type of public policy activity to determine tactics, timing, players needed, message, and resources required. Following is an example of a strategy at the state level.

The (fictitious) Jane Doe Foundation realizes that there is a small but significant stream of state government funding that school districts may apply for to help pay for school-based tutoring programs. The Foundation learns that the governor's proposed budget would eliminate this funding stream to help meet the state requirement for a balanced budget. The Foundation's public policy team decides to reach out to and work with interested nonprofits and community foundations to form a coalition of groups concerned about youth and public school education. The defense of the tutoring program funds becomes a high priority for the coalition during the legislative session. The coalition decides it needs a three-part strategy:

- Organize and mobilize students, parents, and teachers to lobby the legislature to urge preservation of the tutoring funds.

- Educate and urge the media to report on the potential impact of cuts to the tutoring program on youth school achievement.

- Provide research that demonstrates the effect of tutoring on educational achievement to the legislature and illustrates what would be lost in educational achievement without the funding.

Figure 8.   Strategy Choice Process

If the opportunity for change sought requires…	…then the following decision makers should be influenced…	…using the following strategies…	…that may employ the following tactics.
Change in law (also increase or decrease in government budget)	Legislative branch and executive branch	• Lobbying • Media advocacy • Organizing and mobilizing grassroots groups • Fiscal policy research	• Nonprofit coalition hires lobbyist • Foundation supports a public awareness campaign about the impact of budget cuts on human needs • Foundation produces a cost/benefit analysis of the policy proposal • Citizens affected by the legislation are mobilized to serve as leaders and spokespersons
Change to rules or procedures by executive branch agency (e.g. Department of Health and Human Services)	Executive branch	• Administrative advocacy • Organizing and mobilizing grassroots groups • Judicial advocacy (including participation in an agency adjudication)	• Foundation convenes government officials and nonprofits for a conversation regarding proposed rule changes • Foundation supports a petition effort to urge change in agency rules • Foundation funds a legal effort to challenge agency rulemaking through a courtlike proceeding
Challenge to government authority to make a public policy decision	Judicial branch and executive branch	• Litigation	• Foundation supports nonprofit challenge to rulemaking • Foundation funds litigation • Foundation files an amicus brief to support a party to litigation
Change to the level of participation of a community in a civic process (e.g. neighborhood councils, voting, PTA)	Public at large and citizen leaders	• Public education • Media advocacy	• Foundation funds a civic education program by a nonprofit that aims to reach goals (funding public, educational, and governmental cable access television is an example) • Foundation conducts its own direct appeal to the public to participate in nonpartisan activities including attending and speaking at open meetings • Foundation supports emerging neighborhood groups that may not be nonprofits but are able to reach out to the community
New information about the nature of a problem or its impact	Executive branch and legislative branch	• Research	• Foundation commissions a study • Foundation organizes a group to examine a public issue

At this point the Jane Doe Foundation makes a general operating support grant to the organization serving as the fiscal agent of the coalition so member organizations can devote more time to the coalition and acquire general public policy training. Then the Foundation convenes a breakfast for members of the legislative and executive branch to discuss the value of tutoring to educational achievement in a general policy sense, but the foundation is careful not to take a specific position on the a proposed budget bill. Soon thereafter, the education committee of the legislature holds a hearing on tutoring in public schools and invites the Jane Doe Foundation (in writing) to testify about the issue and to make policy recommendations. The Foundation testifies, making use of the exception to the restrictions on foundation direct lobbying. (Note that if this were the Jane Doe *Community* Foundation, it could lobby like any other public charity, as you will learn in Chapter 9.)

Participants in the coalition that are not private foundations will focus on all of the strategies, including lobbying and media advocacy. The Foundation may continue to participate with the coalition to produce nonpartisan analysis and research that refers to, and even argues for or against, specific legislation and is distributed to all members of the legislature, but does not contain any call to action for others to lobby the legislature. (Again, see Chapter 9 for the exceptions to lobbying.) Tactics for defending the tutoring funds might include

- Hiring a former legislator or staff person to play the "inside game" of lobbying key budget committee members of the legislature
- Developing and placing print and radio ads to inform parents that their child's tutoring program might be cut from the state budget
- Helping students develop their own organizing effort to involve students and speak to policymakers in person, via blogs, e-mail, or preferred web sites such as www.MySpace.com
- Organizing a Capitol Hill rally of students, parents, and teachers for the tutoring program
- Presenting scholarly research demonstrating the connection between tutoring and test scores by testifying before a legislative committee

- Holding an award dinner for legislators who are champions for the tutoring funding
- Working with agency staff to reserve a portion of their budget for the tutoring program
- Encouraging corporations to invest in education of the communities they reside in by supporting the tutoring program and advocating for government to continue its role as a partner in support of after-school tutoring

There are many more possible tactics that might be added to this list. Depending on the type of change needed, the policymakers involved, and the strategies chosen, there will be different tactics selected. For example, in public interest litigation, tactical decisions involve whether or not to go to trial, the types of discovery tactics, and, once at trial, the types of expert witnesses to bring. Foundations are not restricted to serving as silent benefactors that have to hide in the shadows. That said, it is important to be conscious and strategic about the political risk that public policy issues and strategies might bring to the foundation and other institutions that are primary players in the process.

Action: Set out strategies and tactics.

Step 10: Determine Political Risk

Almost every foundation's nightmare would be to have a headline in their local paper (or worse, the *New York Times*) that reads "Foundation funds used for illegal political purposes" or "Foundation found to have violated lobbying law." Legal risk can be better ascertained by securing the services of a lawyer who has specific knowledge and training in the lobbying and election-related activities of tax-exempt organizations. In Chapter 9, Lloyd H. Mayer, Esq. addresses this topic more fully, but it is important to know that the more foundations become proficient in understanding the legal rules of public policy and electoral participation, the more they will be able to determine how aggressive they want to be.

Determining political risk involves more than legal questions. It involves public perception and asking questions about the inherent trade-offs that take place by engaging in specific policy shaping tactics on priority policy issues. Some foundations have stated that they are powerful in their communities because of political neutrality and the ability to bring all sides of an issue together. This type of statement presents a powerful reason to avoid the appearance of taking sides on policy matters. But policy participation does not always result in a trade-off of credibility or moral authority for policy success. So long as the foundation or any institution advocates its position with sound information, a legitimate constituency, and reasonable ideas to add to the public debate, then it will likely maintain credibility in the court of public opinion. Among the best people a foundation can turn to for advice about political risk include grantees and experienced political advisors, other foundations that are active in public policy in their own state or city, local newspaper editorial board members (off the record, of course), leading associations including the Forum of Regional Associations of Grantmakers, the Council on Foundations, the National Committee for Responsive Philanthropy, and, possibly, political science professors acquainted with local politics or the issues the foundation is exploring.

The questions that follow will help foundations assess possible political risks associated with their choices.

Foundation political risk assessment questions

1. Does the issue matter to our foundation?

2. If we speak out or engage in policy shaping strategies on a specific issue, who will notice and what will be their reactions?

3. What will be the short-term, mid-range, and long-term consequences of our activities?

4. What concerns do we have about the possible reactions of government officials, donors, media, businesses, grantees, other grantmakers, other constituents, and the public?

5. Is the opportunity to get involved and make a difference worth the potential negative consequences we have anticipated?

6. Have we consulted with all available and appropriate advisors to avoid blind spots?

7. Recognizing any possible challenges, retribution, or other negative consequences, is our participation in this policy debate simply the right thing to do because of what we believe as a foundation? *Remember to connect the policy goal with mission and values to determine alignment.*

8. Can we effectively explain the relationship between our policy actions and our core mission, values, and programs?

9. Have we established clear lines of authority for decisions made within our foundation regarding public policy?

10. Do we have a process in place for dealing with an attack on foundation public policy actions from government, media, or others?

✓ *Action*: Assess the political risk of overall involvement and for each strategy selected. See also the risk assessment checklist in Chapter 8.

Step 11: Allocate Resources

Allocating resources for public policy requires planning for the known and the unknown. Some public policy initiatives are planned for years and then take even more time to realize outcomes. Other public policy issues are annual in nature with heightened activity during the legislative cycle (budgets and appropriations) and electoral activity. Still other activities arise due to unplanned crisis such as the September 11 attack in 2001 or Hurricane Katrina in the Southeast in 2005. Allocating discretionary funding for public policy provides a foundation the opportunity to plan ahead and ensure resources will be ready for inevitable needs.

The allocation of funding for public policy–related grantmaking may be done in two ways: first, by dedicating a portion of each portfolio for public policy–related grants, and second, by dedicating a portion of the foundation's general operating budget for public policy activities.

Managers of donor-advised funds can educate donors of the opportunity and merits of dedicating a portion of the annual payout of grants to be devoted to public policy and civic action by nonprofits that address the donor's intended cause. Community foundations new to public policy–related grantmaking should consult with community foundations that are experienced, including The Boston Foundation and Dade Community Foundation.

✓ *Action:* Establish a general public policy budget for the foundation to advocate as an institution and dedicate a portion of the budget for individual grantmaking areas to be available for public policy and civic initiatives that further philanthropic and grantee goals.

Step 12: Execute and Chronicle Strategy

By the time a foundation has reached Step 12, public policy efforts should be underway. If they are not, then it is now time to begin. Just to review, beginning to engage in public policy or civic activities doesn't necessarily mean jumping to tactics such as sponsoring paid media ads to advance an issue. Rather, it starts with preparation and the will to just get started. Developing internal foundation awareness, learning the public policy process, assigning roles, establishing internal guidelines, developing partnerships, and identifying and choosing strategies and tactics are all steps that may be precursors to action or concurrent with incrementally increasing involvement. It is worth underscoring the importance of either having a person on staff or on the board who understands the public policymaking and other civic processes at your foundation's levels of focus: local, state, national, or international. The foundation can also accomplish this by identifying a person in a partner organization who can serve as a resource to help the foundation formulate its plan.

Chronicling the work

If your foundation is engaging in public policy or civic activity for the first time or is engaging in more substantial activity than ever before, it is important to chronicle your work. Chronicling public policy work means the following:

• *Recordkeeping.* Maintain files of all minutes of committee and board decisions related to public policy activity and grants and grant-related decisions that involve public policy. The importance of recordkeeping is twofold. First, it helps future generations of foundation leaders understand what decisions were made and the considerations for them. Second, in the event of an audit, it is important to be able to show a paper trail that the foundation was making careful, legal decisions.

- *Storytelling.* Write a narrative of your foundation's story in the public policy arena. A narrative, or longer story of the issue and the foundation's role, will help future generations of foundation leaders understand what occurred. It could be helpful and informative for other foundations learning about public policy and civic participation. Your narrative can help the foundation world.

- *Evaluating.* Decide what resources and staff are available for evaluation. If funding allows, a full-scale evaluation can help you determine the effectiveness of your actions relative to your goals and improve both for future efficiencies. (Chapter 10 focuses on evalaution.)

Action: Implement, chronicle, and evaluate.

Conclusion

We hope the steps presented in this chapter will help you prepare your foundation for public policy and civic activity. They are by no means the only way to get started. Furthermore, so long as you obey the law and the rules of your organization there is no one "right" way to do any of the strategies discussed in this chapter. Bob Smucker, former vice president of government relations at Independent Sector and founder of the Center for Lobbying in the Public Interest, observes that "there are as many ways to lobby as there are people who lobby." This statement holds true for all forms of public policy advocacy and civic engagement.

The key points to remember, however, are that alignment between mission and action is absolutely critical and that preparing the foundation internally is essential to sustaining policy participation long enough to realize the rewards. There are many resources available to foundations to help in planning and in implementation of policy related activities. However, because there are so many resources, it is important to be precise in choosing the kind of assistance that is needed. Finally, like all business ventures, public policy involves some risk, but it can be managed through careful planning, establishing a clear chain of command, and using legal counsel experienced with advocacy.

Public policy activity presents an exciting opportunity to engage staff, board, and external partners in new ways and with new purpose. With so many roles one could play, public policy work presents leadership opportunities to advance your mission and help people and causes.

Chapter Seven

Private Foundations:
Encouraging Support for Advocacy

Cynthia M. Gibson, PhD, and Geri Mannion

Voting rights. Campaign finance reform. Welfare reform. Civil rights. Better housing. Access to quality health care. Improving public schools.

What do all of these issues have in common? They (along with many similar issues) have been championed, at least in some part, by organizations supported by foundations that recognized the importance of providing funds for advocacy. Unfortunately, the number of foundations engaged in this work continues to be relatively small.

Although foundations may conduct a wide range of public policy activities (discussed in Chapters 5 and 6), many foundations continue to view these activities as "red flags" and simply refuse to fund anything that smacks of advocacy, even if a nonprofit organization has a stellar record of achievement.

This lack of awareness about what advocacy is and how it can leverage grantmakers' investments, as well as the work of the nonprofits they fund, hurts both funders and their grantees. A 2002 national study, for example, found that the frequency of nonprofit public policy participation is quite low. Consequently, the lack of action by the nonprofit sector stifles what could be a powerful industry in addressing some of the complex problems of our time.[36] It is, after all, often through strategic advocacy

CHAPTER SNAPSHOT

This chapter discusses the following:

- How funding advocacy and public policy participation leverages foundation investments

- Successful strategies used at Carnegie Corporation for encouraging better public policies

- How to encourage funders to embrace public policy–related grantmaking

- How nonprofits can urge foundation support for public policy

- How to incorporate advocacy and public policy funding into grantmaking programs

- The importance of foundation and nonprofit leaders working together

---

[36] OMB Watch, Tufts University, and Center for Lobbying in the Public Interest, "Overview of Findings of Strengthening Nonprofit Advocacy Project," May 2002, http://www.ombwatch.org/snap.

and civic/voter engagement activities that policymakers, the public, business leaders, and others learn about community problems and enact solutions. And after all, many corporations use lobbyists at local, state, and federal levels to advance their agendas. Unlike many in the for-profit business community, most nonprofits do not use all of the available legal freedom they have to shape public policy.

How Funding Advocacy Leverages Investments

A fact that usually elicits surprise when mentioned during public discussions about the nonprofit sector is that foundation and corporate funding constitute only about 10 to 13 percent of support provided to nonprofits.[37] Earned income, individual donations (not counting volunteer time), and government support comprise the rest. Government support is especially important today as nonprofits are shouldering more responsibility for providing an array of human, social, housing, education, and health care services that were once part of the federal social safety net. Moreover, since 1996, welfare reform legislation and other public policies have shifted to local and state governments. Learning how to advocate for regulations, laws, and funding streams that will benefit their constituencies is, therefore, no longer a luxury for nonprofits.

Two public policy strategies at the Carnegie Corporation that have leveraged philanthropic investment for greater public policy benefit are *convening* and *research*.

It is essential for their survival and the survival of those they serve. Foundations that ignore this fact risk lessening the impact of their investments, and, in turn, the potential of solving the problems they are attempting to address through those investments.

So if advocacy is no longer optional for the nonprofit sector, including the foundation world, what approaches to policy participation seem to work?

---

[37] According to the National Center for Charitable Statistics, in 2000, individuals were the main source of income for all nonprofits ($152.07 billion or 75 percent of all revenues), with foundation revenue comprising a mere 12 percent (or $24.5 billion) of all nonprofit revenue sources. Source: National Center for Charitable Statistics (2004). *Note:* Foundations appear as 11.6 percent of estimated total giving to charities in 2004 on page 18 of *Giving USA 2005* (Giving USA Foundation, AAFRC, Glenview, IL). This chapter distinguishes donated revenues from all revenues. As a percentage of all revenues that come to charities including fee income and other streams, foundation donations as a type of revenue might be around 2 percent. See also http://nccsdataweb.urban.org/FAQ/fDetail.php?category=48&itemID=409#finance.

Two public policy strategies at the Carnegie Corporation that have leveraged philanthropic investment for greater public policy benefit are *convening* and *research*.

Evenhanded convening pays dividends

As one of the oldest private foundations in the nation, the Carnegie Corporation also has understood that grantmaking dollars can be leveraged through the support of organizations engaged in research, public education and dissemination, and public policy advocacy activities. This emphasis is particularly effective when foundations have limited grantmaking funds at their disposal and have to leverage them as much as possible. We have found that one of the best ways to do this is to support organizations engaged in advocacy around the issues on which the Carnegie Corporation has focused. We could, for example, fund every literacy program in the country, or we could support organizations working to advocate for education policies that will make it a requirement that all public schools in the country have such programs in place. The latter is a strategy that, arguably, will be less expensive and is likely to result in more systemic change than the former.

In addition to grantmaking, serving as a concerned, evenhanded broker and convener of politically disparate groups can be one of the most valuable roles foundations play in the public policymaking process. Although the Carnegie Corporation can point to several specific examples of how advocacy and public education strategies, coupled with research, analysis and a communications strategy, have been successful in advancing its goals, there are a few that stand out. The Carnegie Corporation's support since the early 1980s of the Aspen Institute's congressional forums on U.S. relations with the former Soviet Union brought together small bipartisan groups of members of Congress to discuss foreign policy issues in a "safe space"—outside Washington, DC and with no news media present. The Institute's forums on Russia convene experts from the United States and elsewhere to discuss nuclear and biological proliferation, U.S. relations with Russia and the post-Soviet states, and other issues of international security. Under the leadership of Dick Clark, former senator from Iowa, these meetings have led to the development of stronger bipartisan relationships and greater awareness of the region and its implications for the United States. In addition to Aspen, the Carnegie Corporation has supported other bipartisan educational briefings for policymakers on a wide range of issues, among them K-12 public education, science policy, and Africa—issues on which the foundation's programs have focused for years.

Using research to drive policy

The Carnegie Commission on Science, Technology, and Government, launched in 1988, is another example of how the Carnegie Corporation incorporated advocacy and public education. Operating over five years, the commission—which comprised a bipartisan group of former policymakers, corporate leaders, and other experts—issued nineteen reports about the importance of incorporating science and technology into government decision making at all levels. The reports not only summarized particular aspects of issues (science and technology in the states, in the environment, in education, etc.) but also included sets of recommendations for public policy consideration. A comprehensive dissemination process, which included several public policymaker forums in Congress, helped to ensure that many of the commission's recommendations were implemented, including the restoration of the cabinet-level position of science advisor to the President by President George H. W. Bush.

More recently, the Carnegie Corporation has supported research, public education, and advocacy on the need to reinstate civic education in the public schools. That process began with an analysis of the issue that helped to frame several meetings with the nation's top scholars and practitioners focused on building or achieving consensus on what constitutes good civic education. Participants also developed a set of policy recommendations that would help move an agenda to instill this kind of education back into schools across the country. The result was "The Civic Mission of Schools," a report endorsed by all sixty-plus participants in these meetings who represented a wide spectrum of organizations from The Heritage Foundation to the American Federation of Teachers. The report has since become a central framing document for scores of organizations, as well as for numerous national and state conferences, including the White House Conference on History, Civics, and Service; the First Annual Congressional Conference on Civic Education; and the National Conference on Citizenship's 50th Anniversary Meeting. Senator Lamar Alexander cited the report in his maiden Senate floor speech, introducing federal-level legislation in support of school-based civic education. The report is also serving as the launchpad for a new national coalition that will advocate at the federal level for increased funds for civic education, as well as provide seed grants to coalitions advocating for civic education policies at state level.

Two years prior to this work, the Carnegie Corporation made a grant to the North Carolina Civic Education Consortium to position itself as a national model for state-level advocacy and education around civic education. Today, the Consortium has become one of the most effective state-based coalitions working on this issue. It brings together a diverse group of stakeholders to advance a strategic approach toward revitalizing civic education in schools and communities. The Carnegie Corporation also gave the Consortium a grant to develop a statewide Civic Index that measured how much young people and adults know about and practice democracy. The results of that survey not only landed on the front pages of every major newspaper in the state but, three weeks later, was cited by several state legislators as the catalyst for introducing a new civic education bill for the state. Several states have since indicated that they will use the Civic Index as an advocacy tool in their own states.[38]

These examples show how the Carnegie Corporation has employed public policy strategies to effectively realize goals. If this approach is so successful, why aren't more funders involved? Attitudes toward public policy and advocacy involvement play a big role. Following are some ways funders can change attitudes about advocacy to fuel increased involvement.

[38] See http://www.civics.unc.edu/civicindex/index.htm.

How Do We Change Funders' Attitudes Toward Advocacy?

Funders' attitudes can be changed through education, education, and more education. The more foundation staff members, administrators, and trustees know about and understand what advocacy is, what is allowed under IRS guidelines, and how it leverages grantmaking funds, the more likely they will consider supporting and incorporating advocacy as an integral component of all their grantmaking initiatives. Providing concrete examples of how these approaches work and, perhaps more importantly, how they can often be more cost-efficient than funding individual programs, cannot be overemphasized, especially in times of increased attention to outcomes, results, and impact. The grant made to the North Carolina Civic Education Consortium, cited previously, is an excellent example of how a relatively small investment in an advocacy effort resulted in a significant policy change—one that will affect thousands of school-aged children in North Carolina, and perhaps beyond, as other states begin to replicate the Consortium's model.

So, what can foundation staff members and nonprofit leaders who already understand the importance of funding advocacy do? They can

- *Educate reluctant stakeholders.* Invite reluctant foundation staff, board, and trustee members to funder briefings organized by others who are supporting similar issues (especially those with whom they have a prior relationship and whose judgment they trust) that highlight the uses and effects of advocacy around those issues. It is important to work with those hosting the event to ensure that there will be substantive discussion about how advocacy tools have been used successfully by nonprofits—the more concrete examples, the better. Meetings should include stakeholders from different sectors (business, public sector, news media, and so on) to discuss how their own views changed because of the advocacy strategies of the nonprofits engaged in this issue. There should be ample time allowed for those not yet persuaded about the efficacy of advocacy to ask questions and explore concerns.

- *Explain nonprofit lobbying laws.* At the kind of briefing described above—or a separate one—have experts in nonprofit law on hand to conduct a training on the dos and don'ts of funding advocacy and answer funders' questions. Some foundations have found the Regional Associations of Grantmakers to be useful forums to educate board members and staff because of their neutral, member service orientation. There are also a few highly reputable law firms with specific expertise in nonprofit and foundation advocacy law that may be a good fit in terms of substance and style for your foundation.

- *Use personal contact to persuade.* Arrange for colleagues (at either the program, administrative, or board level) working on the same issue (and funding advocacy) to have private conversations with funders reluctant to support advocacy so that the latter will have the chance to reveal the internal impediments to supporting advocacy within that particular foundation. One-on-one conversations often are helpful in giving potential advocacy funders the opportunity to learn from more experienced funders about how to overcome internal barriers.

- *Offer multiple ways to participate.* If funders are unable to support advocacy because of internal policies, discuss whether they might be willing to become involved in funder collaboratives or affinity groups on particular issues (such as environment, housing, or children's issues). Funders who work closely and collaboratively on a particular problem may then be able to divide their collective funds in ways that allow some funders to support advocacy and others to support program-related activities. This way, individual funders are able to fund strategies with which they are more comfortable but still reap the benefits from the overall group's efforts, which may include advocacy. This approach may also lead to changes in each other's grantmaking.

- *Prepare for risks.* Ensure that foundation senior staff members and board members are briefed about potential political or other risks that may develop because of support of a particular organization or project. The more a foundation is prepared at all levels for any public or media reaction to its support, the more likely it will be comfortable in recommending ongoing support for advocacy activities of its grantees.

What Can Nonprofits Do to Encourage More Funders to Support Advocacy?

While a lack of understanding may cause some foundations to shy away from funding advocacy, nonprofits may also suffer from this problem. This can reinforce funders' fears. In addition, some nonprofits may be engaging in advocacy-related activities that are not permitted, or they are unaware of what they can and cannot do, which will only exacerbate funders' reluctance to support advocacy.

Therefore, nonprofits should assess whether they have adequately educated themselves and their board members about what advocacy is, what is allowed, and why they are using these strategies.

Program officers in foundations that want to encourage advocacy can share the following tips with current and potential grantees:

- *Obtain appropriate legal and tax advice.* Even if the executive director or members of the nonprofit's board are lawyers, it is a mistake to assume that they are knowledgeable about nonprofit law. In fact, it has been our experience that some of the biggest mistakes in proposals have been written by lawyers who may have expertise on other legal issues but know little about nonprofit law. The same warning applies in dealing with accountants who have to review these forms and related expenditures.

- *File IRS Form 5768, or the "(h) election form."*[39] This is the form that charities file to elect to come under the expenditure test rules that govern lobbying. The expenditures test allows a public charity to spend up to 20 percent of its exempt purpose expenditures on direct lobbying. Nonprofits should note that this has been done in all proposals sent to funders. This alerts program officers that the organization has at least basic knowledge about appropriate lobbying. It also assures the funder that the group is working to protect its own legal status and that of the foundation from which it seeks funding.

- *Understand (and indicate this understanding in proposals) the legal limits on private foundations' support of advocacy activities—including lobbying and nonpartisan voter engagement.* When prospective grantees brag about how their work has "single-handedly resulted in a particular piece

[39] Editor's note: The filing of the Form 5768 is described in Chapter 9.

of legislation" or "defeated a candidate," that raises a red flag with foundations. First, it is usually untrue. Second, it shows a lack of knowledge of the restrictions on what private foundations can and cannot support in terms of lobbying, voter participation, and advocacy.

- *Indicate how the research and reports the organization published as part of an advocacy campaign have helped to educate policymakers and the general public—on a bipartisan or nonpartisan basis—about the need for policy change.* Such research should be rigorous, balanced, offer concrete facts and figures, demonstrate some type of independent oversight, and generally be defensible.

- *Understand that private foundations, such as the Ford Foundation, The Rockefeller Foundation, and Carnegie Corporation, are different from community foundations and public charities.* Each has different IRS restrictions and rules regarding funding lobbying and voter engagement programs. Nonprofits should also be educated about legal issues affecting different types of foundations and can do so by participating in trainings or reading publications by the Center for Lobbying in the Public Interest (CLPI) or the Alliance for Justice. Each helps nonprofits and private foundations navigate the IRS rules and regulations on lobbying and voter engagement activities.

- *Understand what nonprofits can and cannot do in relation to voter engagement activities and elections.* Voter registration and get-out-the-vote activities, in particular, need to be conducted within the strict confines of the IRS regulations, including the principle of nonpartisanship.

Beyond Understanding: Incorporating Advocacy into Grantmaking

Once funders understand the importance of supporting advocacy, how can they incorporate it into their funding strategies and programs? Following are a few suggestions:

- Understand that "advocacy" comprises a wide range of activities that are permitted under law and can be supported individually or in combination.

Funders can, for example, decide to support an organization's efforts to do policy research around an issue that will be disseminated to policy-makers, it can support a public education campaign that involves getting press attention, or it can do both. See Chapter 5 for descriptions of various advocacy-related activities.

- When developing new program areas, conduct an in-depth analyses of organizations working in these areas to assess whether they are undertaking advocacy efforts, what they are doing, and whether their efforts can help "move" an agenda or policy recommendation forward. Include in this analysis how these efforts can bolster the activities of individual organizations or programs the funder might want to support.

- When considering individual programs or organizations for support, include an assessment of whether and to what extent these groups have incorporated advocacy as part of their strategy or program agenda. If they have not, ask why. Some organizations simply have not considered it; others may not know that they can, so your questions will help spur more thinking about it.

- Provide support for groups of organizations working collectively to pursue policy-related goals like using coalitions to leverage even more funds. For example, several foundations, organized by the JEHT Foundation worked collaboratively to fund research, public education, litigation, and advocacy around the issue of former felon re-enfranchisement (the Right to Vote Campaign). This has been an excellent way to combine forces, and, because there is a sufficient pool of funds available, each foundation can direct its funds toward a particular aspect of the campaign.

- Provide general support grants to organizations working in areas of concern to foundations. Carnegie Corporation, for example, often provides general support to organizations that are working solely on an issue that it is concerned about like campaign finance reform. Providing general support grants allows the nonprofit flexibility in many areas and in particular, provides greater legal flexibility both for nonprofits and for private foundations.

- Understand that advocacy is not necessarily synonymous with "legislation" and that changing public opinion by using media strategies can also be an extremely effective advocacy tool. In fact, most experts agree that the most successful advocacy initiatives use both legislative and media strategies to bolster one another. Therefore, foundations should provide support for organizations that understand the importance of media advocacy or strategic communications and are using these to develop key messages that can be disseminated through various outlets toward the goal of changing public opinion in ways that will be more favorable to the organizations' policy goals. Funders can also provide small grants to help organizations get the training they need to become more sophisticated about communications tools and strategies. Groups such as the Communications Consortium Media Center and the SPIN Project, for example, offer such trainings regularly.

- Provide support for nonpartisan voter registration and other electoral activities to engage people around issues and to encourage nonprofits to get involved in the crucial job of improving how our democracy works—and provide this support beyond election years. Encourage nonprofit grantees, especially those with large constituencies or membership bases, to ask their constituencies to engage in activities that will hold political leaders accountable *after* the election. The Voter Engagement Evaluation Project (VEEP), commissioned by the Funders' Committee for Civic Participation and Proteus Fund after the 2004 elections, clearly addresses the feast and famine problem of funding voter engagement activities. In particular, their report makes it clear that planning and funding effective voter engagement programs should start earlier, be ongoing, and be integrated into permanent policy or issue-based work. (The report is available from http://www.proteusfund.org.)

- Provide ongoing internal training sessions for the foundation's staff and board to help them understand the rules of nonprofit lobbying and supporting voter engagement activities. Even staff members who are knowledgeable about this area need refresher courses and to learn whether IRS rules have changed. Foundations can—and should—support advocacy or lobbying training for their grantees as well, especially if the ultimate goal of the organizations they are funding is to influence policy. Foundations should not assume that the nonprofits they fund—even larger and well-known ones—have the appropriate legal and lobbying skills.

- Review grant agreement letters to ensure that there is not overly restrictive language contained in them that would steer nonprofits away from activities in which they are permitted to engage and that foundations are allowed to support. See the Toolkit in Appendix A for sample grant letters that do not overly restrict advocacy.

Foundation and Nonprofit Leaders Must Work Together

Foundation leaders and nonprofit leaders must work together to encourage greater support for public policy and civic activity from the foundation world. Together, they can do much more than either would acting alone. First, they can work together to educate funders that such support is critical not only to the nonprofits that foundations support but to *all* nonprofits and the sector overall. Second, they can emphasize that advocacy should be viewed as an integral part of capacity building and that nonprofits cannot sustain their efforts without having the skills to be effective advocates for their constituencies and missions. Third, they must provide evidence that such strategies work and then continually build on that knowledge to "make the case" to funders, individual donors, and, yes, to the thousands of nonprofits who are reluctant to advocate for their own interests or those of their constituencies. An important part of making that case is demonstrating how and why advocacy can be a more cost-efficient and effective strategy for grantmakers to consider—now and in the future.

The most important thing that funders and nonprofit leaders can do is to stop talking about the importance of "civil society," "democracy," and "civic engagement" and start investing in the real-life implementation of these rather lofty constructs.

The most important thing that funders and nonprofit leaders can do, however, is to stop talking about the importance of "civil society," "democracy," and "civic engagement" and start investing in the real-life implementation of these rather lofty constructs: nonpartisan voter registration and voter engagement activities, grassroots organizing, media campaigns, letter-writing drives, lobbying, and the myriad of other tools nonprofits can and do use to advocate for their interests, issues, and constituents. These activities are not forbidden by law, nor should anyone—funder or otherwise—be uneasy about them since they are part and parcel of a healthy democracy, which encourages freedom of speech, the right to assembly, and other vital freedoms. Just as the other two sectors—the for-profit and public sectors—have the right to engage in these kinds of efforts, so does the nonprofit sector, which Alexis de Tocqueville described so eloquently two centuries ago as being a force for encouraging healthy and vibrant civic life in the United States. It is time for funders—and the nonprofit sector of which they are a part—to embrace advocacy as part of this legacy, rather than running from it.

- - -

Conclusion

Private foundations have an opportunity to strengthen their philanthropy by investing and participating in advocacy. Funding advocacy leverages philanthropic investments by ensuring that laws and the processes for making them do not undermine foundation supported initiatives. Private foundations can also safely and effectively help shape public policy directly by providing general support grants to nonprofit organizations that engage in efforts to influence media and public opinion; by improving citizen participation in solving community problems; and by convening policy decision makers and providing them with credible, focused research that can influence policy outcomes. To become influential in the policy arena, foundation leaders must fully support their organization's policy efforts. Staff can motivate trustees who are hesitant about advocacy by sharing examples of effective advocacy, educating board members about advocacy laws, and demonstrating risk management. The final and perhaps most important message of this chapter holds true for both private and community foundations (discussed next in Chapter 8). Foundations should not talk in the abstract about strengthening democracy; they should do it by funding projects that support their mission and add voices to the debate. If foundations view nonprofits as partners in solving problems and creating opportunities via public policy, then more can be accomplished.

Chapter Eight

Community Foundations and Public Policy

Stuart Comstock-Gay

In 2002, when scores of Minnesota nonprofit organizations were told by the state that their funds for human services would be cut drastically, The Minneapolis Foundation (a community foundation) jumped into action. Within a matter of days, the Foundation joined with the Minnesota Council of Nonprofits to engage in full-bore advocacy work to stop the cuts. The advocacy was almost instantaneous, including assembly of a coalition, newspaper ads, press conferences, and public pronouncements, with The Minneapolis Foundation president in a very public role. The final decision was that cuts were in large part eliminated, and grants made on schedule to statewide nonprofits.

Unique in the foundation world, it can be said that public policy work is an outright obligation of community foundations. In an era when citizens have increasingly abdicated their responsibility to serve the community, community foundations increasingly are urging that civic responsibility be revived and that the public policy arena is a natural extension of community foundation work. Community foundations' traditional leadership role in promoting individual responsibility suggests a similar obligation to provide institutional leadership in public responsibility—the policy arena. And while private foundations face tougher restrictions on their ability to lobby, community foundations can lobby with the same latitude as nonprofits (public charities).

CHAPTER SNAPSHOT

This chapter discusses the following:

- Public policy advocacy: a core function of community foundation leadership

- How advocacy benefits donor goals

- Developing a public policy orientation in the board

- Developing a public policy orientation among donors

- Choosing your issues

- Dealing with risk

- How to build expertise

Community foundations have a unique position in society. They sit at the intersection shared by donors, business leaders, community organizations, and government. Looked to for leadership among all groups, community foundations build tremendous political and social capital alongside their financial capital. And yet, it is too easy for a community foundation to merely build the capital and not use it toward leading the community. Done right, community foundations can strengthen communities by using some political capital in the public policy arena. That's why public policy leadership should, indeed, be considered a basic element of community foundation leadership.

> Community foundations can strengthen communities by using political capital in the public policy arena. That's why public policy leadership should, indeed, be considered a basic element of community foundation leadership.

Moreover, community foundations have resources that can be found nowhere else. Most community foundations have on their boards a cross-section of leadership, with varying political beliefs, different religious convictions, and professional affiliations that touch many, if not most, of the significant fields in the region. And most community foundations have donors that also represent a broad cross-section of the region. All of these people come to the foundation with a goal of making the community better. These foundations are a precious community resource, and public policy work can help them achieve their bigger goals.

Insofar as the mission of a community foundation is betterment of society, it seems foolish to attempt to improve a community only through grants or an occasional report. The rise of national gift funds should not merely challenge community foundations on donor service, but should serve also as a reminder that community foundations need to make sure we are truly providing outstanding service to our communities. That call has been heard. Scores of community foundations across the country are adding lobbying and public advocacy campaigns to their toolbox, either by their direct action or by advocacy grants. In addition, convening organizations and community leaders around public issues is increasingly recognized as a basic element of the complete community foundation portfolio.

While The Minneapolis Foundation example above is perhaps the most dramatic, there are dozens of inspiring stories. A convening effort by the

Hutchinson (Kansas) Community Foundation led to a reevaluation of the county's child protective services practices. A seven-year effort by The Rhode Island Foundation led from support of community health providers to a partnership with the State Department of Human Services, which resulted in Medicaid legislation that allows the state to insure more low-income children by partnering with private employers. And there are many more fine examples.

How can a typical community foundation move from the status quo to supporting advocacy? The change starts at the top—with the board.

Developing a Public Policy Orientation in the Board

Board support will make any public policy endeavor much more successful. While it is not always critical for board members to know the ins and outs of every grant, public policy is a different endeavor, and it behooves the foundation to have the board fully aware of and engaged with the work. First, the board brings broader community credibility to advocacy work because boards include a variety of community leaders with various contacts. If you do take on public policy work, especially on controversial issues, you should assume that board members will field calls from public officials and community members about your work. And you want them to be prepared and supportive of the foundation when that happens.

Additionally, depending on the interests of the board members, they can be a tremendous resource in moving forward a particular agenda. A president or staff member of a community foundation has some clout, merely based on institutional affiliation. Board members have additional clout based on their reputations, business relationships, political activities, and community involvement. The best board members will be willing to call officials on behalf of the issue, recruit other supporters the cause, and help you develop more effective strategies.

Finally, it is especially important to have a supportive board when you first begin public policy work. Some in the community will think public policy work is a betrayal of neutrality, and you want your board to understand that it is not a betrayal and why it is useful and important work.

Introducing the board to public policy work

For some foundations, the path to public policy engagement is difficult and requires extensive work and time with the board. While staff may think it's obvious that the foundation ought to expand into the public policy arena, the board may not see it that way. Because many community foundations have a tradition that is based on grantmaking and donor advising and because those roles are viewed as politically neutral, it may seem to some that public policy work is a violation of that neutrality. This is of course not the case. Yet every decision to make one grant or another is supporting one type of work over another. The move to public policy work is merely a more comprehensive approach to the issues that matter to a foundation. Nonetheless, it may take some time to build up the board's comfort level (and indeed the comfort level of staff) for public policy work. The best way to do this is to talk about desired results and outcomes. As long as the foundation is focused on making grants, it will be hard to move to new work, but shortly after the foundation talks about outcomes—such as the number of children receiving health care or the amount of low-income housing available—the board will quickly see the shortcomings of grants.

> Every decision to make one grant or another is supporting one type of work over another. The move to public policy work is merely a more comprehensive approach to the issues that matter to a foundation.

Therefore, to develop board members' comfort with public policy work, focus on outcomes and not grants. Select an issue of concern and identify an outcome that the board wants—say, after-school programs for every child in the metropolitan area. The board will quickly see that the foundation's money alone would do very little to achieve that outcome. When developing the New Futures substance abuse program, the New Hampshire Charitable Foundation began with a challenge. A donor had provided a major grant to the Foundation with the intention of having an impact on substance abuse programs in the state. Because of the significance of the gift, the Foundation created a task force of experts who reviewed a wide range of uses to which the funds could be put, including policy analysis, grants to service providers, training, and direct advocacy. The Foundation board, reviewing the range of options available, agreed that leadership development and policy advocacy were the best ways the Foundation could affect policy change and, accordingly, created a new organization for just that purpose.

Sometimes the barrier is not the work itself, but the term "public policy." Some years ago, during discussions at the New Hampshire Charitable Foundation about whether or not to engage in more public policy work, some board members were extremely reluctant. During the course of discussion, when specific activities were discussed—report generation, funding of advocacy by nonprofits, testimony in city councils and legislatures, convening of public leaders on important issues, writing op-eds—one of the resistant board members said, "I'm happy for us to do these things. In fact, they are precisely what we should do. But I don't want this foundation to be doing public policy work." The learning here is, don't get hung up on words. Sometimes words get in the way of good work. So don't call it public policy if it gets in the way. Talk about the work that needs to be done. And do it.

Strengthening board commitment to public policy

Some board members may never get comfortable with a public policy orientation. If that's the case, it may take some time to bring on new board members. And that work will require a nominating committee that believes in the public policy. Following are a set of recommendations to strengthen your board in its advocacy role and change the board over time.

- Ask the board to create a public policy task force to investigate how the work might be done. Make sure to staff the board adequately and bring to the task force the right kind of experts who can explain how policy work can be done the right way.

- Have other community foundations that have entered the public policy arena talk to your board representatives about why they do policy work and why it works for them.

- Include in your board orientation a full discussion of the many approaches to foundation problem solving, including an explicit discussion about public policy work. If a potential board member resists, consider carefully whether that person is an appropriate board member.

- When identifying seats for the board, include two members with experience in the critical legislative arena for your foundation (for example, city council, state legislature, or county board). They will help with your board-level strategy discussions. It is important to have at least two people to balance each other out and to better ensure a broad perspective on the elected body. And if your legislature is particularly partisan, you want representatives from both sides of the aisle.

- If the board does not want to pursue full public policy agenda right away, stage your entry into the endeavor.

- Include on your board, members with different perspectives. If you are a more liberal board, make sure you have conservative voices. If conservative, include liberal voices. It will keep you honest and neutral.

- Listen to your board. If the board resists a particular action, pay attention. Many foundation staffers find that if they push hard enough, the board will go along. But if a board is seriously resistant on a public policy matter, there may well be good reason. Consider the board as a group, the first test of a new policy or action. Reconsider your approach if members resist.

Learn to engage in the full range of public policy activities

Even when the board sees that grants alone won't achieve your mission, most people will naturally resist new work because it is new and, therefore, uncomfortable. If a board has a history of simply reviewing and approving grants, that board may chafe at the idea of presenting testimony to city council or taking a public position on funding of after-school programs. Consider the whole range of public policy work and start with those things that are closest to what you've done before. Here are a variety of tactics to engage in public policy, starting with those that should be least challenging to a board and leading to those activities that will be most challenging to board members who resist public policy work. By working through this list, boards are likely to find that they can embrace each successive level of engagement as important to their work.

- Publish reports that provide important community data. Whether it's a social capital benchmark survey or a survey on poverty levels in your region, publish it as simple public education.

- Publish the report, but add policy recommendations. Don't make recommendations from the foundation, just provide recommendations provided by others.

- Convene leaders in the field—public and private—to discuss the issue and the policy recommendations, with the goal of achieving consensus for public policy.

- Fund somebody to keep the discussion going, continue the research, or research additional solutions. Or do it yourself.

- Provide a grant to an organization to advocate for policy changes.[40]

- Go on talk shows, write an op-ed, or meet with editorial boards to discuss the policy changes needed.

- Lobby your legislature.

As the community foundation successfully completes work in one activity, the next will become that much easier. While it is suggested that a community foundation will want to work its way up to active lobbying, it should be understood that each of these activities will be appropriate at different times and for different issues. Once your community foundation has gained comfort in all of them, you will be best able to identify the approach that best suits the issue at hand. Remember the outcome you seek: *The work is not solely about grants, it's about better communities.*[41]

---

[40] For some foundations, a staged way to engage in advocacy is to fund other nonprofits doing the work instead. Because community foundations are public charities and not private foundations, they can provide grants specifically earmarked for lobbying. When making these grants, however, it is important to do so intentionally and with full understanding of the law because grants earmarked for lobbying will count against the community foundation's total allowable lobbying expenditure limits if they elect to follow the expenditure test rules described in Chapter 9. Otherwise, the earmarked grant will count against the community foundation's undefined limit for what is a "substantial" amount. Again, see Chapter 9. Some community foundations, for instance, encourage nonprofits to apply for grants to engage in advocacy. When doing so, it is recommended that the community foundation has elected to come under the expenditure test rules by filing Form 5768 with the IRS, a process known as making the 501(h) election.

[41] The report *Foundations and Public Policymaking: Leveraging Philanthropic Dollars, Knowledge, and Networks* (University of Southern California, The Center on Philanthropy and Public Policy, October 2003), by James M. Ferris, discusses three stages of public policy work: 1) agenda setting, where issues are described and desired results identified; 2) policy setting, the process of creating a proposed policy, developing a strategy to make it reality, and getting that policy passed; and 3) implementation, which is simply putting the new policy into place, whether through agency action or otherwise. Most foundations will find agenda setting and implementation the easier elements of the process and the central section (policy setting) the most difficult. Policy setting has the greatest burden for community foundation, as this is the one part of public policy work in which private foundations cannot easily engage.

Developing a Public Policy Orientation among Donors

One of the truly exciting parts of public policy work in community foundations involves individual donors. Many community foundation donors believe they can only make simple grants with their funds. Take advantage of the opportunity to use these relationships to forward a public policy agenda. Many community foundations find that not only do they bring public policy work to donors' philanthropy, but donors bring their public policy agendas back to the foundation. In fact, many donors will demand this. Consider the many donors who express their frustration at the level of progress being made by their grants to organizations they care about. By helping them see that their philanthropy can be used to change the system, you are helping them be better philanthropists and achieving your mission of improving the community.

Of course, sometimes it is the donors themselves who push the foundation. In the Greater Milwaukee Foundation, it was an advised fund donor who convened a meeting of local foundations to discuss how they were helping families in the child welfare system. That discussion initially led the group to establish a committee to discuss systems reform, followed by meetings with judges and public officials, a conference with national and local leaders, and ultimately sweeping changes in how the courts handled cases. The committee then made a grant to an organization to write a policy paper on possible improvements to the entire child welfare system. The paper led to meetings with the committee and state officials and ultimately to statewide policy changes.

Donors can make the work more focused, can push new efforts, and can broaden the constituency for policy changes. Private foundations don't have the privilege of working with individual donors. Community foundations do have that privilege and, indeed, that obligation.

Following are some methods to move donors toward public policy work.

- During briefings for donors on your interest areas, make sure to include a policy discussion. For example, if you are conducting donor site visits to a community theater, make sure to have someone talk about how government arts funding policies are affecting their work. And make sure the donors also hear how the community foundation can help with that problem.

- Invite donors to briefings from public policy leaders. Ask the chair of the city council, or the mayor or senate president, to talk with your donors about important issues. Invite agency heads. This does many things. It shows donors that the foundation is connected to movers and shakers. It shows public officials that the foundation is connected to movers and shakers. It shows both that they have something in common.

- When bringing new donors into the foundation and talking with them about how you can help them with their philanthropic interests, make sure to include public policy work in the discussion. Make sure to tell them that their advised fund can go toward not just programmatic grants, but toward advocacy in their issue area.

- In newsletters to donors, include policy discussions. Most foundations talk about great grants. Talk occasionally about great public policy–oriented grants and how they made a difference.

- In your organizational assessment, talk not only about numbers of grants and dollars, but about public policy affected and how many new dollars resulted for the community. Share your findings with donors.

- If you have a donor who wants to engage in public policy work, create a house party with other donors, where the public policy donor can talk about why he or she decided that advocacy-related grantmaking is worthwhile.

- Listen to donors when they ask for more. The foundation will become a better organization as a result.

Choosing Your Issues

Public policy work is not an end in itself but merely a means toward your goals. It's another tool. And the more you use the tool (or really tools, since there are many different activities), the better you'll be at it. Ultimately, you'll find yourself combining lobbying with grants and reports, and convening in a seamless fashion. Even so, because of the added concern about public policy work, you will want to decide when and where to use your public policy skills. There are many ways to do this, and books have been written about this work. Some community foundations have developed formal public policy decision-making processes.[42] Others find it a much more informal process. Whatever you decide, it is best to be clear in your expectations about when you'll engage in public policy and when not. And be open to all the many ways public policy engagement may come to you. Here are some typical starting points:

Strategic analysis of community needs. Some community foundations may engage in a full strategic analysis of community needs and decide that one or another issue warrants public policy involvement.

Crisis. The Minneapolis Foundation example in the beginning of this chapter showed a community foundation responding to a need at the moment. This means of adopting an issue is preferably done by an experienced public policy foundation.

Donor initiation. In some cases, donors will ask you to engage in public policy, or you will find that to achieve the goals of a donor-advised fund, you will need to move into public policy.

Response to community request. Once you begin public policy work, you can expect to be approached by supporters and friends to weigh in on their issue, even though they have no formal connection to the foundation. Caution is key, so your community foundation is not improperly influenced by outsiders.

Next generation of work on an issue you're already addressing. It is not at all uncommon for a foundation to discover that it needs to move into public policy to succeed at something they've already been working on.

The point here is that public policy is not a simple tool you pull out once and never use again. It's a tool that you'll need at different times for different reasons.

---

[42] See the Rochester Area Community Foundation document, "Rochester Area Community Foundation: Public Policy Handbook," which describes that foundation's protocol for engaging in public policy.

Risks and How to Minimize Them

As with any good work you do, there are risks involved. This is also true with public policy work. Grantmaking alone is a relatively safe endeavor. People like your organization because you give money to good causes. You know many people in many different walks of life. You have links with nonprofits, wealthy donors, private companies, other grantmakers, and people in government service. You know a little bit about many things going on in the community. And what agency that receives a grant is going to be outright critical? If you stick to grantmaking, few people will be critical. Depending on how aggressive you become in public policy work, this can change.

If you take serious positions about public policy, somebody—and maybe many somebodies—will disagree. This section is not intended to frighten a community foundation away from the work. The goal is to prepare for criticism and minimize the degree of criticism you receive.

As the saying goes, "Politics ain't bean bag." People have strong opinions about public policy and rightly so. For a community foundation entering the public policy world, attention to important constituencies is critical. In particular, the risks with donors and elected officials deserve special attention.

Minimizing risks with donors

Most community foundations have donors from across the political spectrum. That's the pitch of community foundations—"We're here for everybody." But if you take a position urging harsher enforcement of drunk-driving laws, assume that your donors who head the state grocers' association, or who own a beer distributor, or run a chain of restaurants, may not be happy. If you take a position urging increased taxes, any number of donors may object. There are a number of actions you can take to minimize the disquiet felt by your donors:

- *Orientation of donors.* When introducing donors to the foundation, make sure to talk about the many different ways you work, including public policy advocacy. Help them understand that you not only make grants to a wide variety of organizations, but that the institution itself occasionally takes public positions on policy matters.

- *Alert donors before beginning a campaign.* Before you release significant public positions, contact your key donors, especially those who might disagree with the position. Tell them what you'll be doing and why. It's a simple courtesy.

- *Keep donors informed during and after specific campaigns.* Get back to your donors—through newsletters or other means—to tell them what happened, why you did it, and the benefit for the community that will result.

- *Communicate regularly.* Always maintain regular communications with donors about the various activities you're doing, so they don't hear from you *only* when you're doing something they don't like.

Additional thoughts about bringing donors into the public policy process are below.

Minimizing risks with elected officials

When an elected official or agency director who has viewed you as an ally suddenly finds you on the opposite side of an issue, he or she may get quite upset. Often the upset feelings stem from two sources. One is simple disagreement. A second and often more powerful concern is with being blindsided. Don't ever surprise an elected official (or a donor, for that matter). Adopt the strategy of no surprises. Here are a number of steps to reduce the surprise and reduce negative reactions:

- *Meet with officials regularly.* Identify the key elected officials—mayor, governor, city council, congressional representatives—and schedule annual briefings. Tell them what you're involved with, ask them to share their major concerns, and make sure they know the many ways in which you operate—including public policy work. Likewise, if your foundation is particularly involved with health and human services issues, hold annual meetings with the secretary of the department—or whoever matters most to your work.

- *Respond to calls from officials.* Jack Valenti, who served as the president of the Motion Picture Association of America for over thirty years, had an ironclad policy to respond to every call from a congressperson within twenty-four hours. Do it, and if you can help them with their projects, do so.

- *Be a partner to officials.* If key elected officials are seeking a partnership on some project, find ways to engage with them when possible. Without betraying your principles and without taking on public responsibilities, you will surely find some way to help them. The New Hampshire Charitable Foundation makes it a point to engage in some manner of partnership with every governor and has done so for almost twenty-five years.

- *Contact officials before you go public with specific positions.* Tell them what you'll be doing and saying, and tell them why. Don't let them hear from a reporter first. This is true whether they will be on your side on a question, on the other side, or neutral.

Risk assessment checklist

Given the risks to public policy work, how do you assess whether or not to move beyond grants to public policy work? The following questions can help guide a community foundation in its decisions about when to engage in public policy advocacy:

❑ Does the action serve the mission of the foundation?
  Advice: Be clear about how the action serves the mission. If it does not, ask yourselves why you are even considering involvement.

❑ Is the issue important?
  Advice: Be careful about using political capital on a minor issue.

❑ Will foundation involvement on this issue make a difference, or will we simply be another minor voice in a large movement?
  Advice: If the foundation's involvement doesn't matter, *Don't* get involved. Once you start weighing in on public issues, you will be asked to do so regularly. Be judicious. If you take a position on everything, you become far less useful to anybody. At the same time, "making a difference" can mean many different things, including a) convincing an agency to change its position or an elected body to pass new legislation; b) putting an issue on the public agenda when it hasn't been there before; and c) strengthening an important nonprofit organization in its work by giving it more credibility.

❑ Will public involvement in this issue make it harder to achieve another policy goal?
Advice: Don't win the battle and lose the war. If you can influence a particular agency's behavior on a small piece of work, but at the price of the agency director blocking a bigger initiative down the road, you may want to back off.

❑ How will other donors react?
Advice: If you will lose donors or if the work will turn potential donors away, consider the work carefully. It may still be worth it, but consider the risk in advance.

❑ Is the foundation prepared to be in this for the long term?
Advice: Few things are more frustrating—or more likely to create mistrust—than an organization that makes a big splash when entering a movement and then backs off when it becomes difficult. Public policy work takes time. Either commit to the effort for however long it takes, or make clear to your colleagues at the beginning what the extent of your involvement will be. If you can't do either of those, don't start.

❑ Will involvement betray the foundation's neutrality?
Advice: Community foundations lose their clout if they become stalking horses for a political movement. That doesn't mean you should avoid controversy. It does mean you should avoid partisanship.

❑ Is the foundation prepared to take criticism?
Advice: No matter how much communication you have with donors, elected officials, and colleagues, some people will be unhappy about the work. Make sure you're prepared for it.

Building Policy Expertise

The day you start working for a foundation is the day your ideas suddenly become brilliant, your insights insightful, your jokes funny, and your sense of style world-class. It doesn't take long for a good foundation staffer to recognize that it's not true, it's merely the distorting influence of lots of money. One of the great dangers of using new public policy tools may be the temptation to think you know what you're doing. Just as foundations hire investment consultants to manage their portfolios, look to the appropriate experts to help with public policy work. Those experts can be contractors, or if the foundation is moving into a broad range of public policy work, you may want to hire staffers with that expertise. The skills may reside in the people you have now, but don't assume that.

The community foundation's great assets include institutional credibility, political neutrality, and financial resources. Of course, the staff and board also have personal credibility and a variety of skills. But the specific skills needed for public policy work are not instinctive. So get trained or get expert help. In every step of the public policy process, consider what resources and skills are needed and whether you have them, can get trained for them, or need to hire them. Three specific areas where you should seek help include compiling reports, making policy recommendations, and lobbying.

> **One of the great dangers of using new public policy tools may be the temptation to think you know what you're doing. Just as foundations hire investment consultants to manage their portfolios, look to the appropriate experts to help with public policy work.**

Reports

Whether you are hiring local universities or research centers, be clear with those you hire what kind of report you want. If it's merely data analysis, ask for that. If you want policy recommendations, ask for that. But also make sure to look at previous reports by the same writers and researchers. A person skilled at crunching survey numbers may have little idea how to turn the numbers into policy recommendations. For example, in 2000, when thirty community foundations engaged in a national social capital benchmark survey, each foundation had an academic partner. However, some academics simply compared local data with national data, while others compared the data and made recommendations about future changes in community work. The Community Foundation of Greater Greensboro coupled the social capital benchmark survey with a community economic study conducted by McKinsey to create Action Greensboro, a collaborative project of funders and nonprofits seeking major change in the region's economic infrastructure.

Making policy recommendations

While policy recommendations can usefully come from outside the political infrastructure or the agency you're intending to affect, it helps tremendously to have political strategists as part of the design stage. Your recommendations are more likely to get consideration if they are at least written with an understanding of political realities.

Lobbying

For real impact on legislation, there's no replacing savvy lobbyists. The best ideas in the world will founder without someone to help manage the process. Contract with a lobbyist or get one on your committees. They can tell you who works well with whom, where the power on your issues lies, and what arguments are likely to win and lose. And they can help you count the votes. When the Greater Des Moines Community Foundation sought to pass endowed tax credits to help build more community foundations in the state, it not only hired a marketing firm, it hired a lobbying firm to build a bipartisan group of state legislators who would spread the word. The lobbyists recommended that by limiting the benefit to any one county, all counties would be more likely to receive benefit and the legislation would be more likely to pass. And it did. In a particularly tight 2003 session, the legislature passed a bill that provided $1 million over three years to foundations.

Stories of Successful Initiatives

Following are brief descriptions of three community foundation public policy initiatives, all of which touch many of the concepts described above. There are, of course, hundreds of stories from around the country.

In 2002, The Boston Foundation identified a lack of low-income housing as a critical problem for the metropolitan area. With the help of grantees in the housing field, a housing collaborative was established to study the problem and produce a report. The Foundation funded a local university to conduct a thorough analysis of the problem—including data about the scope of the problems and projections of the future of housing in the region—as well as a series of policy recommendations. After two years of work, in the fall of 2003, a report was jointly issued by The Boston Foundation, the housing collaborative, and Northeastern University. In early 2004, legislation was introduced to the Massachusetts legislature to implement the recommendations in the report. In this case the Foundation helped to set a public policy agenda by identifying a problem, convening interested parties, funding organizations working on the issue, funding research to scale the issue, and supporting in the same report an agenda for change in policy.

In 2003, the Battle Creek Community Foundation became the lead partner in developing a regional public policy council with a goal of engaging on issues that have an effect on matters affecting Michigan nonprofits. The council trains nonprofits on effective advocacy, educates nonprofits on issues of relevance, and advocates to policymakers on behalf of nonprofits. The council also plans to schedule annual legislative briefings to push its agenda. Some community foundations are more comfortable with advocacy around nonprofit issues than they are with other advocacy, believing that community foundations have a special obligation to stand up for the nonprofit community.

Beginning in 1997, the New Hampshire Charitable Foundation invested over half a million dollars per year from a new substance abuse fund to a new statewide substance abuse policy and leadership program. New Futures was intentionally designed with an advocacy element and by 2000, it was submitting testimony, making public statements, creating reports, lobbying legislators, and activating a new grassroots lobby to press for changes in state substance abuse laws, among them beer-keg registration and creation of a state-funded Governor's Task Force on Substance Abuse.[43]

— — —

---

[43] In 2002, NHCF decided to turn New Futures into a freestanding nonprofit organization, funded in large part by the Foundation. (The board voted to turn what was a board-directed fund into a designated fund for New Futures.) In spite of the Foundation's eagerness to engage in public policy work, this step was taken to ensure that New Futures could pursue the most aggressive positions it felt were necessary without concern about the impact on the Foundation.

Conclusion

As community foundations become more professional, better respected, and more influential, it is important that they become smarter about their work. Irving Goffman famously critiqued hospitals and warned that the business of hospitals was to be better hospitals, when the real business of the hospitals should be to provide health care. Likewise, the business of community foundations cannot be simply to be a community foundation. The mission of almost every community foundation is some version of strengthening its community. To achieve that mission, community foundations need to turn their focus to outcomes. And it is very rare that a grant alone will achieve the desired outcome. At the same time, community foundations serve as a critical neutral meeting place for everybody in the community.

As community foundations all across the country enter the public policy arena, much good can result. For those new to the field, consult with others who've already been there. Seek professional assistance. Take risks. And make the community better.

Chapter Nine

The Legal Rules for Public Policy and Civic Impact by Foundations

Lloyd H. Mayer, Esq.

Foundations have significant legal opportunity to support and participate in activities that shape public policy, strengthen civic participation, and foster social change. There are rules that must be adhered to, but that should not stop any foundation from seriously considering the wide range of public policy–related actions that might be effective strategies for achieving mission-related purposes.

This chapter explains the legal rules that allow private foundations and community foundations to advocate for public policy changes and encourage involvement in elections. With only a few limitations, foundations may make grants to support public policy shaping activities (often called "advocacy") and nonpartisan voter participation. They may also directly engage in these activities as organizations, again with a few limitations.

The chapter has three parts. Part 1 focuses on private foundations and covers common myths; grantmaking involving lobbying and other forms of public policy activity; grantmaking involving nonpartisan voter education; legal risk assessment; reporting and accountability; participation in public policy; and voter education. Part 2 covers community foundations, including grantmaking for public policy activities (including lobbying); grantmaking for nonpartisan voter education; participation in public policy; and voter education. Part 3 explains

CHAPTER SNAPSHOT

This chapter discusses

- The law regarding private foundations (Part 1); community foundations (Part 2); and the lobbying rules expenditure test (Part 3)

- Federal legal rules for grantmaking for public policy and civic activity

- IRS rules governing lobbying by nonprofits

- Exceptions to lobbying definitions that allow for private foundation participation in legislation-related activities

- Rules pertaining to coalitions

- Rules for making grants to organizations that are not 501(c)(3) charities

- Managing legal risk

- Legal resources on foundation advocacy

the federal lobbying rules expenditure test, including pros and cons of the expenditure test governing community foundation and charity lobbying; a list of legislation-related activities that are not considered lobbying and that are available to all foundations; definitions of lobbying; lobby expenditure limits; and how to make the 501(h) election to come under the expenditure test rules.

In addition, the Toolkit found in Appendix A provides sample grant letters for various situations. The Toolkit also provides an executive summary of the legal rules regarding foundations and advocacy. This is meant to be copied and distributed as needed in your organization. The executive summary and sample letters are also posted on the publisher's web site at the following address:

http://www.FieldstoneAlliance.org/worksheets
Access Code: W458pip07

There are a few terms that have very specific meanings in this chapter that you should know before we begin:

Charity: A *charity* is an organization that is tax-exempt under section 501(c)(3) of the Internal Revenue Code and is *not* a private foundation. Such organizations are sometimes also referred to as "public charities." Except for churches and other houses of worship, a charity should have a letter from the IRS stating that it has these characteristics. Community foundations are charities.

Note that in the rest of this book, we use the term "nonprofit" to refer to the organizations that are most typically grantees of community and private foundations. But in this chapter, the term "charity" refers to nonprofit organizations exempt from taxation under section 501(c)(3) of the Internal Revenue Code *excluding* private foundations. Community foundations, in contrast, *are* considered charities under 501(c)(3). The usage of terms in this chapter is specific and is due to the need to differentiate private foundations from other nonprofit organizations exempt from taxation under 501(c)(3).

Non-charity: Any organization other than a charity or a private foundation. A non-charity might be a 501(c)(6) trade association, a 501(c)(5) labor union, a 501(c)(4) civic organization, or other organizations including a school, government program, or business.

Advocacy: Seeking to influence public policy. Advocacy includes educating the public and policymakers about issues of public concern, attempting to influence the development of governmental agency rules and regulations, attempting to influence legislation, and litigating on public policy issues. All lobbying is therefore advocacy but not all advocacy is lobbying.

Nonpartisan Voter Participation: Seeking to encourage citizens to participate in elections without indicating support for or opposition to any particular candidate. Nonpartisan voter participation includes voter registration drives, get-out-the-vote (GOTV) efforts, and educating voters about issues and candidates. Note that these activities are categorized as civic strengthening activities in Chapter 5.

More terms specific to lobbying are introduced in Part 3 of this chapter—to introduce them here would complicate an already complex topic! See also the Glossary at the end of the book.

Finally, we ask your tolerance and patience with this chapter. Legal information is essential to everyone, but exciting to only a few rare birds. If you are one of the latter, pull up a perch and enjoy the chapter. For the rest of you, the information in this chapter (and in the executive summary located in the Toolkit) will help you sort through what's legal and not and should help convince you that whether yours is a private or community foundation, there are many ways you can legally be involved in advocacy. For the fine details, of course, consult an attorney knowledgeable with the laws referenced here.

PART 1. What Private Foundations Need to Know about the Law

Myths versus realities

Myth: Private foundations can't make grants to organizations that lobby.

Reality: Private foundations may make grants to organizations that lobby. A private foundation can make

- A general support (that is, unrestricted) grant to any charity

- A grant to a charity for a specific project that involves lobbying if the grant does not exceed the non-lobbying portion of the project's budget

- A grant to a non-charity that lobbies if the foundation follows certain procedures to make sure the grant funds are used only for charitable purposes

Myth: Private foundations cannot make grants to organizations involved in voter participation efforts.

Reality: Private foundations may make grants to organizations that are involved in voter participation efforts. A private foundation can make

- A general support (that is, unrestricted) grant to any charity

- A grant to a charity for a specific voter participation project other than voter registration as long as the project is nonpartisan

- A grant to certain charities for nonpartisan voter registration projects conducted over more than one election cycle and in at least five states

- A grant to a non-charity for a specific nonpartisan voter participation project other than voter registration if the foundation follows certain procedures to make sure the grant funds are used only for charitable purposes

Myth: Private foundations cannot make grants to non-charities.

Reality: A private foundation may make a grant to a non-charity if the grant funds will be used for charitable, educational, or similar purposes and the following requirements are met:

- A *pre-grant inquiry* to confirm the grantee is capable of using the funds properly
- A *written grant agreement* limiting the use of the funds to permitted purposes and requiring documentation to confirm that use
- At least annual *written grantee reports* on the use of the grant funds
- *Reporting to IRS* of certain information about the grant on the private foundation's annual IRS Form 990-PF

Myth: Private foundations cannot, themselves, advocate on public policy issues.

Reality: A private foundation may advocate on public policy issues as long as it does not engage in lobbying, which is communicating with government officials or the public about specific legislation. A private foundation may also communicate with the public about specific legislation if the foundation does not call on the public to act by, for example, calling their representative. Finally, the following types of communications are not considered lobbying even if they discuss specific legislation:

- *Nonpartisan analysis, study, or research*: material that provides a sufficiently full and fair exposition of legislation to allow the recipient to form his or her own conclusions, distributed to persons on both sides of the legislation, that does not include a direct call to action urging the reader to contact government officials about the legislation
- *Technical assistance*: an oral or written response to a written request for information from a legislative committee, subcommittee, agency, or other governmental body
- *Self-defense*: a communication with a government official (but not the public) about specific legislation that could affect the foundation's existence, powers, duties, tax-exempt status, or right to receive tax-deductible contributions
- *Jointly funded project*: a communication with a government official (but not the public) about specific legislation to fund a project that may be funded by both the private foundation and the government

Myth: Private foundations cannot themselves engage in voter participation activities.

Reality: A private foundation may itself engage in voter participation activities as long as such activities are strictly nonpartisan. Such activities include candidate forums, candidate questionnaires, get-out-the-vote (GOTV) efforts, issue education or advocacy, legislative scorecards, and voter guides. The one exception is voter registration, which a foundation generally will not be able to do itself.

What private foundations *can't* do

There are three limitations that apply to the advocacy activities of private foundations:

1. *No support of specific lobbying efforts.* Private foundations generally may not support specific lobbying efforts. Congress enacted this ban in 1969 as part of a larger set of restrictions on private foundations, apparently because of perceived improper interference by one or more foundations in local legislative decisions.

2. *Support of nonpartisan voter registration drives only if certain conditions met.* The 1969 restrictions permit private foundations to support nonpartisan voter registration drives only if they do so by making grants to charities that meet certain financial tests and also do voter registration in five or more states and for more than one election.

3. *No support of partisan voter participation efforts.* Private foundations may not support partisan voter participation efforts. This means that a private foundation may not support or oppose the election of a particular candidate to public office or support or oppose a particular political party. This is a restriction that Congress has imposed on both charities and private foundations.

A private foundation that violates these rules can face significant penalties, including the loss of its tax-exempt status. This section will therefore also explain how to manage risk when supporting advocacy and nonpartisan voter participation.

What private foundations *can* do

Fortunately, there is far more that private foundations can do than they can't do. Despite the general legal prohibition on private foundations in making grants specifically for legislative lobbying, private foundations can support charities that engage in lobbying and many other forms of public policy as part of the services they provide to society.

Grantmaking that involves lobbying

Private foundations that want to make grants to nonprofits that, in turn, engage in lobbying have two grantmaking approaches at their disposal under the law. First, the *general support grant*, which is the most flexible type of foundation grant, provides support for the general operations of a nonprofit and leaves the organization the most discretion as to what to do with it. Second, if a private foundation does wish to support a particular project within a nonprofit that happens to have a lobbying component, then the *project-specific grant* is appropriate. Following is a discussion of both types of grants.

1. General support grants

A private foundation may make a general support grant to a charity even though the private foundation knows the charity is engaged in lobbying or nonpartisan voter participation efforts. A general support grant is one that is not for a specific project or activity of the charity, including any specific lobbying or voter participation activities.[44] Because the grant is not designated by the foundation for any specific project or activity, the charity in its discretion may use the grant for its lobbying or voter participation activities.

> *Example:* The John and Jane Doe Family Foundation wants to support efforts to improve access to AIDS drugs in inner-city neighborhoods. The Inner City AIDS Initiative is a charity involved in such efforts, including lobbying in support of legislation to provide funding for the purchase of such drugs for inner-city residents with AIDS. The Foundation may make a general support grant to the Initiative that is not earmarked for any specific purpose. The Initiative may use the grant for its lobbying efforts.

---

[44] Treas. Reg. § 53.4945-2(a)(5), (6)(i).

Example: The John and Jane Doe Family Foundation knows that the Inner City AIDS Initiative engages in nonpartisan voter education, voter registration, and get-out-the-vote efforts to encourage victims of AIDS and their friends and family to participate in elections. The Foundation may make a general support grant to the Initiative. The Initiative may use the grant funds for its nonpartisan voter participation efforts.

Note: By making a general purpose grant to a charity that will conduct a voter registration drive, a foundation does not also have to ensure that such a drive is ongoing in five states, as must occur in situations where the grant is earmarked for a nonpartisan voter registration drive.

See the Toolkit for a sample grant letter for a general support grant. If a private foundation chooses to provide a general support grant in response to a grant application that requests funding for a specific project or set of activities, the grant letter should make it clear that the grant is not earmarked for any of the specific activities listed in the proposal but, instead, is for the general support of the organization.

2. Project-specific grants

A private foundation may make a grant for a specific advocacy project of a charity if

- The charity provides a project budget (described on page 177) showing that the non-lobbying expenditures of the project (including those for any activities that fall within the nonpartisan analysis and technical assistance exceptions to lobbying described on pages 200–201, Exceptions to the lobbying definitions) are equal to or greater than the amount of the foundation's grant. There also must not be an agreement between the private foundation and the charity that the grant will be used for lobbying.[45] OR

- The project does not involve lobbying (that is, no grassroots or direct lobbying communications). OR

- The project falls into either of the following two exceptions to lobbying: (1) nonpartisan analysis, study, or research; or (2) technical assistance for governmental bodies such as agencies, departments, or legislative committees or subcommittees.

---

[45] Treas. Reg. § 53.4945-2(a)(6)(ii).

Here's an example of a specific project budget that is within the guidelines.

Example: The Inner City AIDS Initiative operates the Detroit Project. The Project has a budget of $100,000, of which $77,600 will be spent on non-lobbying activities such as public education about AIDS. The John and Jane Doe Family Foundation may make a grant to the Inner City AIDS Initiative specifically for the Detroit Project of up to $77,600 as long as the Foundation and the Initiative do not have an agreement that the grant will be used for lobbying.

Here's the budget for the project:

Inner City AIDS Initiative—Detroit Project

Category	Non-Lobbying	Lobbying	Total
Salary	$30,000	$7,500	$37,500
Benefits	$7,500	$1,875	$9,375
Payroll Taxes	$2,295	$574	$2,869
Printing	$30,000	$10,000	$40,000
Postage	$6,000	$2,000	$8,000
Office Supplies	$1,600	$400	$2,000
Telephone	$205	$51	$256
	$77,600	$22,400	$100,000

A private foundation may rely on the project budget provided by a charity unless the foundation has reason to believe the budget is inaccurate.[46]

See the Toolkit for a sample grant letter for a project-specific grant to help better communicate with prospective and current grantees regarding the foundation's requirements of the nonprofit with respect to reporting on a specific project with lobbying and non-lobbying components.

[46] Treas. Reg. § 53.4945-2(b)(6)(iii).

Words to Watch for When Reviewing Grant Applications

A grant proposal requesting funding for a specific advocacy project often will not clearly state that the project involves lobbying. If any phrases similar to the ones below appear in the proposal, a private foundation should ask whether the project involves lobbying:

- Influence or reform public policy
- Advocate a policy position
- Educate or influence legislators, decision makers, policymakers
- Influence context of decision making for policymakers
- Affect the public policy debate
- Grassroots advocacy
- Encourage activism or public discussion
- Mobilize public opinion on a policy issue

- Media campaigns
- Encourage citizen participation, petition drives
- Promote, advocate, counter, oppose, support, or defend a governmental action
- Prepare or distribute a policy or legislative agenda
- Prepare or distribute a legislative strategy
- Technical assistance on advocacy
- Prepare or distribute model legislation

A private foundation can also ask potential grantees to state in their grant proposals whether their project involves lobbying, as defined by the Internal Revenue Code and, if it does, to provide a budget dividing the project expenses between lobbying and non-lobbying.

Grantmaking that involves other forms of public policy activity (but not lobbying)

A private foundation may make a grant for a specific advocacy project that does not involve any lobbying but does involve other forms of public policy advocacy. For example, a project advocating to an agency about a regulatory change does not involve lobbying because a regulation or administrative rule is not legislation. Educating the public or government officials about a general issue also is not lobbying because it does not involve legislation.[47]

Example: The Forest Service is considering changing the Roadless Area Conservation Rule, which bars virtually all road building and logging on millions of acres of national forests. The John and Jane Doe Family Foundation may make a grant to Environment First! to fund its efforts to convince the Forest Service not to change the rule. This grant is not for lobbying because the Roadless Area Conservation Rule is not legislation.

[47] Treas. Reg. § 53.4945-2(d)(4).

Example: Environment First! wants to send letters to members of Congress explaining the need for scientific research on sources of renewable energy. The letters do not reflect a view on any specific legislative proposal, although there is legislation pending in Congress that would provide tax credits to encourage scientific research Environment First! supports. The John and Jane Doe Family Foundation may make a grant to fund the preparation and distribution of the letter because it does not refer to specific legislation.

Funding specific nonpartisan voter participation projects of charities

A private foundation may support *nonpartisan* voter participation activities, including

1. Candidate forums

2. Candidate questionnaires

3. Voter registration (subject to certain restrictions)

4. Get-out-the vote (GOTV) efforts

5. Issue education or advocacy

6. Legislative scorecards

7. Voter guides

Grantmaking for each of these activities is described below.[48]

The key requirement is that these activities must be strictly nonpartisan—they must *not* indicate support for or opposition to any candidate for elected public office. A private foundation cannot support any activities that would tend to support or oppose a particular candidate. For example, a private foundation cannot endorse a candidate or make a contribution to a candidate's campaign.

A private foundation also cannot more subtly support or oppose a candidate for elected public office. For example, a private foundation cannot allow one candidate to use its conference center without making it available on the same terms to that candidate's opponents. A private foundation also cannot

[48] The IRS has also provided a fact sheet regarding these and similar activities. FS-2006-17 ("Election Year Activities and the Prohibition on Political Campaign Intervention for Section 501(c)(3) Organizations") is available at http://www.irs.gov/newsroom/article/0,,id=154712,00.html.

make grants to support voter participation efforts only in "battleground" states or districts with close congressional races. The IRS has indicated that this prohibition extends to candidates for election and voter registration drives in other countries.[49]

1. Funding candidate forums

A private foundation may make a grant to fund a nonpartisan candidate forum. To be nonpartisan, the forum must have these characteristics:

- All legally qualified candidates are invited (there is some leeway to exclude candidates with only minimal support based on independent polls);

- At least two candidates (or their representatives) attend for each position;

Words to Watch for in Voter Participation Grants

For voter participation project grants, grantees should be asked to confirm *in writing* that grant funds will not be used in a partisan way. To quote the Code, get confirmation that the funds "will not be used to pay for the expenses of participating in or intervening in (including the publishing or distributing of statements) any political campaign on behalf of (or in opposition to) any candidate for public office, within the meaning of section 501(c)(3) of the Internal Revenue Code." This confirmation could be in either the grant proposal or the grant agreement.

Grant proposals requesting funding for specific election-related projects often don't clearly state that the projects involve partisan activities. If any phrases similar to the ones below appear in the proposal, a private foundation should ask whether the project involves partisan activities:

- Educate candidates
- Evaluate candidates' positions
- Educate voters
- Mobilize our constituency or membership to vote
- Use the election to raise the prominence of our issue
- Ask candidates to pledge or commit to support
- Candidate forum or debate
- Voters' guide

- Candidate questionnaire
- Analyze or summarize or report on candidate materials or promises
- "Bad vote" advertisements
- Encourage participation in elections
- Prepare or distribute a election agenda or strategy
- Provide technical assistance to candidates

---

[49] James F. Bloom, Edward D. Luft, and John F. Reilly, "Foreign Activities of Domestic Charities and Foreign Charities," FY1992 Exempt Organizations Continuing Professional Education Technical Instruction Program, available at http://www.irs.gov/pub/irs-tege/eotopick92.pdf on page 14.

- The questions are prepared and presented by an independent nonpartisan panel or, for a forum that has been widely advertised to the public, the questions are from the audience;

- The topics discussed cover a broad range of issues of interest to the public and appropriate to the public office involved—for example, limiting a school board candidate forum to educational issues would be appropriate and limiting a congressional candidate forum to a broad subject area such as civil rights would be acceptable, but not limiting a congressional candidate forum to such relatively narrow topics as housing or employment discrimination;

- Each candidate has an equal opportunity to present his or her views on the issues discussed; and

- The moderator does not comment on the questions or otherwise make comments that imply approval or disapproval of any of the candidates or their positions.[50]

The IRS has also stated an organization's activities are nonpartisan, and so fundable by a private foundation, if the organization invites all of the candidates for a particular office to speak at sequential meetings, rather than all appearing at the same meeting, as long as the meetings meet certain requirements. Those requirements include each meeting providing essentially the same opportunity to reach the public, each candidate being given an equal opportunity to speak, questions being asked by the attendees of each candidate on a wide variety of topics, and no comments being made by representatives of the organization indicating a preference for a particular candidate.[51]

2. Funding candidate questionnaires

A private foundation may make a grant specifically to fund a nonpartisan candidate questionnaire. To be nonpartisan, the questionnaire must have the following characteristics:

- The questionnaire is sent to all candidates for a given office, who are given a reasonable amount of time to respond and an opportunity to explain

---

[50] Rev. Rul. 86-95, 1986-2 C.B. 73.

[51] FS-2006-17; (IRS Publication 1828 ("Tax Guide for Churches and Religious Organizations), available at http://www.irs.gov/pub/irs-pdf/p1828.pdf, on page 9.

their positions if the questions provide a limited set of answers (such as yes/no, support/oppose);

- The charity publishes all responses, with any editing disclosed and unbiased (for example, cutting off responses after they reach a word limit that was communicated to the candidates);

- The questions and any other description of the issues are clear and do not indicate a bias toward the charity's preferred answers;

- The charity does not compare the responses to its preferred answers or otherwise grade or rate the answers;

- The questions are selected on the basis of their interest to the public at large and cover a wide range of issues relevant to the elected public office at issue; and

- The charity does not edit the candidates' responses (except to cut off a response to conform to a length limit, if needed).[52]

3. Funding voter registration

Private foundations may make grants to support nonpartisan voter registration drives, but only if the grantee meets certain requirements. These additional restrictions apparently arose because of controversy over a Ford Foundation grant to the Congress on Racial Equality for voter registration in heavily African American areas of Cleveland during Carl Stokes's closely contested campaign for mayor.

A voter registration drive is an effort to encourage eligible people to register to vote if they have not already done so. It includes handing out voter registration cards, conducting media campaigns encouraging people to register, providing a web site with information about registering to vote, and similar activities. These activities may focus on a particular demographic group if that group has historically been discriminated against. Such groups include, for example, most ethnic minority groups. This is true even if the group tends to support one political party over another.[53]

A voter registration drive does not include other election-related activity. For example, it does not include get-out-the-vote and voter education

---

[52] Rev. Rul. 78-248, 1978-1 C.B. 154, as amplified by Rev. Rul. 80-282, 1980-2 C.B. 178.

[53] See, e.g., PLR 9540044 (July 6, 1995) (women, particularly minority women); PLR 9223050 (Mar. 10, 1992) (homeless); PLR 8822056 (Mar. 4, 1988) (minorities, low-income people, recent immigrants, undereducated people, and young people).

efforts that are separate from helping people to register. It also does not include training people how to conduct voter registration drives, as long as such training does not include providing them with sufficient copies of materials and forms to actually conduct the drives.

The grantee must have these characteristics:

- Be a charity or a private foundation;
- Do voter registration drives that are nonpartisan, not confined to one specific election, and carried on in five or more states;
- Eighty-five percent of its income (after the deduction of fundraising expenses) is spent directly for the active conduct of the activities constituting the purpose or function for which it is organized and operated (including reasonable and necessary administrative expenses);
- Eighty-five percent of its support (other than gross investment income) is received from tax-exempt organizations, the general public, and/or governmental units, and not more than 25 percent of the support is received from any one exempt organization, and not more than 50 percent of the total support (including gross investment income) is gross investment income (calculated over the current year and the four previous years); and
- Contributions for voter registration drives, including from private foundations, are not subject to conditions that they may be used only in specified states, possessions of the United States, or political subdivisions, or other areas of any of the foregoing, or the District of Columbia, or that they may be used in only one specific election period.[54]

Any activity that is more than nominal should satisfy the five-state requirement. It is therefore not necessary for the grantee to spread its voter registration resources equally across at least five states or even to allocate its voter registration resources in proportion to the voting age populations of those states.

[54] IRC § 4945(d)(2), (f); Treas. Reg. § 53.4945-3(b).

4. Funding get-out-the-vote (GOTV) efforts

A private foundation may support get-out-the-vote (GOTV) activities if these activities are strictly nonpartisan. These activities are still considered nonpartisan if they focus on a particular demographic group if that group has historically been discriminated against. Such groups include, for example, most ethnic minority groups. This is true even if the group tends to support one political party over another.

TIP

Documenting grants for voter registration

To confirm that the voter registration drive requirements are met, a private foundation should require any grantee that is asking for funds for a voter registration drive to confirm in writing that it has the required characteristics. Some grantees may have a letter from the IRS stating that they have these characteristics, but such a letter is not required.

A private foundation may not, however, support GOTV efforts based on party affiliation or positions on candidates. For example, a private foundation may not support a GOTV effort that screens the people it will take to the polls by first asking them what party they belong to or whether they support or oppose a particular candidate.

5. Funding issue education or advocacy

A private foundation may fund issue education or advocacy that is focused on *issues* as opposed to *candidates*. For example, a private foundation may fund a media campaign that reminds voters about the important issues of concern to them that will be decided by the politicians they elect to office, as long as no mention is made of any particular candidate or political party.

The one exception is if in a particular race an issue has become one of the key distinctions between the candidates. For example, assume that in a particular state the legislature recently failed to pass a defense of marriage law that would overturn a previously enacted civil union law, but only because of a technical error, and so the bill is expected to pass in the next legislative session. There is an intervening gubernatorial election, and one of the key public distinctions between the two candidates is that one has pledged to veto the bill and the other has pledged to sign it "as my first act in office." Under these circumstances, making a grant for a media campaign shortly before the gubernatorial election that focuses on the importance of permitting or not permitting civil unions is *not* allowed, even if the campaign itself does not refer to the election or mention any of the candidates.

A private foundation may also fund education or advocacy that mentions a candidate under certain circumstances. For example, a private foundation may fund an educational communication that has the following characteristics:

- The communication is timed to coincide with an upcoming official act by the candidate—for example, for a candidate who is currently a legislator such an act would include a scheduled vote on a specific bill, and for a candidate who is currently a governor such an act would include a decision whether to stop a scheduled execution;

- The communication identifies the candidate solely as a governmental official who is in a position to act on this specific event, not as a candidate;

- The communication identifies the candidate's position only on the public policy issue that is the subject of the official act; and

- The candidate's position on that issue has not been raised as distinguishing the candidate from others in the campaign.[55]

6. Funding legislative scorecards

A private foundation may pay for a legislative scorecard if that scorecard is not a disguised attempt to support or oppose particular candidates. To meet this requirement, the scorecard should have these characteristics:

- Is published on a regular basis—that is, in both election and non-election years;

- Is published on a timetable unrelated to the election cycle—for example, for the organization's annual meeting or after each legislative session;

- Includes the voting records of all members of the legislative body representing the region in which the publication is distributed;

- Does not identify individual legislators as candidates;

- Does not refer to an upcoming election;

- Reports on votes on a broad range of issues;

- Does not express the organization's agreement or disagreement with particular votes—for example, by pluses or minuses—unless the distribution is very circumscribed—for example, only to the organization's membership—and the publication acknowledges the "inherent difficulty of evaluating legislators on simply a few selected votes." [56]

[55] Rev. Rul. 2004-6, 2004-4 I.R.B. 528; FS-2006-17.
[56] Rev. Rul. 80-282, 1980-2 C.B. 178.

The legislative scorecard also cannot be lobbying. This usually means it cannot include a call to action such as "Call your Representative to make sure that H.R. 305 passes next year."

7. Funding voter guides

Private foundations may make grants for voter guides, but those guides must be completely nonpartisan. For these purposes, a voter guide is a document that identifies the candidates for one or more elected positions and provides information about those candidates. To be nonpartisan, these guides generally must be limited to providing clearly nonpartisan information about the upcoming election, including polling place locations and hours, the names and party affiliations of the candidates who will appear on the ballot, and so on. The positions of candidates on various issues should not be included, as the selection of the issues and the characterization of their positions will almost certainly result in a bias for or against particular candidates.

Unusual grantees: Funding coalitions

A private foundation may also be asked to fund a coalition advocacy effort. Usually such efforts are overseen by a single charity that collects the funds and is accountable for their use to all participants in the coalition. A coalition effort is treated as a specific advocacy project of the charity that is managing the funds, even though in fact many organizations may have influence on how those funds are spent.

Coalitions and voter participation

A private foundation may make a grant to support voter participation activities conducted by a coalition of organizations, but such activities must be nonpartisan. Therefore, care must be taken when a coalition involves non-charities. In that situation the grant or other support that will be controlled by the coalition must meet the requirements described below for grants to non-charities. An alternative and simpler arrangement is to make the grant to a participating charity for possible use by the coalition at the discretion of and under the control of the charity. In that situation, the rules for funding specific nonpartisan voter participation projects of charities described above (starting at page 179) apply.

A private foundation should not make a grant to or otherwise support the activities of a section 527 organization, as such organizations by definition are engaged in partisan activities. A private foundation should also not make a grant to develop, for example, a mailing list if the foundation knows the recipient charity intends to provide that list at no charge to a non-charity, including a section 527 organization. In both of these cases, the foundation will have engaged in partisan activity if it makes the grant.

Unusual grantees: Funding non-charities

A private foundation can also generally make grants for advocacy to non-charities, but only if four requirements are met:

- A pre-grant inquiry;
- A written grant agreement with certain terms;
- Regular reports from the grantee; and
- Reporting certain information on the foundation's annual Form 990-PF.

Each requirement is described below.

Pre-grant inquiry

Before making the grant, the private foundation must make a sufficient investigation to assure a reasonable person that the non-charity will use the grant for charitable or other exempt purposes. Topics that generally should be covered in such an investigation include the identity, history, and experience of the non-charity and its managers; the knowledge of the private foundation about the non-charity and its management; and any other readily available information concerning the management, activities, and practices of the non-charity. This requirement is generally satisfied if the non-charity has previously received grant funds from the private foundation and properly used and reported on the use of those funds.[57]

Written grant agreement with certain terms

The private foundation and the non-charity must enter into a written grant agreement. In the agreement, the non-charity must agree (i) to repay any portion of the amount granted which is not used for the stated purposes of the grant; (ii) to submit full and complete annual reports on the matter in

---

[57] Treas. Reg. § 53.4945-5(b)(2)(i).

which the funds are spent and the progress made in accomplishing the purposes of the grant; (iii) to maintain financial records that are available for the grantor to review; and (iv) to not spend any of the funds on activities listed in section 4945(d) (lobbying; political activity; grants to individuals that do not comply with section 4945(d)(3); grants to organizations that do not comply with section 4945(d)(4); and activities with a purpose other than a charitable, educational, or other exempt purpose). The agreement must also describe the purposes of the grant.[58]

Regular reports from the grantee

The grantee must provide the grantor with reports that describe the use of the grant, compliance with the terms of the grant, and the progress made by the non-charity toward achieving the purposes for which the private foundation made the grant. The non-charity must provide such reports on an annual basis within a "reasonable period of time" after the close of each of the non-charity's annual accounting periods during which any portion of the grant remains outstanding. In addition, the non-charity must provide a final report within a reasonable period of time after the close of the non-charity's annual accounting period during which it expends the last of the grant.[59]

Reporting certain information on the foundation's annual Form 990-PF

The private foundation must report certain information to the IRS about the grants with its annual Form 990-PF. For each year in which grant funds are paid, grant funds are outstanding, or a report from the non-charity is outstanding, the private foundation must report for each grant to a non-charity: (i) the name and address of the non-charity; (ii) the date and amount of the grant; (iii) the purpose of the grant; (iv) the amounts expended by the non-charity based on the most recent report received from the grantee; (v) the dates of reports received from the non-charity; (vi) the date(s) and results of any verification of the non-charity's reports; and (vii) whether, to the knowledge of the foundation, the non-charity has diverted any of the grant funds from the purpose of the grant. Information contained in reports from the non-charity that are received after the close of the foundation's tax year but before the Form 990-PF is filed does not need to be included in that year's report to the IRS.[60]

---

[58] Treas. Reg. § 53.4945-5(b)(3).
[59] Treas. Reg. § 53.4945-5(b)(c).
[60] Treas. Reg. § 53.4945-5(d).

See the Toolkit in Appendix A for a sample grant agreement with a non-charity.

Making grants for specific nonpartisan voter participation projects of non-charities

A private foundation may also make grants to non-charities for nonpartisan voter participation projects. Such grants must meet the same requirements as grants to non-charities engaged in advocacy. Such grants also may not be for voter registration, as grants for voter registration may only be made to charities or other private foundations that meet the requirements listed above.

A private foundation may not make grants to non-charities that only exist to engage in partisan political activities. Such non-charities include registered political committees, commonly known as political action committees, or PACs. Such non-charities also include all section 527 organizations—that is, organizations that are tax-exempt as political organizations under section 527 of the Internal Revenue Code.

Legal risk assessment when supporting advocacy and nonpartisan voter participation

A private foundation that violates these legal rules can face two different types of federal tax penalties. A private foundation that inadvertently funds lobbying or nonpartisan voter registration in violation of these rules is subject to a 10 percent penalty tax on the amounts spent.[61] The private foundation is also required to "correct" the violation. Correction entails recovering the improperly spent funds if possible and taking whatever other corrective action the IRS may require—usually instituting procedures and policies to prevent future violations.[62] Failure to correct will result in additional taxes on the foundation and possibly on its directors, officers, and other managers.

A private foundation that willfully and knowingly violates these legal rules, or funds either partisan voter participation activities or a substantial amount of lobbying, can lose its tax-exempt status.[63] In the event of a willful

---

[61] IRC § 4945(a)(1).
[62] IRC § 4945(i)(1); Treas. Reg. § 53.4945-1(d).
[63] IRC §§ 501(c)(3), 507(a).

and knowing violation of these rules, a private foundation may also be required to pay to the federal government the lesser of the taxes saved by any donors to the foundation or the value of the net assets of the foundation.[64]

To manage these risks, private foundations should

- Learn to identify the terms listed on pages 178 and 180 that indicate a potential grantee may be asking for funding for lobbying or partisan political activity and ask the grantee for more information when needed;
- Follow up with potential grantees as necessary if those terms are present;
- Document that grants have been made in compliance with these rules, as suggested above; and
- Review rules with legal counsel.

Reporting and accountability

Now that you are beginning to get the broad sense of what is illegal, what kinds of grantmaking are permissible, and how to manage legal risks, you will be better prepared to implement policies and procedures in grantmaking that improve and maintain accountability to the board, donors, government regulators, and the public.

Private foundations *directly* advocating for public policy

A private foundation can also, itself, engage in advocacy that it is permitted to fund through grants. For example, a private foundation may advocate on general public policy issues or for regulatory or other changes that do not involve legislation.

A private foundation may also directly engage in advocacy that falls within the exceptions regarding the nonpartisan analysis, study, or research or the technical assistance for government bodies. These activities are described in Part 3 of this chapter, page 200.

---

[64] IRC § 507(a), (c).

No Need to Require That Grant Funds Not Be Used for Lobbying

The rules for both general support grants and project-specific grants to charities means that a private foundation does not need to require that its funds not be used for lobbying in its written grant agreement with the charity grantee. For general support grants, it is sufficient that the foundation have confirmed the charity status of the grantee and not have any reason to believe that this status is at risk. For project-specific grants, it is sufficient that the foundation receive a budget from the charity grantee showing that the foundation's grant is equal to or less than the non-lobbying portion of the project's budget. This is true even if the foundation knows that one or more other, unrelated private foundations are providing the rest of the funding for the project (and so, inevitably, some of the funds from at least one of the private foundation funders will be used to fund the lobbying portion of the project budget). This result may seem counterintuitive, but it is the legal rule.

Reports from Grantees

It is natural for a grantee to highlight its legislative victories in its reports to its private foundation funders. To counter the risk that the grantee, by doing so, might mistakenly create the impression that the private foundation earmarked its funds for lobbying activities, a private foundation that has provided a project-specific grant should ask the grantee to also confirm in its report that the grant continues to meet one of the following two requirements:

1. The specific project funded had total non-lobbying expenditures that were at least as much (if not more) than that grant; OR

2. The grant was used only for advocacy activities that were not lobbying.

A private foundation may also directly influence legislation under two additional exceptions:

1. *Self-defense.* A private foundation can communicate with governmental officials (but not the public) about specific legislation that could affect the foundation's existence, powers, duties, tax-exempt status, or right to receive tax-deductible contributions.[65] For example, a private founda-

---

[65] Treas. Reg. § 53.4945-2(d)(3).

tion could press members of Congress to reduce the net investment income tax on foundations or to oppose an increase in the required payout amounts by private foundations.[66]

2. *Jointly funded project*. A jointly funded project is a project that is, or may be, funded by both a private foundation and the government. A private foundation may advocate in support of, for example, appropriations legislation that would provide the government funding. For example, if a private foundation agrees to match any government funding for a particular public park, the foundation can contact government officials to encourage them to pass legislation providing funding for the park. This exception only applies to communications with government officials, not to communications with the public.[67] There is no particular requirement regarding the size of the foundation's proposed grant as compared to the amount of government funding.

Private foundations *directly* conducting voter participation

A private foundation may, itself, engage in nonpartisan voter participation activities that it is permitted to fund through grants. The only exception is that a private foundation may not, itself, engage in a voter registration drive unless it satisfies the financial requirements for private foundation funding of such drives.

Private foundations in sum

Private foundations have the legal ability to foster impressive and lasting change by using legal avenues to fund and engage in advocacy. They have two forms of grants at their disposal (general support and project-specific) that can be used to help nonprofits develop capacity and deploy various policy and civic oriented tactics. Private foundations may also become direct players by engaging in all of the forms of policy participation except lobbying, plus they may also become highly influential in the legislative process through important exceptions to the definition of lobbying, including research.

---

[66] Editor's Note: The self-defense exception is even more important for private foundations due to the increasing number of legislative issues that relate to the operations and governance of foundations.

[67] Treas. Reg. § 53.4945-2(a)(3).

PART 2. What Community Foundations Need to Know about the Law

Good news! The federal law governing nonprofit advocacy and lobbying allows community foundations to become highly active in the public policy process. In nutshell, community foundations may

- Do all of the grantmaking activities allowed private foundations; and
- Make grants specifically for lobbying; and
- Conduct all of the public policy and civic strengthening activities that charities can.

This section presents the legal rules for public policy grantmaking and participation by community foundations. It first provides an overview of the legal rules pertaining to public policy or advocacy-related grantmaking by community foundations. Second, it discusses the rules governing community foundations' direct involvement in lobbying and other public policy activities.

Community foundation grants for public policy and civic strengthening projects

Community foundations may make grants to charities that lobby and conduct other types of public policy activities as part of their activities similarly to private foundations. Community foundations usually make one of two types of grants: general support grants and project-specific grants. The following explains how they may be used as vehicles to support public policy and civic strengthening activities. A community foundation may

1. Make general support grants to charities engaged in public policy and nonpartisan voter participation efforts;

2. Make grants for specific public policy projects of charities and other nonprofits; and

3. Make grants for specific nonpartisan voter participation projects of charities and other nonprofits.

1. General support grants

Community foundations may make general support grants to charities engaged in advocacy or voter participation without any restrictions. A community foundation may make such grants from its general funds or from a donor-advised fund, on the advice of a donor. The only requirement is that the community foundation and the charity may not have an agreement that the grant will be used for specific activities. Otherwise the rules relating to grants for specific projects apply.

2. Specific public policy–related projects

Community foundations, unlike private foundations, may support a limited amount of lobbying. The form of support may be money, all of which is for lobbying, or through a specific project that has a lobbying component. However, when a community foundation gives money to an organization that is for legislative lobbying, the lobbying expenditures of that organization count against the annual amount of lobbying expenditures allowed by the community foundation under the IRS code.

Funding a charity's public policy project: If a community foundation wants to fund a project that has a lobbying component but does not want to fund the lobbying part, it can specifically earmark the grant for non-lobbying activities only.[68]

Funding non-charities' public policy projects: A community foundation grant to a non-charity for a specific public policy project that has a lobbying component will be considered a lobbying expenditure by the community foundation in the amount of the non-charity's *total* lobbying expenditures. Again, if the community foundation does not want to fund the lobbying part of the public policy project of the organization, it may specifically earmark the grant for non-lobbying activities only.[69]

The next question is, How much money may a community foundation spend on legislative lobbying in a one-year period, whether those expenditures are through a grantee organization that is lobbying or through the community foundation itself? The answer depends on which set of lobbying expenditure rules the community foundation has chosen to follow.

---

[68] Treas. Reg. § 56.4911-3(c)(1), (2).
[69] Treas. Reg. §§ 56.4911-3(c)(3), 46.5911-4(f)(3).

The choice of rules is either a clear "bright-line" rule with fixed limits, or a more amorphous rule with significant gray areas. These rules are described in detail in Part 3 of this chapter.

3. Grants for specific nonpartisan voter participation projects

A community foundation may make grants to both charities and non-charities to support voter participation activities. The only restriction on community foundation grants for specific nonpartisan voter participation projects is that such activities must be nonpartisan. The nonpartisan standard for a community foundation is the same as the standard that applies to a private foundation. Therefore, a community foundation may make a grant to support a nonpartisan candidate forum, a nonpartisan candidate questionnaire, a nonpartisan voter registration drive or get-out-the-vote effort, and nonpartisan issue advocacy or legislative scorecards that do not support or oppose a candidate for elected public office.

Community foundation direct participation in public policy and voter education activities

A community foundation may directly do any and all forms of public policy and civic activity that it is permitted to fund through grants. Such activities include lobbying and nonpartisan voter education.

Previously mentioned was the choice of federal lobbying rules that community foundations, and all other charities under 501(c)(3), can follow. These rules include the default rule and the expenditure test, as explained below.

The default rule—"insubstantial" lobbying: The default tax rule governing lobbying by community foundations (and all charities) is that a community foundation may only engage in lobbying as an insubstantial part of its activities.[70] Unfortunately, how much money or activity that exceeds an "insubstantial" part has never been clearly defined.

The generally preferred choice—the expenditure test: It is recommended that most charities, including community foundations, choose the set of rules called the "expenditure test" by making what is called the 501(h) election.

---

[70] IRC § 501(c)(3).

(See Part 3 of this chapter that explains the 501(h) election of the expenditure test rules governing lobbying.)

In a nutshell, the expenditure test offers three advantages to the "insubstantial" lobbying rule: clarity, latitude, and safety.

1. *Clarity*: A community foundation that makes the 501(h) election will also be subject to the clearest definition of lobbying available under the tax code. A community foundation or charity is only lobbying when it communicates with intention to influence specific legislation. (See the definitions in Part 3 of this chapter for the specific definition of lobbying.) In addition, there are several important exceptions to the definition of lobbying that include activities that are directly related to legislation. See Part 3 on the "expenditure test."

2. *Latitude*: Community foundations may spend up to $1 million per year, depending on the size of their budget. The annual amount that a community may spend on lobbying is based on a sliding scale. See Part 3 for the expenditure test rules and limits.

3. *Safety:* The IRS has stated publicly on a number of occasions that the choice to make the 501(h) election and follow the expenditure test rules does not, in itself, expose the organization to an increased risk of an audit.[71]

Community foundations in sum

Community foundations have the same legal latitude to engage in public policy and voter education as charities. This means that they have *greater latitude* than private foundations in that community foundations can lobby. Community foundations, like all other charities, have a choice of rules they may follow to govern lobbying activities. By default they fall under a rule that allows no more than an insubstantial amount of money and activity to be devoted to lobbying annually. Increasingly, community foundations, like other charities, are electing to adhere to the expenditure test rules that provide clarity in terms of definitions and expenditure limits and still provide plenty of latitude to spend. In terms of grantmaking, com-

---

[71] See the letter from Thomas Miller of the Internal Revenue Service to Charity Lobbying in the Public Interest (now Center for Lobbying in the Public Interest), June 26, 2000, referencing the instructions in the Internal Revenue Manual. The letter is available at http://www.clpi.org/Lobbying_and_the_Law.aspx. Note: The letter to CLPI is not considered authoritative in the same manner as an IRS general counsel memorandum or other official guidance disseminated to the public.

munity foundations have greater latitude than private foundations in their grantmaking for public policy because they may earmark grants for lobbying by grantees. However, their grantees' expenditures on lobbying with community foundation money accrue toward the community foundation's lobby expenditure limits. Community foundations can engage in the same wide array of civic and voter education activities that all other charitable organizations can, so long as they are nonpartisan.

PART 3. The Expenditure Test: Taking the 501(h) Election

The expenditure test was created by the 1976 Tax Act, and the IRS regulations were made final in 1990. In brief, the expenditure test is a set of IRS rules that define lobbying (as distinct from other advocacy activities), provide expenditure limits for lobbying, and apply penalties for excessive expenditures. The catch is that 501(c)(3) organizations, excluding private foundations, must choose or affirmatively "elect" to follow them. If a charity or community foundation does not elect to come under the expenditure test rules, they are by default under an older but very current IRS rule that no substantial part of a 501(c)(3) organization's annual exempt purpose expenditures may be spent on lobbying annually. This older rule has some negative attributes that are leading nonprofits to elect the expenditure test: The older rule lacks a clear definition of lobbying and no definition of how much money is "substantial."

This section of the book proceeds by explaining the expenditure test, including its definition of lobbying, important exceptions to the definition, the lobby expenditure limits scale, the pros and cons of the expenditure test, and the penalties for violations.

Definitions specific to lobbying

Lobbying: An attempt to influence legislation by communicating either with government officials or employees (direct lobbying) or with the public (grassroots lobbying).[72]

---

[72] IRC § 4911(d); Treas. Reg. § 56.4911-2(a)(1).

Legislation: 1) An action of a legislature, including acts, bills, resolutions, legislative vetoes, approval of nominees, and ratification of treaties; 2) legislative proposals that have yet to be introduced; and 3) ballot initiatives, referenda, constitutional amendments, and other matters submitted directly to the public for approval.[73]

Direct lobbying: A communication with

- A legislator or legislative employee that a) refers to specific legislation and b) reflects a view on that legislation;
- An executive branch official or employee that a) refers to specific legislation, b) reflects a view on that legislation, and c) the principal purpose of the communication is to influence legislation; or
- The public that a) refers to a ballot initiative, referenda, constitutional amendment, or other matter submitted directly to the public for approval, and b) reflects a view on that initiative, etc.[74]

Grassroots lobbying: A communication with the public that a) refers to specific legislation, b) reflects a view on that legislation, and c) includes a call to action.[75] A call to action is not required if the mass media rule, described below, applies.

Call to action: A communication includes a call to action if it:

- Tells the recipient to contact a government official or employee about legislation;
- Provides the address or telephone number of a legislator or employee of a legislative body;
- Provides a petition, tear-off postcard, e-mail, etc. addressed to a government official or employee; or
- Specifically identifies a legislator who will vote on the legislation as opposing the communication's view on the legislation, as being undecided on the legislation, as being a member of the committee or subcommittee considering the legislation, or as being the recipient's representative; this does not include, however, naming the main spon-

---

[73] Treas. Reg. § 46.4911-2(d)(1).
[74] Treas. Reg. § 56.4911-2(b)(1).
[75] Treas. Reg. § 56.4911-2(b)(2).

How to Choose the Expenditure Test by Making the 501(h) Election

A community foundation may make the 501(h) election by filing the simple one-page IRS Form 5768. As long as a community foundation files the form before the end of its fiscal year, the election will apply for the entire year. The community foundation may also revoke the 501(h) election at any time by filing the form again. The revocation will be effective for the community foundation's next fiscal year. This form can be found at http://www.irs.gov or in the Toolkit, page 242.

When There Is No Call to Action, It's Not Lobbying

Remember, communications with the public are *not* "lobbying" if they do not include a call to action. A private foundation may, therefore, make a grant to pay for such communications. For example, a private foundation may make a grant to pay for an ad stating "We need to repeal the PATRIOT Act now or America will never truly be free again!" as long as the ad does not include a call to action. The only exception is if the communication refers to highly publicized legislation within two weeks of a legislative or legislative committee vote on the legislation (see the description of the "mass media" rule discussed below).

sor or sponsors of legislation in order to identify it (for example, the "McCain-Feingold bill").[76]

Mass media rule: The mass media rule applies only when legislation is highly publicized and the communication is made within *two weeks* of a legislative or legislative committee vote on the legislation. Legislation is highly publicized if it has received frequent coverage on television and radio and in general-circulation newspapers in the two weeks preceding the vote. If this rule applies, a paid television, radio, billboard, or general-circulation newspaper or magazine advertisement is presumed to be grassroots lobbying if it refers to the legislation and reflects a view on that legislation (no call to action required) or if it refers to the general subject of the legislation and includes a call to action. An organization may overcome this presumption if the paid advertisement is a type of communication regularly made by the organization without regard to the timing of legislation or that the timing of the paid advertisement was otherwise unrelated to the upcoming legislative action.[77]

---

[76] Treas. Reg. § 56.4911-2(b)(2)(iii).
[77] Treas. Reg. § 56.4911-2(b)(5).

Foreign legislation: Lobbying includes communications with foreign government officials or citizens about foreign legislation that otherwise meet the above definitions and does not fall within one of the exceptions.[78]

Exceptions to the lobbying definitions

There are exceptions to the lobbying definitions that enable private foundations and community foundations to fund or take part in certain legislation-related projects. The exceptions aid community foundations in that they can also fund and do the excepted activities, and in that the expenditures of organizations they have funded to do such activities do not count toward the community foundation's lobbying expenditure limits. Normally, if community foundations are doing or funding lobbying they must count such expenditures toward their own lobbying limits under the tax law. Finally, since the section 501(h) limits are based solely on expenditures, lobbying activities that do not involve expenditures, such as the efforts of volunteers, can occur in an unlimited amount.

The following legislation-related activities are *not* prohibited for private foundations and do not count as lobbying for community foundations (but would be permissible anyway).

1. *Nonpartisan analysis, study, or research.* Preparations of nonpartisan analysis, study, or research—as well as distribution to the public or government—is NOT considered lobbying, even if the analysis argues for or against specific legislation. The analysis must (a) provide a sufficiently "full and fair exposition" of the legislation to allow the recipient to form his or her own conclusions; (b) be distributed to persons on both sides of the legislation; and (c) not include a "direct call to action."[79] A full and fair exposition means providing a factual basis for the conclusions reached and arguing in a reasoned fashion for the conclusions from that basis.[80] A direct call to action is (1) telling the recipient to contact a government official about legislation; (2) providing the address, e-mail, or telephone number of a legislator or employee of a legislative body; or (3) providing a petition, tear-off postcard, etc. addressed to a government official. For example, scholarly research and academic papers will

---

[78] See Rev. Rul. 73-440, 1973-2 C.B. 177.
[79] Treas. Reg. § 53.4945-2(d)(1).
[80] See Rev. Proc. 86-43, 1986-2 C.B. 729.

almost always fall within this exception. An analysis, study, or research that argues for or against specific legislation and is later distributed with a direct call to action will become grassroots lobbying unless the primary purpose in preparing it was not for use in lobbying or six months has passed since it was prepared.[81]

Example: No to Gun Violence, a charity, asks the John and Jane Doe Family Foundation for a grant to produce a lengthy report by two university professors on the comparative dangers of families owning handguns versus owning rifles and other types of firearms. No to Gun Violence expects the report to demonstrate that handguns result in a much higher rate of intra-family gun violence, all other factors being equal. No to Gun Violence also expects the report to conclude with a specific legislative recommendation regarding limiting ownership of handguns. The report will be distributed through normal academic channels and to the press and public and will not include or be accompanied by a direct call to action. The John and Jane Doe Family Foundation may make this grant because it is for nonpartisan analysis, study, or research.

2. *Technical Assistance for Governmental Bodies.* An oral or written response to a written request for information from a legislative committee, subcommittee, agency, or other governmental body is NOT considered lobbying.[82] The written request must come from the body itself or someone authorized to speak on the body's behalf, such as the chairman of a legislative committee, and not from only an individual legislator or government employee.

Example: The Chair of the Judiciary Committee of the California Assembly has asked the executive director of No to Gun Violence to testify before the Committee on legislative options for reducing gun violence. No to Gun Violence asks the John and Jane Doe Foundation for a grant to cover the cost of the executive director's travel to California to testify. While there, she will also meet with several major donors and local gun control advocates, but she will not meet with government officials regarding legislation or otherwise engage in lobbying. The John and Jane Doe Foundation may make the grant because to the extent it relates to legislation, it qualifies as technical assistance.

---

[81] Treas. Reg. §§ 56.4945-2(d)(1)(v), 56.4911-2(b)(2)(v).
[82] Treas. Reg. § 53.4945-2(d)(2).

Lobby expenditure limits

A community foundation that makes the 501(h) election will usually be able to engage in a greater amount of lobbying. This is because once the 501(h) election is made, the lobbying limits are based on a sliding scale that starts at 20 percent of a community foundation's first $500,000 of expenditures and declines from there to 5 percent of expenditures above $1.5 million. Of this amount, only one-quarter can be spent on grassroots lobbying. Lobbying expenditures are capped at $1 million for community foundations with annual expenditures of $17 million or more. The sidebar below shows the sliding scale.

The Section 501(h) Election Limits on Lobbying

Expenditures	Overall Ceiling	Grassroots Ceiling
Not over $500,000	20% (up to $100,000)	5% (up to $25,000)
$500,001 to $1,000,000	$100,000 + 15% of excess over $500,000	$25,000 + 3.75% of excess over $500,000
$1,000,001 to $1,500,000	$175,000 + 10% of excess over $1,000,000	$43,750 + 2.5% of excess over $1,000,000
$1,500,001 to $17,000,000	$225,000 + 5% of excess over $1,500,000	$56,250 + 1.25% of excess over $1,500,000
Over $17,000,000	$1,000,000	$250,000 *

Expenditures include any amounts paid by a community foundation to advance charitable purposes, plus lobbying expenditures and some fundraising expenditures. Expenditures do not include investment management expenses, expenses related to the conduct of any unrelated trade or business, amounts paid for outside fundraising services, and expenses related to a "separate fundraising unit" within the organization, defined as a group of two or more employees devoting a majority of their time to fundraising activities.** Expenditures that must be treated as capital expenditures under applicable tax rules may not be treated as exempt purpose expenditures, but an organization may claim a reasonable depreciation allowance with respect to capital assets used in exempt purpose activities as exempt purpose expenditures.***

* IRC § 4911(c).
** Treas. Reg. § 56.4911-4(b), (c).
*** IRC § 4911(e)(4); Treas. Reg. § 56.4911-4(b)(7), (c)(5).

Advantages and disadvantages of the 501(h) election of the expenditure test for charities and community foundations

Advantages

- The election provides clear limits based on expenditures only. The substantial part test does not have a clear limit and is based on all of the relevant facts and circumstances, not just the level of lobbying expenditures.

- It subjects an organization to only financial penalties for minor violations, not loss of tax-exempt status. The only penalty for violating the substantial part test is loss of tax-exempt status.

- The 501(h) election provides a precise and narrow definition of lobbying that excludes many advocacy efforts. The substantial part test does not provide such a definition and may, therefore, include a larger set of advocacy activities.

Disadvantages

- The 501(h) election caps the permitted amount of lobbying for large organizations at $1 million in expenditures, of which only $250,000 can be used for grassroots lobbying. The substantial part test may therefore permit more lobbying for the largest organizations (with annual expenditures of $17 million or more).

- The 501(h) election requires the aggregation of the lobbying expenditures of affiliated organizations. Organizations are generally affiliated if one organization is able to control action on legislative issues by the other because of interlocking governing boards or provisions in the controlled organization's articles of incorporation, bylaws, or other governing documents.[83] The substantial part test applies to each organization by itself.

Penalties

A community foundation that violates these legal rules can face two different types of federal tax penalties. The penalties can be financial or they can be revocation of the foundation's tax-exempt status.

---

[83] Treas. Reg. § 56.4911-7(a)(1).

A community foundation that has not made the 501(h) election can lose its tax-exempt status and face a 5 percent tax on its lobbying expenditures if lobbying becomes a substantial part of its activities.[84] The IRS usually will settle a case without revocation if the violation was inadvertent. When the IRS does choose to settle for a sanction short of revocation, it will frequently do so by 1) imposing a fine equal to a percentage of the tax the community foundation would owe if it were treated as a taxable entity during the years in question, and 2) requiring the community foundation to adopt administrative procedures sufficient to prevent future violations.

A community foundation that has made the 501(h) election is subject to a penalty tax equal to 25 percent of the amount by which its exceeds either its overall limit on lobbying expenditures or its limit on grassroots lobbying expenditures. The community foundation will not lose its tax-exempt status unless it exceeds either the overall or grassroots lobbying expenditure ceiling by more than 50 percent over a four-year period, however.[85]

A community foundation that engages in partisan political activities can lose its tax-exempt status. It can also be subject to a 10 percent tax on the amounts expended on such activities and its managers can be subject to a 2.5 percent tax (up to $5,000) on the same amounts.[86] The IRS also can immediately terminate a community foundation's tax year and assess tax for willful and flagrant violations of the prohibition and can seek an injunction in the event of flagrant violations.[87]

The best way to manage the risk is to follow the same steps as a private foundation:

1. Learn to identify the terms listed above that indicate a potential grantee may be asking for funding for lobbying or partisan political activity;

2. Follow up with potential grantees when those terms are present;

3. Document that grants have been made in compliance with these rules, as suggested above; and

4. Review with legal counsel.

— — —

[84] IRC §§ 501(c)(3), 4912.
[85] IRC § 501(h)(1).
[86] IRC § 4955.
[87] IRC §§ 6852, 7409.

Legal Resources and Legal Counsel

Additional free and low-cost legal resources on how foundations can support advocacy and nonpartisan voter participation efforts can be found at:

- Alliance for Justice: http//www.allianceforjustice.org/foundation/index.html

- Center for Lobbying in the Public Interest: http//www.clpi.org

- Council on Foundations: http//www.cof.org

- Independent Sector: http//www.independentsector.org/programs/gr/advocacy_lobbying.htm

A private foundation or a community foundation may not, however, find its particular questions regarding support advocacy or voter participation answered by these general legal resources. The foundation should, in this case, consult with an attorney who specializes in advising tax-exempt organizations on their advocacy and election-related activities. The stakes are too high—substantial financial penalties and possible loss of tax-exempt status—to ignore these issues until the IRS is on the doorstep. Any of the above organizations can provide a referral to an attorney with expertise in this area.

Conclusion

For many years, myths about the law governing foundation advocacy served to deter participation in policymaking and civic activities or at least contribute to overly cautious behavior. The reality is that there is significant legal latitude for foundations to unleash financial resources to reach goals through the public policy process and to strengthen our democracy.

Private foundations may not be able to fund or engage directly in lobbying, with some important exceptions. However, they have legal avenues for funding public policy at their disposal. Community foundations, in contrast, have greater latitude than private foundations: they follow the charity rules that allow them to lobby under the expenditure limits and to make grants for all forms of advocacy, including lobbying. Similar to any regulated business, the rules may seem somewhat complicated, but chapters like this one—and the written work of foundation technical assistance organizations—will help foundations and their legal counsel understand the law. Seek legal counsel that has expertise in the area of foundation advocacy to help you establish and maintain an internal legal framework for public policy philanthropy.

Chapter Ten

Evaluating Public Policy Grantmaking

John Sherman and Gayle Peterson

In 2003, private foundations spent more than $490 million on public policy grantmaking. Did this significant investment make a difference? What was the impact? Was it worth the investment? What was learned?

This chapter will help grantmakers answer these vital questions. Designed as a practical, tactical tool, it explains the process of public policy evaluation—the why, who, what, when, and how—to better inform decision making. It is a useful primer for both experienced foundations (with specific goals, objectives, outcomes, and indicators for success) as well as the novice who wants to learn more. Just as important, it is useful to grantees. Grantmakers and grant recipients learning together can yield powerful results through participation in public policymaking.

To begin the discussion, it is important to provide definitions.

- *Grantmakers* develop programs to realign public and private goals toward policy outcomes. Grantmakers participate in policymaking directly or through the work of grantee organizations. *Grantees* are the change agents. Policy goals are achieved through their hard work.

- *Policy evaluation* assesses public policy education, advocacy, and civic efforts of grantmakers and grantees from the local community level to the expansive federal level.

CHAPTER SNAPSHOT

This chapter offers a practical primer on

- Why, who, what, when, and how to evaluate public policy grantmaking

Evaluation enables grantmakers and grantees to move beyond intuition to tangible results. Foundations that want to measure effectiveness, impact, and relevance of public policy projects use evaluation for answers and direction.

Evaluation assesses the effectiveness of policy change efforts while measuring impact and providing lessons learned to hone future collective strategies.

Why Evaluate?

Before a foundation puts a public policy evaluation in motion, it must understand why evaluation is important. Program evaluation for policy can elicit knowledge about processes and outcomes—information more powerful than simply answering the question of whether a policy change effort is a win or a loss. Evaluations provide grantmakers and grantees with opportunities for learning about the *processes* used to create policy change as well as the *outcomes* of those processes. Evaluation goes beyond whether a policy change occurred to uncovering vital lessons for foundations and their grantees.

Knowing why one should undertake evaluation and for whom the evaluation is targeted is critical in determining *what* to evaluate. Public policy evaluation can aid

- Measurement of grantee contribution toward the success of passage or implementation of a public policy
- Determination of public policy approach relevance toward achieving the goals of the foundation or a specific program
- Capture of specific strategies and processes that contribute to public policy success and the reasons for success or failure
- Understanding of grantee(s) capacity (individually and collectively) to conceive and implement pubic policy initiatives and ensure the long-term success of such activities

How Evaluation Works

The Headwaters Group believes that the evaluation process should be determined by the reasons grantmakers want to evaluate—including the intended audience and uses for the insights gained. Before we address public policy evaluation, here is a brief overview of how evaluation works.[88]

---

[88] Editor's note: Fieldstone Alliance offers two publications on the uses of evaluation. These include *A Funder's Guide to Evaluation: Leveraging Evaluation to Improve Nonprofit Effectiveness* by Peter York and *The Manager's Guide to Program Evaluation: Planning, Contracting, and Managing for Useful Results* by Paul Mattessich.

Program development evaluation should be integrated early in the process rather than as an afterthought. Evaluation is easier when it is integrated into a program from the outset.

The W.K. Kellogg Foundation's use of logic models[89] and The Pew Charitable Trusts' focus on evaluation in the earliest stages of program planning[90] exemplify an integrated planning–evaluation approach to grantmaking.

The process of evaluation is dynamic. It contributes to thoughtful grantmaking, and to refining programmatic and grantee strategies by building on knowledge gained from the evaluation. Figure 9, Evaluation as Part of a Dynamic Learning Loop, below, illustrates the dynamic qualities of evaluation.

Figure 9. Evaluation as Part of a Dynamic Learning Loop _____

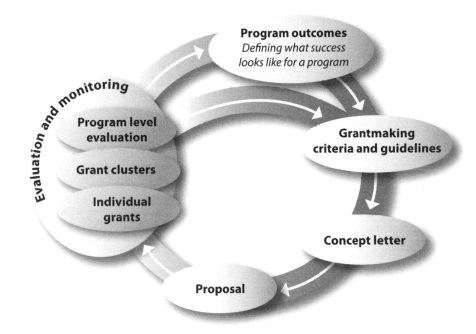

[89] W.K. Kellogg Foundation, Logic Model Development Guide (Battle Creek, MI, January 2004), http://www.wkkf.org/Pubs/Tools/Evaluation/Pub3669.pdf#search=%22Logic%20Model%20Development%20Guide%22.

[90] The Pew Charitable Trusts, *Returning Results: Planning and Evaluation at The Pew Charitable Trusts* (Philadelphia, January 2001), http://www.pewtrusts.com/pdf/returning_results.pdf.

Critical elements of dynamic learning include

- *Program outcomes:* Evaluation starts with defining what success looks like for a program—what specific outcomes the foundation wants to achieve. The optimal time for these to be established is at the beginning of a new program, not once it has been launched.

- *Grantmaking criteria and guidelines:* Program success, defined through clearly articulated outcomes, is then communicated to grantseekers via the grant application guidelines and criteria.

- *Concept letter and proposal:* Concept letters and proposals are expected to demonstrate how the proposed projects will address one or more of the program's outcomes and how the projects will be evaluated.[91] Because outcomes (highlighted as the cornerstone of the grant guidelines) direct the acceptance or rejection of concept letters and proposals, they can be quickly assessed. By using the outcomes as the standard (or one of the standards) for determining the fit of a concept letter and proposal with the intent of a program or initiative, a set of feedback loops is established. For example, if few concept letters address the outcomes, there may be an issue with the way in which the outcomes are communicated in the grant application criteria or guidelines. Foundation staff can assess individually and collectively whether their process for accepting or rejecting concept letters is working. If a large number of proposals are being invited based on concept letters that do not adequately address the outcomes, the concept letter review process may be faulty.

Foundation boards have the opportunity to examine and learn whether they, in fact, support proposals that address outcomes or if they support proposals that do not address the outcomes (in which case the evaluation becomes muddier or, at least, the evaluation questions change).

- *Evaluation (project- and cluster-level):* Well-defined outcomes communicated effectively through the grant application process can lead to much clearer and easier evaluations. Evaluators have a clear set of outcomes with which to measure the individual grants and the cluster of related grants. These results are then fed back to the grantees (to inform their

---

[91] Private foundations may not articulate specific lobbying outcomes as grant criteria or outcomes of a partisan nature as part of grant guidelines. However, guidelines may call for broad policy outcomes including expanding the number of Americans with health insurance, or increasing the number of Americans who understand their voting rights.

learning about the strategies and processes) and to the grantmaker (to inform its learning and improve the next iteration of grantmaking).

Considerations and Cautions Distinct to Evaluation of Public Policy Related Projects

Public policy evaluation needs to follow the same standards and processes that any other form of evaluation does. However, there are some important evaluation considerations relevant to typical policy projects.

1. *Know which phase of public policy change the project is focused on.* There are several specific phases of the public policy process. (See Chapter 6, The Public Policy Process, page 96.) This is a fairly obvious point, yet without explicit understanding of the phases of the public policy process, evaluation can focus on the wrong phase, thus providing useless data and inappropriate findings. The evaluation methodologies identified in this chapter can be applied to any of the phases of the public policy process. Among the key phases include:

   - Identifying public problems or opportunities
   - Determining who is affected and involved in the issue
   - Gathering information about what options and solutions exist
   - Bringing key players together for deliberation and discussion
   - Planning for public policy and civic action
   - Building the capacity of groups that will engage in advocacy
   - Organizing and mobilizing activities to influence government decision makers or other stakeholders to agree to a policy change or new way of doing civic business
   - Working with agencies and other groups to put the agreed-upon change into place
   - Evaluating and tracing results

2. *Policy change does not happen quickly* regardless of the phase. The evaluation needs to account for this. More importantly, the project's time frame must be reasonable for the targeted policy change. An effective evaluation will identify such issues, the reasons for them, and whether or not they could have been foreseen by the grantee or the foundation.

3. *Policy change is messy.* Cause and effect and direct attribution of a grantee's work to the policy change can often be difficult to ascertain and measure. External factors, policy changes at other levels of government, and the ever-changing faces of policymakers can play havoc with the best-laid strategies and timelines. The evaluation (and evaluator) needs to be flexible and adaptive to account for these changing conditions.

4. *Consult the appropriate decision makers.* A necessary ingredient to making policy and civic change happen is power. An evaluation of whether a grantee is influential in the policymaking process requires information from government officials, corporate officials (if a business is the target of advocacy), or other decision makers. The evaluator should be careful to be precise about whom to interview. Depending on the strategies used, the evaluation should gather the opinions of the specific decision makers. Examples include legislators who are members of the committee of jurisdiction for that issue, the specific agency staff including the commissioner who makes policy rules, and the chiefs of editorial boards.

5. *Think about the short- and long-term impact of the public policy work on your organization and its allies.* Whether the first battle is won or lost, effective advocates know how to use resources including coalition power, political capital, and financial strength effectively over the long term—where lasting victories are secured.

Who should be involved in the evaluation

Who will benefit and learn from evaluation? The audiences targeted for evaluation are likely beneficiaries. When the organization being evaluated is an active partner in the entire process, more learning occurs because the organization can identify what it wants to learn from the evaluation. Thinking about how the final evaluation document might be used may also inform who should be involved.

Figure 10. Examples of What to Evaluate

Why Evaluate	What to Evaluate
What was the contribution of grantees to the outcome of the grant-funded public policy effort? (Examples: policy formation, coalition building, executive branch advocacy, or influencing the media.)	Evaluate the grantee's performance in the context of the other factors impacting the outcome of the public policy initiative. (Examples: changes in priority by the legislative branch or executive branch or shifts in public opinion.)
Does the public policy approach actually have an impact on the goals the foundation wants to achieve (or the goals that a specific program aims to achieve)?	Evaluate the relative contribution of a grantee's public policy initiative to meeting program goals.
Which specific strategies and processes contributed to the success or failure of a public policy activity? Why and how did these strategies contribute to the success or failure?	Evaluate the strategies and processes used by grantees to achieve public policy change.
Are the grantees now better able to conceive and implement pubic policy initiatives? Are they better able to ensure the long-term success of the public policy initiatives they successfully implement?	Evaluate the relative difference in these capacities before the public policy initiative and after the initiative was enacted.

What should be evaluated

Policy evaluation needs to target the aspects of a public policy grant or program that a foundation wants to know more about. Figure 10 illustrates examples of what to evaluate in a process-based policy evaluation, based on the reasons why a policy change initiative is to be evaluated.

Evaluators and grantmakers need to determine *at what scale* the evaluation should take place. They need to decide either to evaluate grantees case by case (an *individual evaluation*) or to evaluate many grantees that are involved in similar activities, such as all those within a grantmaking program (called a *cluster evaluation* or *initiative evaluation*). In the case of policy work, the latter might include evaluating all the grantees that are participating in a policy-focused grantmaking initiative.

When evaluations are conducted at the individual grant level, the grant's amount and duration are the criteria most often used in determining the intensity of an evaluation. Some foundations simply monitor individual grants to ensure compliance with the grant agreement. Others want cursory, internally conducted evaluations for grants less than a certain size and independent third-party evaluations for larger grants. Most, however, request evaluation of individual grants but do not indicate how the evaluation should be done.

When clusters of grantees are evaluated, some foundations create formal evaluation processes at the inception of the grantmaking program (or the grantmaking initiative within a program). These are communicated to grantees and are often approved by the foundation board. Sometimes these evaluations are conducted internally, especially if there is a large evaluation staff. Other times they are conceived and conducted by a third party. In either case, the level of resources committed to the evaluation correlates with the size of the grantmaking budget for the initiative.[92]

When to evaluate

Evaluation can occur at any time and for any duration of a program. As discussed earlier, it is preferable to engage in evaluation from the beginning of a program.

Formative evaluations are performed to help inform the program's activities and strategies, thereby offering the grantees and grantmaker opportunities to alter their efforts accordingly. These evaluations can occur at any time during the program. *Summative* evaluation is focused more on the outcome of the program and determining whether, why, and how collectively the program achieved its objectives.

Evaluation should identify ways to improve performance, identify the lessons learned, and measure progress toward the program's (or individual grant's) objectives. The issue of *when* to evaluate should be based on

- Why the evaluation is being conducted and the needs of those being served by it

---

[92] A general guideline is to estimate costs for evaluation at between 5 to 10 percent of the overall budget; thus, up to $10,000 could be spent on a $100,000 grant or $5 million on a $50 million initiative.

- The duration of the program (a single-year program would probably only need a summative evaluation, whereas a multiyear program may need evaluation annually or biennially)

Evaluation Tools and Approaches

Public policy evaluation methodologies vary.[93] Good results can come from various approaches, four of which are described here. Grantmakers can evaluate

1. Grantee performance, including content and context research and key informant interviews
2. Strategy-level success
3. Specific strategy indicators
4. Grantee capacity

1. Grantee performance

Ruth Holton of The California Wellness Foundation notes, "It can be difficult to attribute a policy achievement to the actions of specific grantees…frequently such change is the result of a combined effort of several organizations and political factors outside the control of the grantees."[94] To understand the contributions of the grantees, the contribution and interplay of other factors external to grantees' efforts must be understood. It is important to account for the content of their efforts as well as the context. These external factors and their contribution to performance can be identified through:

- *Media research* to understand the publicly acknowledged forces at play.

- *Review of internal and official documents* of policymakers and the policymaking body. These materials offer the official legislative, administrative, and judicial history of the policymaking effort. At the least they can better prepare the evaluator for the next step (interviews) and at the most

[93] An excellent resource on this topic is The California Endowment's *The Challenge of Assessing Policy and Advocacy Activities: Strategies for a Prospective Evaluation Approach*, October 2005, available at http://www.calendow.org/reference/publications/pdf/npolicy/51565_CEAdvocacyBook8FINAL.pdf.

[94] Ruth Holton, *Reflections on Public Policy Grantmaking*, Report from The California Wellness Foundation (Woodland Hills, CA, May 2002), 4, http://www.tcwf.org/pdf_docs/reflections/may2002.pdf.

can shed important light on the workings, priorities, and machinations of the public policymaking body (whether it is legislative, administrative, or judicial).

- *Key informant interviews.* Most often the most productive and informative sources of evaluation data are the key informant interviews—grantees, the policymaking decision makers or their key staff (often more useful and more insightful), and third-party observers. This qualitative data set provides the richness of the policymaking landscape. Though often data is contradictory, through a sufficient number of interviews across a number of types of interviewees, an evaluator can triangulate on some basic truths about the information he or she seeks. Third parties are those who are following the specific public policy in question such as the media, lobbyists, and individuals from organizations that may not be engaged in the specific policy issue but are politically savvy.

2. Strategy-level success

Often, a foundation or its grantees involved in public policy use more than one strategy to meet an overall goal. When working with evaluators, a key consideration for foundations is to ensure that the evaluator is prepared to evaluate each strategy or tactic to create a comprehensive evaluation report.

Another important aspect of evaluating grantees' success is how the grantees adapt strategically to changing events in the world of public policy and politics. For example, a group of grantees may have set a certain goal, but, because of changes in priority by government, the original outcomes could not be reached during the period of the grant. Consequently, the evaluation might focus on what choices and decisions were made to advance the original goal in light of the uncontrollable obstacles faced by the grantees.

3. Specific strategy indicators

When assessing strategies, evaluators usually rely on key informant interviews. Depending on the specific strategies used, they may also employ other evaluation techniques. Often in public policy initiatives, foundation and grantees use media campaigns, grassroots mobilization, and "grass tops" mobilization. There are various evaluation approaches suitable for each. Note that the expense of evaluation can vary significantly depending on the tools used. Grantees and foundations should consider the cost of evaluation relative to the project budget when making choices about evaluation approaches.

Media campaigns. Media campaigns are diverse in their focus, messages, and intent. Regardless, there are specific evaluation methodologies that are often employed to measure the impact of media campaigns on the target audience and on the actions taken due to the media exposure. In addition to including questions on media impact and influence in key informant interviews, evaluators have devised simple yet sophisticated surveys to track media impact. If this is a strategy a foundation is using, then it needs to be sure the evaluator has experience in assessing media.[95]

Outreach and mobilization of the grassroots. Grassroots mobilization efforts usually target individual members of organizations participating in the public policy initiative or organizations considered sympathetic to the public policy change. The activities may be done through meetings, newsletters, e-mails, phone calls, and door-to-door efforts. Assessing the impact of each of the outreach and mobilization strategies, as well as the overall contribution of the grassroots effort on the public policy outcome, can be equally important in determining whether the initiative was successful and why.

Key informant interviews are important, especially with the decision makers as they can indicate the impact of the grassroots mobilization on their decisions. But interviews may be insufficient. Evaluators should also survey the target audience (that is, the grassroots) regarding how their actions related to the ways they were informed.

Outreach and mobilization of the "grass tops." These are the opinion, civic, religious, and political leaders who can deliver messages to policy decision makers. These individuals are less likely to be surveyed; thus, interviews will probably be the only way to access them. The impact of efforts to mobilize these leaders is uncovered mainly through interviews with the decision makers and their staff.

---

[95] An excellent resource on evaluating media and communications work is *Lessons in Evaluating Communications Campaigns* by Julia Coffman, Harvard Family Research Project. It can be obtained at http://www.gse.harvard.edu/~hfrp/content/pubs/onlinepubs/lessons/lessons.pdf.

4. Grantee capacity

Assessing the capacity of individual grantee leaders and individual grantee organizations as well as the collective capacity of grantees is a challenging arena. Much has been written on building capacity of organizations and ways in which to evaluate capacity. Paul Connolly and Peter York have described a continuum of capacity building evaluation based on the capacity building activity and time frame for the desired outcomes.[96] Associated with each are a set of evaluation questions and methodologies. Grantmakers for Effective Organizations and several nonprofit organizations have also developed or addressed evaluation of capacity building, partnerships and collaborations including the Urban Institute, the Environmental Support Center, and the Institute for Conservation Leadership.[97]

Figure 11 summarizes these evaluation approaches and relates what is to be evaluated with how it should be evaluated.

What to Consider When Hiring an Evaluator

A question that often accompanies *how* to evaluate is *who* should do an evaluation. Three possible parties are foundation staff; a third party, external evaluator; or the grantees and others involved in and affected by the effort (often called a "participatory evaluation").

Hiring an external evaluator

Here are general guidelines for hiring an outside evaluator for a public policy–related project:[98]

- Find out if the consultant has had experience evaluating public policy or other civic initiatives sponsored by a foundation.

---

[96] Paul Connolly and Peter York, "Evaluating Capacity-Building Efforts for Nonprofit Organizations," *OD Practitioner* vol. 34, no. 4, 2002, http://www.tccgrp.com/know_art_evaluating.html.

[97] Evaluating capacity building is not without its challenges. Kennard T. Wing notes some of the key unresolved issues in such evaluations, including identifying what is to be built or improved upon and determining standard units of measurement. See Wing's article "Assessing the Effectiveness of Capacity-Building Initiatives: Seven Issues for the Field," *Nonprofit and Voluntary Sector Quarterly* vol. 33, no. 1, March 2004, 153–160.

[98] More information on the contracting of evaluators can be found in *The Manager's Guide to Program Evaluation: Planning, Contracting, and Managing for Useful Results* by Paul W. Mattessich, 2003, available at http://www.fieldstonealliance.org.

Figure 11. Evaluation Tools and Approaches _____

What to Evaluate	How to Evaluate It
Evaluate grantee performance in the context of other factors impacting the outcome of the pubic policy initiative	1. Research other factors via media, internal and official documents, records of policymakers, or key informant interviews 2. Conduct key informant interviews (grantees, policymakers or their staff, or third-party observers)
Evaluate the relative contribution of a grantee's public policy initiative to meeting program goals	1. Evaluate other efforts to meet program goals 2. Conduct key informant interviews (grantees, policymakers or their staff, or third-party observers)
Evaluate the strategies and processes used by grantees to achieve public policy change.	Assesse each strategy via 1. Key informant interviews 2. Specific strategy indicators of success (media campaigns, grassroots outreach and mobilization, or "grass tops" outreach and mobilization)
Evaluate the relative difference in these capacities before the public policy initiative and after the initiative is enacted.	Assess capacity of individual grantee leaders and individual grantee organizations, as well as the collective capacity of grantees

Figure 12. Types of Evaluators* _____

Evaluator	Benefits	Drawbacks
Foundation staff	• Knowledge of the program, board, grantees, and context	• Lack of perspective and objectivity • Lack of evaluation skills • Time-consuming
External consultant	• Evaluation skills • Should know issues and policy context	• Lack of understanding of foundation culture, grantee culture, and context
Participants**	• Understand context and grantee culture • Understand how best to use evaluation results (if participants are among the intended users)	• Lack of perspective and objectivity • Lack of evaluation skills

* The W.K. Kellogg Foundation has created a checklist for selecting an evaluator on page 63 of its Evaluation Handbook. A copy of the handbook is available online at http://www.wkkf. org/pubs/Tools/Evaluation/Pub770.pdf#search=%22Evaluation%20Handbook%22.

** For more information on participatory evaluation see Cornell University's web page at http:// people.cornell.edu/pages/alr26/parEval.html. It provides definitions and links to several key organizations and individuals active in participatory evaluation.

- Carefully review a potential evaluator's written reports. Are the reports written clearly? Would you feel comfortable submitting the evaluator's reports to the foundation's board of directors?

- Discuss possible measures of process and outcome. Get a sense of whether your ideas and the evaluator's ideas about measures are likely to mesh.

- Have the evaluation candidate give a five-minute presentation on anything. It will help you determine whether the evaluator also might be effective in communicating to your board of directors, program committee, or other key internal audiences.

— — —

Conclusion

Foundations constantly seek to improve knowledge of grantees, programs, and the ways in which the external world influences both. In public policy grantmaking, the process for increasing knowledge via evaluation is to

- Start and end the evaluation knowing *what* is to be learned and *why* and *how* the information will be used

- Ground *how* the evaluation will be designed and implemented around clear mission, goals, objectives, and outcomes

- Design *how* the evaluation is undertaken and *what* is to be learned based on the needs of grantmakers and grantees

- Understand *when* evaluation learning will be most useful to grantees and grantmakers, and make sure the evaluation is completed within that time frame

The concepts in this chapter are summarized in an operational checklist in the Evaluation Checklist, located in Appendix A, page 243.

The Power of Public Policy

This book has introduced many of the reasons why private and community foundations choose to become involved in shaping public policy and civic activity. The authors and contributors to this book agree that foundations cannot afford to ignore the fact that public policy decisions and the quality of civic life are of great importance to philanthropy. We also hope that you find ideas for your own foundation's involvement based on the examples of other foundations, the lessons about how to prepare for policy and civic activity, and explanations of the legal rules and associated risks and opportunities.

No one ever argues about whether businesses should or should not be trying to influence public policy. It is simply a matter of fact that laws and policies and citizens' willingness to influence government directly affect business operations, profitability, liability, rights, and duties. Foundations, as a kind of business, are no different except that they have a higher duty to the public and those they serve. This higher duty is not well served when foundations ignore the tools of public policy, civic participation, and advocacy. It is ironic that so many private and community foundations pride themselves on having state-of-the-art program design, evaluation, marketing, financial planning, executive compensation, communications, and research, while overlooking the leverage available to them through policy initiatives. This book advocates that public policy and civic engagement should be among the core business functions of foundations and of philanthropy. Ongoing debate is the nature of foundations' role in public policymaking. However, most agree that almost every time a foundation grant is made from an endowment or donor-advised fund there is a legal or public policy dimension to it. During the consideration of a grant, or in talking with a prospective grantee, or when meeting with your peers in the foundation world, we hope that after reading this book you will always ask, What are the public policy and civic aspects of this work? How might our foundation improve the ultimate goals and outcomes of the work through public policy and civic activity?

Those who start and operate foundations are extraordinary people. They are change agents who invest in ideas and opportunities that help people succeed and make communities better. Like foundations, government is also working to make life better for all and uses law and policy as its main tools. For too long foundations and government have been like ships passing in the night, carrying full loads of complementary cargo but not seeing each other, not understanding each other, and often even avoiding each other.

Let this metaphor be a fixture of the past in the foundation world. Use this book to help your foundation achieve a new relationship with government. Use it to accomplish your mission. Assert your power to shape the rules that govern. Inspire and enable people to find and use their own voices in the democratic process.

Appendices

Toolkit

Executive Summary: Legal Rules for Private and Community Foundation Involvement in Public Policy and Civic Activity

The following bulleted points are designed to provide a quick reference list regarding the legality of foundation funding of public policy and advocacy-related activities and policy participation by foundations. Please use it as a handout at meetings of directors, trustees, and anyone you think would benefit from knowing the legal rules pertaining to public policy–related philanthropy. An online version of this document can be downloaded from the publisher's web site at the following URL:

http://www.FieldstoneAlliance.org/worksheets

Access Code: W458pip07

A private foundation may

- Make a grant to a charity

  - for general support (that is, an unrestricted grant), even if the charity uses the grant funds for lobbying or nonpartisan voter participation efforts;

  - for a specific advocacy project, if the charity provides a project budget showing that the non-lobbying project expenditures are at least as much as the grant;

  - for a specific voter participation project, not involving voter registration, as long as the project is nonpartisan; and

  - for a specific voter participation project involving voter registration as long as the project is nonpartisan, the voter registration takes place over more than one election cycle and in at least five states, and the charity meets certain financial support tests.

- Make a grant to a non-charity, including a foreign nongovernmental organization that has not been recognized as a charity by the IRS

  - for a specific advocacy project if the foundation conducts a limited pre-grant inquiry, has a grant agreement with certain terms, receives reports on the use of the grant, and reports certain information to the IRS; and

  - for a specific nonpartisan voter participation project, not involving voter registration, if the same conditions are met.

- Directly advocate for public policy as long as such advocacy is not lobbying or falls within the self-defense, technical assistance, jointly funded project, or nonpartisan analysis, study, or research exceptions.

- Directly encourage voter participation, other than through voter registration, as long as such encouragement is nonpartisan.

A community foundation may

- Make a grant to a charity
  - for general support (that is, an unrestricted grant), even if the charity uses the grant funds for lobbying or nonpartisan voter participation efforts;
  - for a specific advocacy project, including if that project involves lobbying, as long as the community foundation does not exceed its permitted level of lobbying; and
  - for a specific voter participation project, as long as the project is nonpartisan.

- Make a grant to a non-charity
  - for a specific advocacy project, including if that project involves lobbying, as long as the community foundation does not exceed its permitted level of lobbying; and
  - for a specific voter participation project, as long as the project is nonpartisan.

- Directly advocate for public policy, including by lobbying, subject to one of the two following limits on lobbying:
  - the default limit that the lobbying not be more than an insubstantial part of the community foundation's activities; or
  - the optional sliding percentage scale limit on expenditures for lobbying, starting at 20 percent of the first $500,000 in total charitable expenditures (5 percent for grassroots lobbying) and ultimately reaching a maximum of $1 million ($250,000 for grassroots lobbying) with $17 million or more in annual charitable expenditures.

- Directly encourage voter participation, as long as such participation is nonpartisan.

For additional legal resources, see the end of this appendix.

Sample Grant Letter from a Private Foundation to a 501(c)(3) Nonprofit for General Support

Following is a sample letter a private foundation might use as a template when making a general support grant to a 501(c)(3) public charity. Notably, it does not place any unnecessary restrictions on the use of the foundation grant. Too frequently, letters of this nature from private foundations have been written in such a manner as to restrict permissible public policy activities. The John and Jane Doe Family Foundation is fictional.

Dear Mr. Smith:

The John and Jane Doe Family Foundation is pleased to provide the Inner City AIDS Initiative with the enclosed general support grant in the amount of $10,000 to fund your charitable operations. By cashing or depositing the enclosed check, the Initiative agrees to the following terms:

1. To use the grant solely for charitable, educational, or other purposes provided in section 170(c)(2)(B) of the Internal Revenue Code;

2. To continue to qualify as a tax-exempt organization under section 501(c)(3) of the Code and not as a private foundation as defined in section 509(a) of the Code while any grant funds remain unspent; and

3. [Any other desired conditions, such as requiring the grant to be spent by a particular date, requiring the grant to be repaid if either of the first two conditions are violated, requiring one or more reports on the use of the grant, or providing the Foundation with access to financial records showing the use of the grant].

Beyond the rights and obligations specifically stated in this letter, the John and Jane Doe Family Foundation disclaims any legal right to control or otherwise influence the Initiative's use of any funds provided pursuant to this agreement. Furthermore, it is expressly understood that by making this grant the Foundation has no obligation to provide additional funding to the Initiative. This is the entire agreement between the Initiative and the Foundation concerning this grant and may be modified only by a written agreement between the Initiative and the Foundation.

On behalf of the Foundation, I extend my best wishes for your success.

Best regards,

Jane Doe

President

Sample Grant Letter from a Private Foundation to a 501(c)(3) Nonprofit for a Project-Specific Grant

Following is a sample grant letter that would be sent from a private foundation to a 501(c)(3) public charity, that has been awarded a grant for a specific project, part of which involves lobbying. In the case of a specific project that contains a lobbying component, a private foundation is allowed to provide a grant up to the amount of the non-lobbying part of the project. The letter below does not discuss the lobbying part of the specific project but only the part that it is funding, and in doing so does not inadvertently restrict the grantee. The John and Jane Doe Family Foundation is fictional.

Dear Mr. Smith:

The John and Jane Doe Family Foundation is pleased to provide the Inner City AIDS Initiative with the enclosed project grant in the amount of $77,600. The purpose of the grant is to fund the Detroit Project, as described in the project proposal and budget attached to this letter. By cashing or depositing the enclosed check, the Initiative agrees to the following terms:

1. To use the grant solely for charitable, educational, or other purposes provided in section 170(c)(2)(B) of the Internal Revenue Code;

2. To continue to qualify as a tax-exempt organization under section 501(c)(3) of the Code and as not a private foundation as defined in section 509(a) of the Code while any grant funds remain unspent;

3. To return to the Foundation any portion of the grant funds and interest thereon which are not used for the purpose of this project grant, as described above; and

4. [Any other desired conditions, such as requiring the grant to be spent by a particular date, requiring one or more reports on the use of the grant, or providing the Foundation with access to financial records showing the use of the grant].

Beyond the rights and obligations specifically stated in this letter, the John and Jane Doe Family Foundation disclaims any legal right to control or otherwise influence the Inner City AIDS Initiative's use of any funds provided pursuant to this agreement. Furthermore, it is expressly understood that by making this grant the Foundation has no obligation to provide additional funding to the Initiative. This is the entire agreement between the Initiative and the Foundation concerning this grant and may be modified only by a written agreement between the Initiative and the Foundation.

On behalf of the Foundation, I extend my best wishes for your success.

Best regards,

Jane Doe

President

Sample Grant Agreement with a Non-501(c)(3) Organization

This is a sample letter to be used with an organization that is not a charitable organization. It covers a broader range of grantee activity including the restriction on the use of foundation funding for voter registration. It also protects the foundation by including language stating that the non-charity nonprofit may not use the grant for lobbying but does not restrict other forms of permissible advocacy. The John and Jane Doe Family Foundation is fictional.

Dear Mr. Smith:

The John and Jane Doe Family Foundation is pleased to provide the Farm Values Advocacy Fund with the enclosed project grant in the amount of $50,000. The purpose of the grant is to fund the Rural Education Project, as described in the project proposal and budget you provided. By cashing or depositing the enclosed check, the Fund agrees to the following terms:

1. To use the grant solely for charitable, educational, or other purposes provided in section 170(c)(2)(B) of the Internal Revenue Code;

2. To return to the Foundation any portion of the grant funds and interest thereon that are not used for the purpose of this project grant, as described above, or are used in violation of any of the other terms of this agreement;

3. During the period in which any portion of the grant remains unexpended, to show those funds separately on the Fund's books for ease of reference and verification, to keep written records of receipts and expenditures under the grant adequate to enable the use of the grant to be checked readily, as well as copies of reports submitted to the Foundation, for at least four (4) years after completion of the use of the grant, and to make these records available to the Foundation or its designees for inspection at reasonable times upon request;

4. Not to use the grant for any attempt to influence legislation as described in section 4945(e) of the Internal Revenue Code;

5. Not to use the grant for any attempt to influence the outcome of any specific public election or to carry on, directly or indirectly, any voter registration drive, except as provided in section 4945(f) of the Code;

6. Not to use the grant to make any grants to other organizations—except United States public charities described in sections 501(c)(3) and 509(a) of the Code—unless the Fund receives the prior written approval of the Foundation and complies with applicable United States tax law with regard to such grants as set forth in section 4945 and elsewhere in the Code;

7. Not to use the grant to make grants to individuals for travel, study, research, or similar purposes unless the Fund receives prior written approval from the Foundation and complies with section 4945(g) of the Code as if the grant were made by a private foundation such as the Foundation;

8. To provide full and complete annual reports accounting for the expenditure of all of the grant; the annual reports must include a narrative account that confirms compliance with the terms of the grant and describes what was accomplished by the expenditure of the grant in achieving the goals of the grant, and a financial statement itemizing how the grant was spent; these annual reports must be provided within three months after the conclusion of the Fund's yearly accounting period for every year in which the grant has been expended or retained;

9. Upon completion of the use of the grant, to submit a full and complete final narrative and financial report to the Foundation covering all expenditures made from the grant and describing the progress made toward the goals of the grant; the final report must be provided within a reasonable time after the conclusion of the Fund's yearly accounting period in which use of the grant is completed, and in no case later than three months after the end of such accounting period; and

10. [Any other desired conditions, such as requiring the grant to be spent by a particular date].

Beyond the rights and obligations specifically stated in this letter, the John and Jane Doe Family Foundation disclaims any legal right to control or otherwise influence the Farm Values Advocacy Fund's use of any funds provided pursuant to this agreement. Furthermore, it is expressly understood that by making this grant the Foundation has no obligation to provide additional funding to the Fund. This is the entire agreement between the Fund and the Foundation concerning this grant and may be modified only by a written agreement between the Fund and the Foundation.

On behalf of the Foundation, I extend my best wishes for your success.

Best regards,

Jane Doe

President

IRS Letter for Foundations about Public Policy Participation and Civic Engagement

Following is a letter from the Internal Revenue Service to Charity Lobbying in the Public Interest, now the Center for Lobbying the Public Interest (CLPI) in Washington, DC. CLPI asked the IRS to provide in writing answers to frequently asked questions about the legal rules governing private and community foundations' legal latitude to make grants that relate to public policy. It is reprinted with permission. Please use the letter with your foundation's board, legal counsel, executives, donors, staff, inquiring parties, or anyone you think should know more about the legal latitude permitted foundations in the public policy arena. In addition, CLPI has prepared a memorandum that explains the content and specifically some of the legal language in the letter. The memorandum is available at http://www.clpi.org/Lobbying_and_the_Law.aspx and is called "IRS Letter on Funding Nonprofits That Lobby EXPLAINED."

DEPARTMENT OF THE TREASURY
INTERNAL REVENUE SERVICE
WASHINGTON, D.C. 20224

TAX EXEMPT AND
GOVERNMENT ENTITIES
DIVISION

Date: **DEC 0 9 2004**

Contact Person:
    Ward L. Thomas
Identification Number:
    50-09822
Contact Number:
    (202) 283-8913

Charity Lobbying in the Public Interest
2040 S Street NW
Washington, DC 20009

Dear Sirs:

   We have considered your request dated February 10, 2003 on behalf of a public charity involved in educating other charities about the role of lobbying as a means of achieving their philanthropic missions. You request information on lobbying and influencing public policy by private foundations. The public charity has compiled a list of recurring questions that, if answered by the IRS, would assist in correcting misconceptions in this area. The questions are addressed below.

   1. May private foundations make general support grants, other than program-related investments, to "public charities" that lobby?

Yes, private foundations may make grants, other than program-related investments, to public charities (i.e., organizations described in sections 509(a)(1), (2), or (3) of the Internal Revenue Code) that lobby, with certain restrictions. The tax rules include explicit safe harbors for general support grants that meet the requirements of section 53.4945-2(a)(6)(i) of the Treasury Regulations. Provided that such grants are not earmarked in whole or part for lobbying, they will not be taxable expenditures.

   2. Does the same answer apply whether or not the public charity has made the election under section 501(h) of the Code governing its own lobbying expenditures?

Yes.

– 2 –

Charity Lobbying in the Public Interest

3. What constitutes "earmarking" of a grant for lobbying?

"Earmarking" a grant for lobbying is making a grant with an oral or written agreement that the grant will be used for lobbying.

4. Absent any specific agreement to the contrary, will the recitation in a grant agreement that "there is no agreement, oral or written, that directs that the grant funds be used for lobbying activities" be sufficient to establish to the satisfaction of the IRS that there has been no earmarking for lobbying?

Yes, absent evidence of an agreement to the contrary.

5. Is a foundation required to include a specific provision in its grant agreements that no part of the grant funds may be used for lobbying?

A specific provision is required only if the grantee organization is not a public charity, or if the private foundation earmarks the grant for use by an organization that is not a public charity.

6. Under what circumstances can a foundation make a grant to a public charity for a specific project that includes lobbying?

A private foundation can make a grant to a public charity for a specific project that includes lobbying pursuant to sections 53.4945-2(a)(6)(ii) and (iii) of the regulations if (1) no part of the grant is earmarked for lobbying, (2) the private foundation obtains a proposed budget signed by an officer of the public charity showing that the amount of the grant, together with other grants by the same private foundation for the same project and year, does not exceed the amount budgeted, for the year of the grant, by the public charity for activities of the project that are not lobbying, and (3) the private foundation has no reason to doubt the accuracy of the budget.

7. In the response to the preceding question, does it matter that the public charity's proposal indicates that it will be seeking funds for the specific project from other private foundations without referring to other, additional sources of funds?'

No, the specific project grant rules in section 53.4945-2(a)(6)(ii) of the regulations do not require the private foundation to concern itself about the other sources of funding for the project in such situations.

– 3 –

Charity Lobbying in the Public Interest

8. What if, in the conduct of the project, the public charity actually makes lobbying expenditures in excess of its estimate in the grant proposal?

If the requirements of section 53.4945-2(a)(6)(ii) and (iii) of the regulations are met (no earmarking, budget shows non-lobbying equal to or greater than grant, and no reason to doubt accuracy of budget), then the private foundation will not have made a taxable expenditure under section 4945(d)(1) of the Code for that year, even if the public charity makes lobbying expenditures in excess of the budgeted amount. However, knowledge of the excess may provide a reason to doubt the accuracy of subsequent budgets submitted by the public charity.

Section 53.4945-2(a)(7)(ii) of the regulations, Example (13), illustrates the situation where a private foundation makes a second-year grant payment after the public charity exceeded its lobbying budgeted amount in the first year of the grant. In that case, although the private foundation did not have a taxable expenditure in the first year, it did have a taxable expenditure in the second year when the public charity again exceeded its lobbying budgeted amount. Similarly, if the public charity's exemption is revoked for excess lobbying after receiving the grant, there is no adverse consequence to the private foundation unless it directly or indirectly controls the public charity or has knowledge of the change in status before making the grant.

9. In determining whether a foundation grant has been earmarked for lobbying, do the definitions of lobbying in sections 56.4911-2 and 3 of the regulations govern?

Section 53.4945-2(a)(1) of the regulations provides that the definitions of section 56.4911-2 and section 56.4911-3 apply without regard to the exceptions contained in section 56.4911-2(b)(3) and section 56.4911-2(c). Instead, similar exceptions are provided in section 53.4945-2(d). Note that the special rules for membership communications under section 56.4911-5 do not apply to private foundations.

10. Private foundations are required to make "all reasonable efforts" under section 4945(h) of the Code to ensure that grant funds subject to expenditure responsibility (for example, a grant to a section 501(c)(4) organization) are not used for lobbying. Assuming grant records reflect that a grantee has been made aware of the applicable lobbying definitions and the grantee's report on the use of grant funds reflects activities that are legislation-related but, as reported, lack one or more of the elements of lobbying under sections 53.4911-2 and 3 of the regulations, is the foundation required to investigate further to discharge its responsibilities?

Section 53.4945-5(c)(1) of the regulations provides that a grantor private foundation is not required to conduct any independent verification of reports from grantees unless it has reason to doubt their accuracy or reliability.

– 4 –

Charity Lobbying in the Public Interest

11. May private foundations directly engage in any policy-related activities without incurring liability for private foundation excise taxes?

Yes. Private foundations may engage directly in a wide range of educational activities that influence the formation of public policy but are not lobbying so long as the foundation does not (1) reflect a view on specific legislation in communications with legislators, legislative staff, or executive branch personnel participating in the formulation of legislation, or (2) reflect a view on specific legislation and make a call to action in communications with the general public (and the rule for certain "mass media" communications does not apply). Some communications that may otherwise qualify as lobbying are excepted as nonpartisan analysis, technical advice to a legislative body, or self-defense.

12. What other policy-related activities may foundations fund?

Private foundations may fund discussions of broad social problems, as well as certain public charity membership communications that are not treated as lobbying communications. Further, the special restrictions on lobbying have no effect on contact with executive branch officials in order to influence the development of regulations (and other non-legislative policy positions). "Lobbying" is limited to attempting to influence action by a legislative body.

13. May community foundations engage in or fund lobbying activities?

Community foundations that are public charities may, if they have elected under section 501(h) of the Code, engage in or fund lobbying activities subject to the limitations of section 501(h) and section 4911 or, if they have not, to the extent that the lobbying activity does not constitute more than an insubstantial part of the community foundation's activities.

14. May community foundations make grants to other public charities that are earmarked for lobbying without adverse federal tax consequences?

Community foundations that are public charities may make grants to other public charities earmarked for lobbying so long as the amounts actually earmarked for lobbying are taken into account under the applicable limitation on lobbying expenditures by the community foundation noted in the response to Question 13.

15. May community foundations engage in nonpartisan election-related activities (activities that do not constitute political campaign intervention within the meaning of section 1.501(c)(3)-1(c)(3)(iii) of the regulations) including voter registration, "Get Out the Vote" drives, voter education projects and candidate forums?

Community foundations may engage in non-partisan election-related activities such as voter registration, "Get Out the Vote" drives, voter education projects and candidate forums, provided they do not constitute political campaign intervention under section 501(c)(3) of the Code. Regarding voter registration activities in particular, community foundations that are not private foundations are not required to meet the standards of section 4945(f).

– 5 –

Charity Lobbying in the Public Interest

16. In contrast to public charities, private foundations are subject to limitations under section 4945(d)(2) of the Code on funding nonpartisan "voter registration drives." For purposes of the limitations, does the phrase "voter registration drive" include nonpartisan election-related activities other than registering voters, including "Get Out the Vote" activities, voter education projects and candidate forums?

No.

We believe this general information will be of assistance to you. This letter, however, is not a ruling and may not be relied on as such. If you have any questions, please feel free to contact the person whose name and telephone number are listed in the heading of this letter.

Sincerely,

Judith Kindell

for Joseph J. Urban
Manager, Exempt Organizations
Technical Guidance & Quality Assurance

cc: Thomas A. Troyer
Marcus S. Owens
Caplin & Drysdale, Chartered
One Thomas Circle, NW, Suite 1100
Washington, DC 20005

IRS FORM 5768

Following (on page 242) is a copy of IRS Form 5768. This form can also be found on the IRS's web site at http://www.irs.gov/pub/irs-pdf/f5768.pdf. A community foundation may use this form to make the 501(h) election to come under the federal expenditure test rules governing lobbying described in Chapter 9.

Form **5768**

(Rev. December 2004)

Department of the Treasury
Internal Revenue Service

Election/Revocation of Election by an Eligible Section 501(c)(3) Organization To Make Expenditures To Influence Legislation

(Under Section 501(h) of the Internal Revenue Code)

For IRS
Use Only ▶

Name of organization

Employer identification number

Number and street (or P.O. box no., if mail is not delivered to street address)

Room/suite

City, town or post office, and state

ZIP + 4

1 **Election**—As an eligible organization, we hereby elect to have the provisions of section 501(h) of the Code, relating to expenditures to influence legislation, apply to our tax year ending...and all subsequent tax years until revoked.

(Month, day, and year)

Note: *This election must be signed and postmarked within the first taxable year to which it applies.*

2 **Revocation**—As an eligible organization, we hereby revoke our election to have the provisions of section 501(h) of the Code, relating to expenditures to influence legislation, apply to our tax year ending ....

(Month, day, and year)

Note: *This revocation must be signed and postmarked before the first day of the tax year to which it applies.*

Under penalties of perjury, I declare that I am authorized to make this (check applicable box) ▶ ☐ election ☐ revocation on behalf of the above named organization.

....
(Signature of officer or trustee)

....
(Type or print name and title)

....
(Date)

General Instructions

Section references are to the Internal Revenue Code.

Section 501(c)(3) states that an organization exempt under that section will lose its tax-exempt status and its qualification to receive deductible charitable contributions if a substantial part of its activities are carried on to influence legislation. Section 501(h), however, permits certain eligible 501(c)(3) organizations to elect to make limited expenditures to influence legislation. An organization making the election will, however, be subject to an excise tax under section 4911 if it spends more than the amounts permitted by that section. Also, the organization may lose its exempt status if its lobbying expenditures exceed the permitted amounts by more than 50% over a 4-year period. For any tax year in which an election under section 501(h) is in effect, an electing organization must report the actual and permitted amounts of its lobbying expenditures and grass roots expenditures (as defined in section 4911(c)) on its annual return required under section 6033. See Schedule A (Form 990 or Form 990-EZ). Each electing member of an affiliated group must report these amounts for both itself and the affiliated group as a whole.

To make or revoke the election, enter the ending date of the tax year to which the election or revocation applies in item **1** or **2**, as applicable, and sign and date the form in the spaces provided.

Eligible Organizations.—A section 501(c)(3) organization is permitted to make the election if it is not a disqualified organization (see below) and is described in:

1. Section 170(b)(1)(A)(ii) (relating to educational institutions),
2. Section 170(b)(1)(A)(iii) (relating to hospitals and medical research organizations),
3. Section 170(b)(1)(A)(iv) (relating to organizations supporting government schools),
4. Section 170(b)(1)(A)(vi) (relating to organizations publicly supported by charitable contributions),
5. Section 509(a)(2) (relating to organizations publicly supported by admissions, sales, etc.), or
6. Section 509(a)(3) (relating to organizations supporting certain types of public charities other than those section 509(a)(3) organizations that support section 501(c)(4), (5), or (6) organizations).

Disqualified Organizations.—The following types of organizations are not permitted to make the election:

a. Section 170(b)(1)(A)(i) organizations (relating to churches),

b. An integrated auxiliary of a church or of a convention or association of churches, or

c. A member of an affiliated group of organizations if one or more members of such group is described in **a** or **b** of this paragraph.

Affiliated Organizations.—Organizations are members of an affiliated group of organizations only if **(1)** the governing instrument of one such organization requires it to be bound by the decisions of the other organization on legislative issues, or **(2)** the governing board of one such organization includes persons (i) who are specifically designated representatives of another such organization or are members of the governing board, officers, or paid executive staff members of such other organization, and (ii) who, by aggregating their votes, have sufficient voting power to cause or prevent action on legislative issues by the first such organization.

For more details, see section 4911 and section 501(h).

Note: *A private foundation (including a private operating foundation) is not an eligible organization.*

Where To File.—Mail Form 5768 to the Internal Revenue Service Center, Ogden, UT 84201-0027.

Cat. No. 12125M

Form **5768** (Rev. 12-2004)

Evaluation Checklist

Evaluation Checklist by The Headwaters Group Philanthropic Services

Action	Yes	No	Rationale
Have program goals, objectives, outcomes, and indicators been identified?			
Have reasons to evaluate been identified?			
Contribution of grantees to the success of passage or implementation of a public policy			
Relevance of public policy approach to achieving the goals of the foundation or a specific program			
Contributions of specific strategies and processes to public policy success and the reasons for success or failure			
Increased capacity of grantees (individually and collectively) to conceive and implement a pubic policy initiative and ensure its long-term success			
Has what to evaluate been identified?			
Grantee performance in the context of the other factors impacting the outcome of the public policy initiative			
Relative contribution of the public policy to meeting program goals			
Strategies and processes used by grantees to achieve public policy change			
Relative difference in these capacities, pre-initiative to post-initiative			
Have evaluation expectations been communicated to:			
Foundation board and staff?			
Grant applicants?			
Grantees?			
Have evaluation resources (financial and technical) been identified and provided?			
Internally, including consultants			
Grantees			

Glossary

Much of the glossary was excerpted with permission from OMB Watch's NPAction.org web site, http://www.npaction.org.

Administrative advocacy: An attempt to influence policies within the executive branch such as agency rulemaking, grant programs, or agency budgets. Also known as "regulatory advocacy."

Advocacy: Speaking out on issues of concern. This can mean something as formal as sitting down and talking to your legislator, as intensive as engaging in efforts to change laws or policies, or as simple as telling your neighbor about the impact of a law.

Amendment: A change to a bill or motion, sometimes replacing the entire bill (called a "substitution"). An amendment is debated and voted on in the same manner as a bill.

Appropriations: Basically, a fancy word for budget. A legislature's appropriations committee will craft a bill that lays out how the government's money should be spent for a given time period (usually a fiscal year), which is then voted on by the legislature and signed into law by the president or governor. Often, these bills are huge and contain many "riders."

Authorization: Legislation that formally establishes a program or activity and sets its funding limit. Authorizations are often for a limited time, and programs must be periodically reauthorized, sometimes with changes.

Bill: Legislation drafted for consideration by the legislature. Bills usually must be formally filed with the legislature's clerk and given an identifying number (H.R. 7, for example, is the seventh bill filed in the House of Representatives this session).

Charity: A nonprofit organization that is tax exempt under IRS Code section 501(c)(3) which derives substantial support from the general public or is a religious, educational, medical, or governmental or a charitable support institution. Charities must apply for 501(c)(3) status with the IRS.

Civic engagement: Individual and collective actions designed to identify and address issues of public concern. Civic engagement can take many forms, including efforts to directly address an issue, work with others in a community to solve a problem, or interact with the institutions of representative democracy.[99]

Civic strengthening activities: Actions taken to strengthen the ability of people and institutions to be involved in civic engagement in all its various forms. Such actions may be focused on enhancing skills, motivation, or other capacities of people and institutions. They may also be focused on making improvements to the rules and systems of democracy itself (for example, voter registration rules or voter education programs).

Coalition: A group of organizations working together for a common purpose. Coalition is a term often used by nonprofit organizers and in a political context.

Committee: A group of legislators that develops legislation on specific topics (veterans' affairs, for example) and has jurisdiction over all legislation that deals with its topic. Generally, legislation must pass in a committee before the entire legislative body can vote on it. Committees often schedule public hearings to discuss legislative issues. Most action takes place at the subcommittee level.

Conference committee: The House and Senate appoint members to a conference committee to resolve differences between versions of legislation passed by both bodies. Both chambers then vote on the combined legislation, which is called a "conference report."

Congressional Record: The official transcript of federal House and Senate proceedings. Often includes statements by members that are added directly into the record, and not fully read on the floor in the interest of time and staying awake.

Continuing resolution: Legislation passed by both the House and the Senate permitting executive branch agencies to continue operating in the absence of a budget. In past years, several continuing resolutions have been needed before a federal budget was finally passed.

---

[99] Source: Michael Delli Carpini, Director, Public Policy, The Pew Charitable Trusts, from http://www.apa.org/ed/slce/civicengagement.html#definition.

Cosponsor: When a legislator supports a bill, but is not the primary sponsor, he or she may sign onto the bill as a cosponsor to show support. Legislation can sometimes have hundreds of cosponsors.

Direct lobbying: To present a case for or against a specific piece of legislation and to ask a legislator to vote a certain way. While any citizen can lobby his or her legislators, nonprofits have limits on how much money they can spend on lobbying.

District: The geographic area from which a U.S. House member or state legislator is elected.

Electoral activities: Activities that directly attempt to influence the outcome of an election. Charities are strictly prohibited from engaging in electoral activities, although other types of nonprofits are not.

Electoral advocacy: Efforts to educate voters (such as legislative scorecards) or to register or encourage them to vote. These activities cannot include efforts specifically designed to influence the outcome of an election (see *electoral activities*).

Executive order: An action by the U.S. president or a governor that has the legal authority of a law, often dealing with regulations or the workings of agencies.

Exempt purpose expenditures: Public charities under section 501(c)(3) of the Internal Revenue Code are permitted to spend a percentage of their annual exempt purpose expenditures on lobbying based on the amount of exempt purpose expenditures they make in a year if they have made the 501(h) election (see below). An exempt purpose expenditure includes expenditures made to accomplish the charitable purpose and include program expenditures, compensation paid, a portion of administrative expenditures devoted to the charitable purpose, lobbying expenditures, research costs, cost of communicating with members, depreciation, and certain fundraising costs.[100]

---

[100] Bruce Hopkins, *Charity, Advocacy and the Law* (New York: John Wiley and Sons, Inc., 1992), 186.

Expenditure test: A set of IRS regulations that provides specific definitions of lobbying and sets monetary limits on the amount of money that a charity (including a community foundation) may spend on lobbying each year. (See Chapter 9 for a detailed explanation.) Charities must choose or affirmatively "elect" to follow these rules by taking the 501(h) election.

Filibuster: A delaying tactic used in the U.S. Senate by the minority in an effort to prevent the passage of a bill or amendment. The Senate's rules allow for unlimited debate in some situations, unless a two-thirds vote to end the debate passes. A filibuster results when one or more senators continues to "debate" for as long as possible (sometimes for days).

501(h) election: When a public charity (including a community foundation) takes the "501(h) election," it is choosing to adhere to the IRS regulations that govern lobbying known as the expenditure test.

Grassroots lobbying: Stating a position on a specific legislative proposal to the public, then asking the public to urge their legislators to support that stated position. Nonprofits are limited in the amount they can spend on grassroots lobbying.

Hearing: A meeting in which evidence to support particular points of view can be presented to a committee. A hearing is usually held in conjunction with the consideration of a specific bill and can include experts on a specific topic or members of the public who would be affected by the bill or issue at hand.

House: The lower body of Congress and most state legislatures. House members are elected to represent a geographic district. The U.S. House of Representatives (with 435 voting members and 5 nonvoting delegates) is much larger than the Senate (with 100 voting members). This is also the case in most states legislatures.

Information advocacy: Activities to provide information or ensure the provision of information that can be used to shape policy.

Judicial advocacy: Working for policy change through the legal system, either by lawsuits, amicus briefs, or providing information for legal cases. Also includes efforts to promote a more just and equitable legal system, which may also include legislative advocacy.

Legislative advocacy: Efforts to change policy through the legislative branch. May include formal lobbying in support of or opposition to a bill, the crafting of new legislative language, writing amendments to existing bills, or encouraging others to contact their legislators.

Lobbying: Communications with elected officials or their staff that expresses a position on a pending piece of legislation.

Majority leader: The leader of the majority party in the Senate, elected by his or her peers. In the House, the majority leader is the second in command after the Speaker of the House and is also elected to that post by his or her peers.

Mark up: The process of amending a legislative proposal in a committee or subcommittee. Committee members can offer amendments that, if successful, are incorporated into the language of a particular bill. Legislation may be drastically changed during mark up.

Minority leader: The leader of the minority party in the House and Senate, elected by members of his or her party.

Omnibus bill: A bill related to a specific area that covers many issues or topics. Often, the federal budget is an omnibus bill that deals with many agencies' budgets at once.

Public law: After a bill passes both the House and the Senate and is signed by the president, it becomes a public law.

Public policy participation: The utilization of tactics and strategies to gain access to public decision making and to influence government, media, individuals, and other institutions that make decisions affecting the public.

Regulation: A rule or order that has the force of law, originates from the executive branch (usually from an agency), and deals with the specifics of a program. Congress, for example, may instruct the Environmental

Protection Agency (EPA) to reduce automotive emissions by 5 percent, but the EPA must develop regulations to reach this goal.

Rider: An amendment to an appropriations bill, which may not actually deal with the allocation of government funds.

Roll call: A formal vote on a bill or amendment taken by each legislator announcing "yea," "no," or "present" as their name is read by the clerk.

Senate: The upper body of Congress and most state legislatures. Each state has two senators, elected at-large to serve six-year terms, with one-third of the seats up for reelection every two years. In state legislatures, senators usually represent larger geographic areas than House members.

Speaker of the House: The "leader" of the House of Representatives, elected by the majority party. The speaker controls the calendar and other aspects of the House's activities.

Sponsor: One or more legislators who are the primary writers of a bill. All bills must have at least one sponsor, but many have more than one primary sponsor and a number of cosponsors as well.

Subcommittee: A part of a committee that deals with a specific issue within the committee's jurisdiction (such as the Subcommittee on Disability Assistance and Memorial Affairs of the House Committee on Veterans' Affairs). Most legislation is first developed and voted on at this level, as a full committee will usually not consider legislation until it has passed its subcommittee.

Voice vote: Voting on a bill by acclamation, or asking those in favor to say "yea" and those opposed to say "no." Usually, only noncontroversial legislation without any "no" votes is passed this way (such as renaming post offices), but a voice vote will sometimes be taken before a roll call vote.

Whip: Senator or representative who serves as an internal lobbyist for the Republican Party or the Democratic Party to persuade legislators to support that party's position, and who counts votes for the leadership in advance of floor votes. While the whip is an official position, there may be other members who act as a whip for specific legislation or issues.

Examples of Foundation Public Policy and Civic Activity

This section provides short examples of public policy shaping and civic strengthening activities employed by private and community foundations respectively. Chapter 5 provides definitions of the policy shaping and civic strengthening activities illustrated below. The following stories are shared for several purposes:

- To emphasize that foundations are engaged in advocacy as a key part of serving community and mission

- To illustrate, however briefly, how foundations are funding or doing advocacy using various strategies

- To provide ideas for you as a foundation interested in public policy, civic engagement, and advocacy

Don't worry too much about whether the examples that follow are state-of-the-art tactics, or whether the particular activity described has produced the intended results. Some of the examples are ongoing efforts. Some of the examples have progressed or changed since the time of this writing. Also, the examples that follow are not to be taken as examples of how foundations have complied with the law. More facts are needed than available to present illustrations of legal compliance. (See Chapter 9 for information on relevant laws and, of course, consult legal counsel.)

Although the brief illustrations that follow emphasize each foundation's usage of a specific strategy, know that probably additional strategies may also be used and that grantee views often drive what kind of role the foundation ultimately plays—as a grantmaker, convener, or other. Foundations should look to the nonprofits and community members they work with, in addition to their own mission and board, when determining the course of action they take in the policy and civic arenas.

Public Policy Shaping Activities

Foundations as institutions and through their grantees have numerous opportunities to improve communities, bring people together and make better rules for our society through sustained participation in public policy. Following are examples of how several foundations have shaped or are shaping public policy to advance mission and community goals.

Convening Stakeholders on Public Policy

Grand Rapids Community Foundation convenes leaders to create child welfare policy

When the Grand Rapids Community Foundation (GRCF) convened segments of the community to discuss pressing issues ten years ago, child abuse and neglect were at the top of the list. Based on their finding, GRCF launched Perspective 21, an initiative designed to change the way child protective services did business in Kent County, Michigan. GRCF's image as a neutral, nonpartisan organization enabled the foundation to bring stakeholders with differing viewpoints to the table. In addition, new voices and organizations were invited to participate. A forty-member leadership group, consisting of representatives from organizations with a stake in child welfare, developed a list of sixteen recommendations aimed at improving services for abused and neglected children. The Perspective 21 recommendations continue to foster new collaborations and partnerships and have significantly improved child protective services.

Woods Fund of Chicago's Policy Conference on Ex-Offenders results in legislation and consensus

In 2002, this private foundation funded a conference hosted by the Chicago Urban League on the reentry of ex-offenders. The conference brought together over 250 people including practitioners, researchers, advocates, policymakers, and community residents. It resulted in the formation of two grassroots organizing groups, policy papers, and legislation by then State Senator Barak Obama (IL) to reinstate professional licenses of ex-offenders who committed nonviolent crimes, thereby giving formerly incarcerated persons an opportunity to secure economic self-sufficiency by applying their skills.

Partnerships and Coalition Building

East Bay Community Foundation's (ECBF) Land Use Partnership results in favorable zoning for more affordable housing

Brentwood, California is a historically agricultural community that now has the distinction of being one of the fastest-growing cities in California. ECBF's Livable Communities Initiative (LCI) worked with city staff, farmers, local businesses, residents, and others to establish the Agricultural Enterprise Program. The Program gives farmers the option of selling conservation easements on their land to a land trust or exchanging their development rights for the right to build more densely in the built-up areas of Brentwood. In addition, LCI has partnered with a regional open space protection group and a local faith-based organization to build the capacity of lower-income residents, predominantly Latino farm workers and their families, to participate in local land use planning decisions. A key success was the implementation of an inclusive zoning ordinance—through a unanimous vote by the city council—that ensures that at least 10 percent of every new housing development will be affordable to low-income households in Brentwood.

Ms. Foundation's partnership with Packard Foundation empowers youth to advocate on sex education policy

In 2001, the Ms. Foundation for Women developed New Partners, New Initiatives: Improving Youth Access to Sexuality Education and Services, a program designed to increase community-based advocacy for improved access to sexuality education and services for young people by groups representing non-typical advocates. This three-year initiative, in partnership with The David and Lucile Packard Foundation, provided funds, technical assistance, networking, and learning opportunities to six groups in underserved communities (three in Washington and three in Arizona). The project seeks to galvanize existing but silent support and bring new actors into the movement to secure reproductive freedom in this country. As an example, Odyssey Youth Center in Spokane, Washington, started as an anonymous teen drop-in center and has emerged as a strong advocate in local policy and advocacy efforts related to sexuality education. The group took a stand against a Teen Aid–sponsored abstinence rally in a Washington school district. The group drafted a letter of concern to the American Civil Liberties Union, handed out flyers about comprehensive sexuality education at the event, and had youth members write letters to local newspapers. Odyssey youth have also become involved with statewide advocacy efforts tracking legislation and visiting local elected officials to educate and advocate around sexuality issues and legislation facing youth in their communities.

Public Policy Capacity Building

Rose Community Foundation funding creates new senior health policy position in governor's office

When the Rose Community Foundation learned that the governor was open to expanding his agenda to include health policy issues in 2000, it made a grant directly to the governor's office to hire a senior policy analyst for health care. The role of the position is to serve as the point person for health-care advocates and stakeholders; to provide recommendations on the administration's position on health-care legislation; and to develop, coordinate, and implement a statewide health-care agenda. A key feature of this grant is that there are no strings attached in terms of specific health policies to advance. As a grantee, the Colorado Governor's Office of Policy and Initiatives is required only to have a health-care agenda that is defensible in terms of solid information and analysis. After three years of funding this position with grants totaling approximately $215,000, the grant helped elevate the importance, quality, and coordination of health policy in state government.

Z. Smith Reynolds Foundation's flexible funding approach builds capacity of environment and health groups, resulting in new clean air policy

The Z. Smith Reynolds (ZSR) Foundation's trustees are firm believers in providing general operating support to grantees. For several years in the late 1990s and early 2000s, ZSR provided general operating and project support to a variety of North Carolina environmental organizations working on clean air issues. While ZSR did not require that the groups work together, the organizations quickly realized that there was greater power as a collective body. The organizations also realized the need to reach out to new allies, such as the health community, in order to add a stronger voice for the enactment of better clean air policies. The organizations educated the public, the media, and elected officials about how North Carolina's air was among the worst in the nation. In 2002, the North Carolina legislature passed the Clean Smokestacks Act which requires North Carolina power plants to significantly reduce nitrogen oxide (NOx) and sulfur dioxide (SO2) emissions. This was a huge victory for the people of North Carolina, and now many of these same organizations are working with the North Carolina attorney general to encourage other states in the region to make similar changes. Also, six of these organizations, recognizing that strength lies in coordination and collaboration, have formed a team of their executive directors called Playing to Win, which focuses on clean water issues. ZSR and the Beldon Fund have provided multiyear support for Playing to Win to hire an economist, augment its legal work (including a lawsuit against the North Carolina Rules Review Commission), expand its grassroots outreach, conduct message polling, and learn how to target members and districts by using Geographic Information Systems.

Public Interest Research and Dissemination

The Boston Foundation's housing research motivates policymakers and media on affordable housing issues

In 2002, The Boston Foundation commissioned research for the first annual Greater Boston Housing Report Card to highlight a lack of new housing production and the impact of soaring housing prices that resulted. The Foundation used the Report Card to convene a new entity called the Commonwealth Housing Task Force, which brought together bankers, developers, and affordable housing advocates and officials in a sector-wide "big tent" approach to address the state's affordable housing crisis. The Task Force surfaced the idea of a strategy providing zoning overlay districts for the construction of so-called smart growth housing in town centers and along existing transportation lines.

Legislation (known as Chapter 40R) for this housing was passed in June of 2004. Subsequent legislation passed in November 2005 (Chapter 40S) held towns harmless for increases to local school budgets caused by 40R housing. The Foundation's Housing Report Card has continued to focus attention on housing and its impact. A *Boston Globe* lead editorial called the Commonwealth Housing Task Force's effort "the most impressive plan to increase the housing stock in Greater Boston since the run-up in prices began two decades ago." In the nine months since the regulations for 40R were implemented in March 2006, seven towns have signed up for 40R housing, more than thirty towns have expressed interest in the plan, and two thousand housing units are planned.

The Foellinger Foundation funding of research on transit leads to new advocacy and coordination among nonprofits and government

In August 1996, the Foellinger Foundation awarded grant funds to the City of Fort Wayne, Indiana, to support a transit needs assessment. The assessment examined the mobility needs of the community, analyzed the issues surrounding service delivery, and made recommendations for an improvement program. In December 1997, the Foundation's board approved a grant to Turnstone (a local nonprofit organization) to serve as the fiscal sponsor for a task force formed to study the needs of the transit dependent. In October 1999, the working task force reformed as a new entity, the Community Transportation Network (CTN), and applied for 501(c)(3) status. The Network hired a transportation/mobility manager who began work in June 2000. Today, the Community Transportation Network is a 501(c)(3) organization that serves Fort Wayne and Allen County, Indiana. CTN is a cooperative organization of private and nonprofit transportation providers; public transportation providers; community planning department staff members; city, county and state government representatives; and consumers and funders. CTN will serve as an advocate and coordinate safe, fiscally responsible community transportation services for persons who are transit dependent.

Public and Consumer Education

The Boston Foundation lends support to an awareness-to-advocacy campaign for early childhood education

Strategies for Children is the sponsor of the Early Education for All (EEA) Campaign, a long-term effort to make high-quality early childhood education and full-day public school kindergarten accessible to all Massachusetts children. The campaign is based on the argument that most intellectual, personality, and social growth takes place by age five, and that education during those early years is essential to both educational and economic achievement in later life. The campaign uses four key strategies to build support for its position: 1) increasing public awareness about the value of early education; 2) involving many geographic communities and constituencies; 3) supporting alliances among many interest groups (such as union officials, private industry leaders, child care providers, and advocates); and 4) aligning existing resources to improve efficiency and effectiveness, as well as advocating for additional funds. The campaign has made much progress since its birth in 2000. It has been largely responsible for the creation of a new state-level board and Department of Early Education and Care in 2005 to administer the state system. The Department is also charged with creating a universal preschool program along with overseeing the care workforce system.

In February 2004, the Massachusetts Speaker of the State House of Representatives declared universal early education to be one of his top five policy priorities. In June 2004, legislation was approved to establish a new state-level consolidated Department of Early Education and Care. An Early Education and Care Advisory Council including the commissioners of the state's Department of Education, the Office of Child Care Services, and the Department of Public Health, was created to integrate the fragmented systems of early education and child care that currently exist. It is mandated to administer the state's early education and care system, develop a kindergarten readiness assessment system and evaluation approach, and oversee the early education and care workforce system. The Campaign has also been successful in increasing voter support through the use of print advertisements in newspapers and television commercials. A 2003 poll found that 73 percent of Massachusetts voters support publicly funded early education, compared to only 33 percent in 1999.

In 2006, a bill to provide universal preschool education in the Commonwealth received unanimous support in the legislature. Vetoed by the outgoing governor, it is expected to pass in the new legislative session.

The Arnold Fund's support triggers greater public understanding of smart growth

The Arnold Fund near Atlanta, Georgia, has invested in the community's ability to engage in and affect issues of growth. It helped to fund Smart Growth Newton County, a community coalition with more than 1,200 mailing-list members that works to raise awareness of growth issues and possible solutions and to help citizens take a role in determining their future. By convening early community meetings, the Fund helped to introduce smart growth principles to county residents who, in turn, through the creation of Smart Growth Newton County, began to understand that while growth was inevitable, efforts could be well spent working for good growth rather than no growth.[3]

Media Education and Influencing

The Minneapolis Foundation's involvement of public relations firm working with nonprofits puts new spin on economic development

In 1998, The Minneapolis Foundation issued an request for proposals (RFP) to spur a new approach to affordable housing advocacy: professional advertising and public relations—never before used in Minnesota to sway public opinion and influence decision makers on the issue. The RFP called for nonprofits to partner with a public relations firm to distill a clear, cohesive message and bring the issue to public attention and onto the radar screen of state legislators. Minnesota Housing Partnership—the statewide collaborative that formed as a result—created billboards, bus signs, radio and print ads, a web site, and a brochure rooted in messages of self-interest—making connections between affordable housing and healthy economic development, children's academic success, and other issues that enjoy broad public support. As one observer noted, "As a result of these advocacy efforts, affordable housing catapulted from relative obscurity to the top of the public policy agenda in a very short period of time. There is now widespread public acceptance of the primacy of this policy issue, as witnessed by the willingness of virtually every local political candidate and official to embrace this goal."

The Wallace Alexander Gerbode Foundation's funding facilitates media awareness of youth advocacy on sexual violence

The San Francisco-based Wallace Alexander Gerbode Foundation's small but strategic grants to Advocates for Youth helps that group continue and develop an effective media and policymaker education center about child abuse and sexual violence through its web site, http://www.advocatesforyouth.org/presspolicy.htm. Media professionals and policymakers may access inspiring stories about young persons engaged in advocacy and the ongoing path to greater self-awareness.

Administrative and Regulatory Advocacy

New Hampshire Charitable Foundation's convening opens opportunities to partner and advocate with government

Through its convening work, the New Hampshire Charitable Foundation (NHCF) has emerged as a key connector across issues and agencies in the state. For example, the New Hampshire Department of Transportation has asked NHCF to play important roles on two major transportation projects. The Foundation was asked to convene and chair a group of state opinion leaders to develop the state's comprehensive long-range transportation plan. Rather than quickly writing a plan to satisfy federal requirements, the agency is approaching this as an opportunity to inspire better land use planning, and to integrate into the state's transportation planning numerous key public services, from health and education to after-school programs, services for non-drivers, and social capital considerations. NHCF is also convening groups to develop a unique technical assistance program to help twenty-three communities deal with increased growth that will result from the state's largest ever public works project, the doubling of the state's principal interstate highway from Boston north.

The Liberty Hill Foundation grantees' leadership in advocating for environmental justice pays off

The California Environmental Protection Agency's (EPA) Advisory Committee on Environmental Justice has been drafting recommendations that are expected to be quickly adopted. Those recommendations require the EPA to address environmental justice concerns for all projects under review, redirect its research and data collection so that appropriate environmental justice concerns are evaluated, take steps to involve greater public participation, and assess "cross media" risks. (In the past, measures taken to fix a pollution problem have sometimes created new pollution problems. Methyl tertiary butyl ether (MTBE), for example, was added to gasoline in order to reduce air pollution, but the underground tanks in which MTBE was stored leaked into nearby soil, causing soil and water contamination.) "These recommendations provide legitimacy to the claims of the low-income communities of color that have been subject to environmental injustice in California," said Dr. Joe Lyou, who sat on the Advisory Committee and is the executive director of California Environmental Rights Alliance (CERA), a Liberty Hill grant recipient.

Carlos Porras, who also served on the Advisory Committee and is executive director of Communities for a Better Environment (also a Liberty Hill grant recipient), added: "If these recommendations had been in effect twenty years ago, we wouldn't have the concentrations of toxic emissions in local communities that we see today… The battle's not over, not by a long shot. The new guidelines will not replace empowered communities. Without holding agencies and industries accountable, these policies do nothing to bring relief." He added, "This is historic. It's a huge win."

Judicial Advocacy and Litigation

Multiple community foundations sign on to an amicus brief in support of first amendment rights

Several community foundations signed on to an amicus brief (friend of the court brief) in support of the Dobbins versus Legal Services Corporation litigation organized by the Brennan Center for Justice and the Council on Foundations to remove restrictions on first amendment rights to focus private donations. The collective judicial advocacy of the organizations that signed on to the brief, including many community foundations, strengthened the unity of opposition of the nonprofit sector to first amendment restrictions. See http://www.brennancenter.org for more information.

Organizing and Mobilizing

The Health Foundation of Greater Indianapolis helps HIV/AIDS Alliance grow from a small voice to a powerful organizing force

Through generous funding by The Health Foundation of Greater Indianapolis, the Indiana HIV/AIDS Alliance was created to allow community and consumer voices to speak together publicly and to create access to policy discussions and opportunities for advocacy in other arenas. The Alliance is currently housed at Step-Up, Inc., a local nonprofit health education agency. The Alliance asserts that advocacy, education, prevention, funding, and the provision of health care and support services for persons living with HIV/AIDS are a necessary part of both primary health care as well as public health and medicine.

On February 23, 2004, a non-budget year for the legislature, the Alliance held its second statewide Legislative Day, "Community Conversation." More than 100 people from across Indiana gathered first at the Indiana Government Center for legislative training and updates. Following the training, participants marched to the statehouse to meet with legislators and voice their concerns about HIV issues in their communities. In the summer and fall of 2004, Step-Up staff and Alliance members will be conducting four additional regional trainings across the state in preparation of the upcoming legislative session. In December 2001, the Alliance was a core group of 25 individuals and organizations that has now grown into a force of over 200 members in 2004. Due to the unwavering support of The Health Foundation of Greater Indianapolis and its CEO, Betty Wilson, Indiana now has a coordinated, effective means to organize and advocate, through the Indiana HIV/AIDS Alliance.

The New York Foundation's funding of start-up organization leads real jobs and empowers a community

Funded by the New York Foundation in its earliest stages as a start-up organization, Community Voices Heard (CVH) is an organization of low-income people, predominantly women on welfare, who are working to improve the lives of their families and communities. Its large membership base was built through one-on-one interviews, community forums, direct actions, public education, grassroots organizing, and leadership development. While focusing primarily on welfare reform, CVH broadly defines its activism to include education, training, jobs, housing, and economic development.

CVH was born just as the impact of the 1996 federal and state welfare reform cuts were being felt at the citywide and local level. They focused on preserving key parts of the New York State welfare programs, and, as tens of thousands of low-income people were being forced to work for their benefits, they advocated for the expansion of educational, training, and work opportunities. Active CVH members planned and executed actions including press conferences, meetings, accountability sessions, and public rallies that addressed inadequacies in proposals to reform welfare in New York State.

As a result of successful organizing and advocacy efforts by CVH and other groups, New York City created a series of publicly funded job programs for Temporary Assistance for Needy Families (TANF) recipients in 2001. The majority of these positions are temporary, entry-level public sector jobs in city agencies, predominantly in the Parks Department and Department of Transportation. These programs place TANF recipients into paid positions cleaning and maintaining the Staten Island ferry terminals, removing debris from highways, painting and maintaining parks, and providing child care and teaching assistance for the after-school programs in the parks. These workers receive approximately $9.45 an hour, are union members, and receive health benefits.

Community Voices Heard has built a local and national reputation for organizing welfare recipients and developing strong leaders. The group continues to make substantial progress in its fight for long-term jobs, living wages, education and training, and access to benefits. It has earned credibility with unions and labor organizations and engaged public officials and policymakers around issues of welfare reform and job creation.

Lobbying and Supporting Nonprofits That Lobby

The Greater Kansas City Community Foundation engages all sectors in lobbying for children

The Greater Kansas City Community Foundation (GKCCF) has identified children, youth, and families as a priority investment area. After a strategic assessment of the landscape, the Foundation determined that the area where the biggest impact could be made was through moving public policy forward and increasing public investment in early learning and before- and after-school programs.

In 2004, GKCCF worked with Kansas Action for Children, a statewide child advocacy organization, and supported its efforts to increase funding for Smart Start Kansas, an initiative that invests funds in local communities to address the needs of children from birth to age five and their families.

A coalition was developed to support an increase in the program from $3.2 million to $10 million annually; this coalition was made of business, civic, nonprofit, faith, and labor leaders. A media campaign funded by two other foundations in the state complemented the work of the coalition. The GKCCF, in partnership with Mid-America Regional Council, was instrumental in engaging over forty large businesses in this coalition and engaging key leaders to voice support for this increase.

The legislature increased funding for Smart Start Kansas to $8.45 million. In a tight budget year, Smart Start was the only program in the state budget that received such a large proportional increase in funding; numerous members of the legislature stated that the widespread support for the increase made it clear that early childhood was a priority for the state.

TIP: Visit the NPAction.org web site (www.npaction.org) and look for Showcase Groups to stay current with nonprofit uses of state-of-the-art advocacy techniques including the use of Internet technology such as blogs, e-cards, flash video, and more.

Civic Strengthening Activities

Foundations are uniquely positioned to inspire, support, and launch projects and initiatives to strengthen participation in the democratic process. Voter participation efforts are most commonly thought of, but in fact there are numerous ways foundations can encourage more volume of civic activity as well as more meaningful opportunities for that engagement. Following are a few examples of how foundations are funding as well as programmatically strengthening civic engagement.

Voter Registration and Get-Out-the-Vote (GOTV)

**The Boston Foundation leads initiative
to increase voter turnout among minorities**

The Civic Engagement Initiative (CEI) was established by The Boston Foundation in 2002 as a three-year, $1 million collaborative to increase voter registration and mobilization in low-income communities and communities of color with low rates of voter participation. Additional funding partners include the Hyams Foundation, Access Strategies Fund, Miller Foundation, and New Community Fund.

CEI provides grant support to community-based organizations, such as community development corporations, health centers, service providers, and ethnic alliances that include voter registration activities as one component of their work. Grantee organizations are given group training and individual consultation on the best practices of running a nonpartisan voter registration drive, voter mobilization efforts on election day, and voter identification technology software and utilization.

Impact has been clear and consistent. In the 2006 Primary Election, turnout rose 10 percent in CEI precincts while turnout in the rest of Boston's districts declined 0.4 percent. In 2004, voter turnout in CEI precincts rose 17 percent. The project has been credited as contributing to Boston's first African American sheriff and its first Asian American city councilor, both elected in 2004.

Ms. Foundation funding critical to increasing voting by young women

Idaho's Women's Network (IWN) is Idaho's largest women-led organization. A grant from the Ms. Foundation for Women will assist the Idaho Women's Network with the Young Women Need to Vote Campaign, an innovative collaboration among the twenty-six IWN organizational members with the shared goal of increasing voter engagement. The organizations will work with IWN to boost young women's voter participation by developing creative ways to provide political education and voter registration to a broader audience. It will also strengthen and build a grassroots base of active, networked leaders who are engaged in community organizing around voter registration, and work with the higher education institutions in the state to increase the voter registrations of young women.

Voter and Candidate Education

Otto Bremer Foundation creates capacity for nonpartisan voter participation by nonprofits in Minnesota

By making civic engagement one of its priority areas, the Otto Bremer Foundation was able to make a grant to the Minnesota Council of Nonprofits to support the launch of the Minnesota Participation Project (MPP). MPP is designed to educate and engage nonprofit organizations and their constituents in civic participation as a means to meeting their missions. The Project has created a variety of web-based tools available to nonprofits and foundations to assist them in becoming active, effective, and legally knowledgeable nonpartisan participants in the electoral process.

MPP operates on the premise that 501(c)(3) charitable organizations are the "sleeping giants" of the democratic process. These community organizations have credibility, trust, and access to potential voters who are often disengaged from the electoral process. As such, they can be the catalyst for a dramatic increase in voter participation through legal, permissible, nonpartisan voter mobilization activities: voter registration, voter education, and get-out-the-vote efforts.

MPP has experienced tremendous success in reaching communities traditionally excluded from the electoral process. Through its sophisticated train-the-trainer program, MPP has recruited a large and active pool of skilled trainers from diverse communities and nonprofit organizations. Currently, MPP trainers are able to present in Hmong, Spanish, Somali, American Sign Language, Deaf-Blind Sign Language, and English. By recruiting trainers from targeted communities and providing both customized "in-house" trainings to individual nonprofits and centralized voter engagement "clinics," MPP is able to address the multiple dimensions of civic engagement with skill, sophistication, and credibility.

Civic Leadership Development

Dade Community Foundation inspires and develops new civic leaders

The Miami Fellows Initiative provides a training ground to create a core group of emerging young leaders who have the breadth of knowledge, depth of understanding, and the network of relationships necessary to be agents of change in Greater Miami-Dade County. The program prepares each class of eighteen to twenty-one fellows to assume leadership roles in a wide variety of settings. Some may serve on boards for the first time, some may run for public office, while others may promote social change through leadership of underrepresented populations. All will use their leadership skills and experience to work in a wide range of environments and service to the community. The program includes six experiential "laboratories" over a two-year period, each representing a chance for the group to engage in in-depth exploration of a significant community and leadership issue, meet and hold discussions with local leaders, visit and learn about diverse neighborhoods and communities, benefit from the insights and perspectives of national experts, and examine the personal relevance of the issues to their lives and futures as leaders. These laboratories included *Outward Bound, Families Neighborhoods and Communities, A Personal Approach to Multiculturalism, Ethical Leadership and the Common Good, International Experience: Engaging Leaders in a North-South Dialogue,* and *The Promise of a Better Tomorrow/Transition.* The fellows also take part in bimonthly evening programs where they can interact informally with dynamic individuals in the community, create new networks of community leaders, and learn about community issues. The fellows also engage in personal development activities and implement community projects of their own creation in order to acquire, integrate, and apply new skills and experiences. The program also includes a mentorship component through which the Dade Community Foundation pairs fellows with local leaders who are committed to grooming the next generation of leaders.

Ford Foundation's Leaders for a Changing World Project recognizes change-makers and fosters new leadership networks

Launched in 2000, the Leaders for a Changing World Project recognizes seventeen to twenty people a year who are working for social change on systemic problems and issues. Many of these previously under-recognized leaders deal with public policy as part of their ongoing activities. The project is carried out by The Advocacy Institute and the Robert F. Wagner Graduate School of Public Service at New York University through a grant for $22 million. An example of one emerging civic leader is Eddie Bautista of New York Lawyers for the Public Interest, who works with community organizers, residents, and organizations on advocacy campaigns designed to bring about positive changes to New York communities and to empower people along the way. Each year, these emerging leaders will collaborate with a research team to develop new insights and understanding about leadership for social change, through working with fellow awardees and telling their own stories. In an effort to facilitate a new conversation about community leadership, awardees will also be part of a media effort to communicate the stories of their efforts and to explore unique approaches to leadership. For more information about Leaders for a Changing World initiative see http://www.leadershipforchange.org.

Research on Civic Activity

The Boston Foundation's civic research leads to quality of life report card

The award-winning Boston Indicators Project is a civic initiative started by The Boston Foundation in the late 1990s in partnership with the City of Boston/Boston Redevelopment Authority and the Metropolitan Area Planning Council. Its goal is to engage the general public, civic and community-based institutions, the media, businesses, and government agencies in better understanding Boston's key challenges and opportunities through shared access to high-quality objective data that is regularly updated.

Every two years, starting in 2000 and continuing through 2030 (Boston's four hundredth anniversary), the project releases the Boston Indicators Report, containing data about Boston and the region in ten categories: civic health, cultural life and the arts, the economy, education, the environment, housing, public safety, technology, and transportation. Data are drawn from the wealth of research and information generated by Boston's many public agencies, civic institutions, academic think tanks, and community-based organizations that contribute their data to the Project. In early 2003, the Foundation created an easy-to-use and unique web site, www.bostonindicators.org, as the primary tool for distributing the Indicators Report. The web site won the internationally recognized Tech Museum Award for its innovative approach.

The Boston Indicators has been highlighted by the U.S. Government Accountability Office as national model of a regional and local indicators project, and the project director has joined the steering committee of the Key National Indicators Initiative, overseen by the Institutes of Science at the request of Congress. Locally, it serves as the data platform for a new civic mechanism known as the John LaWare Leadership Forum—co-convened by the heads of The Boston Foundation, the Boston Federal Reserve Bank, and Sovereign Bank Massachusetts—that creates a data-driven civic agenda and convenes leaders to identify key regional competitiveness challenges.

Carnegie Corporation of New York

With the Center for Information and Research on Civic Learning and Engagement (CIRCLE), Carnegie Corporation of New York coordinated and produced research, meetings, and presentations that synthesized the state of thinking about civic education in the United States. The Carnegie report, titled *From Inspiration to Participation: Perspectives on Youth Civic Engagement,* served as the blueprint for scholars, youth service practitioners, foundations, and the federal government's Corporation on National and Community Service to develop recommendations for civic education at a White House Forum on civics, history, and service in February 2003. Many of the "what works" strategies identified in the report are being carried out and highlighted by CIRCLE through http://www.civicmissionof-schools.org. In addition, ideas from the report were included in legislation introduced by Senator Lamar Alexander of Tennessee.

Civic Education

North Carolina foundations support civic consortia

The Z. Smith Reynolds Foundation and The Cemala Foundation, both in North Carolina, are supporting the North Carolina Civic Education Consortium—a partnership of nonprofits, government agencies, foundations, businesses, and media professionals who are committed to civic education for young people. The Consortium makes small grants of $1,000 to $10,000 for innovative collaborative civic education projects. For example, Boat People S.O.S., a nonprofit organization, was given $7,500 to teach Vietnamese-American youth how to organize events, conduct surveys, and be participants in planning for how community development block grant funds are used in Wake County, North Carolina.

Advocacy as Part of Strategic Philanthropy

The following essay by the William Penn Foundation is an example of how public policy and civic engagement have been adopted as part of one foundation's shift to a new focus—addressing the systems and context surrounding the problems grants are designed to help address. The essay speaks to the use of multiple methods of public policy–related philanthropy and advocacy as an institution. In a candid manner, it shares that public policy engagement helped the foundation maintain relevancy with its constituency and shares how that work is aligned with its core principles. The essay is placed in this appendix to emphasize again that while each strategy for advocacy may be described and employed individually like a single tree with branches, it is important to return to seeing the whole forest, meaning the framework for public policy engagement.

Why and how the William Penn Foundation seeks to influence public policy
Brent Thompson

Reflecting on three decades in philanthropy, Alan Pifer, former president of the Carnegie Corporation of New York, remarked in 1984 that foundations are among the most unique and privileged institutions in American society: they needn't expend energy on raising money, they do not face the demands of making a profit, they cannot be thrown out of office, and they don't answer to a congregation or membership. Absent these pressures, foundations enjoy incredible flexibility and a special ability to take a long-term view. Those of us who work in philanthropy know that our unusual role in society comes with an awesome responsibility—to apply the limited resources entrusted to us for maximum social benefit within our spheres of influence.

For more than fifty years, the William Penn Foundation (WPF) has supported nonprofit organizations in the Greater Philadelphia region. What began as a family trust has grown into a billion-dollar philanthropic organization—the largest Philadelphia-focused foundation. During our half-century of grantmaking, WPF has helped organizations to provide a variety of services for our community. However, by listening to our constituents and community stakeholders over the past decade or so, we have come to believe that WPF's continued relevancy depends upon making an even greater impact on the future of our region. After years of supporting good organizations and programs that often struggled in highly dysfunctional social systems, we began to view reforming those systems and policies as our best opportunity to leverage maximum benefit for our community.

Therefore, in recent years WPF has shifted its focus to more strategic grant-making, with an eye toward changing systems and policies while continuing to fund exemplary organizations and community programs. Using a base of knowledge built over fifty years of working in Greater Philadelphia, we devised a series of grantmaking strategies, which we continually evaluate and revise, designed to effect broad change in our region on a variety of issues.

Today, WPF promotes positive policy and systems change in a number of areas. These include, for example, community development, early childhood education, equity in public education, more rational use of economic development dollars, public support for arts and culture, regional smart growth, and watershed protection. We believe that significant progress in these areas will help to ensure a better future for all those who make Greater Philadelphia their home.

In order to effect change across such a broad range of policy areas, WPF employs a nuanced approach, using a diverse series of tools appropriate to the issue at hand. Some of these tactics and strategies include:

- **Building Knowledge.** Because we believe that advocacy efforts should be grounded in evidence, we support efforts to assemble credible, high-quality data and research that can be used to understand trends, evaluate programs, and in some cases, leverage additional investments in our region. We feel that it is our responsibility to see that this knowledge is communicated and put into practice, and we often support our grantees' efforts to implement or disseminate what they've learned.

- **General Operating Support and Technical Assistance.** We identify good advocates working to change systems and policies and provide them with the core support and technical assistance they need to be healthy and strong in pursuing their missions.

- **Convening/Matchmaking.** Because foundations are free from many of the day-to-day constraints that other nonprofits face, we are often able to view things from the "thousand-foot" level and can spot opportunities for organizations to connect and work together. We use our resources to encourage dialogue and collaboration between organizations in cases where it may be more effective than going it alone or healthier than competition.

- **Bringing Others to the Table.** As one of the major funders in our region, we have the opportunity to speak to other grantmakers about the important issues facing our community and to help organizations and advocates make connections to additional sources of funding.

- **Demonstration Grants.** We often make grants for innovative projects designed to demonstrate better and more effective ways of delivering services.

The roots of our approach can be found in several of WPF's core principles. These values help to guide our efforts to affect public policy in ways that fulfill our mission to improve the quality of life in the Greater Philadelphia region. They include:

- **Long-term focus.** We attempt to strengthen our region's long-term viability and sustainability, rather than confining our efforts to short-term goals.

- **Leverage.** Our work is designed to have a multiplier effect; we seek points of leverage, including alignment of interest across the private and public sectors.
- **Relevance.** We regularly ask our community for information regarding the challenges that our region faces, as well as feedback about the value and effectiveness of our work and the relevance of our planned future directions.

Appendix C

Resources, Organizations, and Publications

Articles, Books, and Reports

(Note: Alliance for Justice publications on foundations and advocacy are listed below under the description of the organization).

Aron, Nan. 2004. Advocacy's Efficacy. *Foundation News and Commentary* 41, no.4 (July/Aug). http://www.foundationnews.org/CME/article.cfm?ID=2953

Arons, David F. 2002. "Lobbying, Advocacy and Nonprofit Management." In *Nonprofit Governance and Management.* 2nd ed. Edited by Victor Futter, Judith A. Cion, and George W. Overton. 369–93. Chicago: American Bar Association Section of Business Law and American Society of Corporate Secretaries.

Avner, Marcia. 2002. *The Lobbying and Advocacy Handbook for Nonprofit Organizations: Shaping Public Policy at the State and Local Level.* St. Paul, MN: Fieldstone Alliance.

———. 2004. *The Nonprofit Board Member's Guide to Lobbying and Advocacy.* St. Paul, MN: Fieldstone Alliance.

Bass, Gary D., David F. Arons, Kay Guinane, and Matthew Carter. 2007. *Seen But Not Heard: Strengthening Nonprofit Advocacy.* Washington, DC: Aspen Institute.

Berry, Jeffrey M., with David Arons. 2003. *A Voice for Nonprofits*. Washington, DC: Brookings Institution Press.

California Wellness Foundation. 2002. *Reflections on Public Policy Grantmaking*. http://www.tcwf.org/pub_reflections/may_2002.htm

Center for Public and Nonprofit Leadership at Georgetown University. 2005. *The Cost of Caution: Advocacy, Public Policy and America's Foundations*. Report from the April 21, 2005, Issue Forum. Washington, DC. http://cpnl.georgetown.edu/doc_pool/IF03CostofCaution.pdf

Coalition of Community Foundations for Youth. 2004. *Policy Matters to Fathers and Families: A Tool for Community Foundations*. Kansas City, MO. http://www.ccfy.org/toolbox/docs/ccfy_Policy_Matters.pdf

Council on Foundations. 1999. *Report of the Public Policy Task Force for the Council on Foundations* (December). Washington, DC. http://www.cof.org/files/Documents/Public_Policy/pubpol.pdf

Covington, Sally. 1997. *Moving a Public Policy Agenda: The Strategic Philanthropy of Conservative Foundations*. Washington, DC: National Committee for Responsive Philanthropy.

———. 1997. How Conservative Philanthropies and Think Tanks Transform U.S. Policy. *Covert Action Quarterly*, no. 63: 6–16.

Egbert, Marcia, and Susan Hoechstetter. 2006. Mission Possible: Evaluating Advocacy Grants. *Foundation News & Commentary* 47, no. 1, (January/February). http://www.foundationnews.org/CME/article.cfm?ID=3545

Ferris, James M. 2003. *Public Policymaking: Leveraging Philanthropic Dollars, Knowledge and Networks*. Los Angeles: University of Southern California's Center on Philanthropy & Public Policy. http://www.usc.edu/schools/sppd/philanthropy

Foundation Center with Independent Sector. 2005. *Social Justice Grantmaking: A Report on Foundation Trends*. New York: Foundation Center. http://www.foundationcenter.org

Funder's Committee for Civic Participation and Proteus Fund. 2006. *Voter Engagement Evaluation Project*. Washington DC: Proteus Fund. http://www.proteusfund.org/pdfs/VEEP-FINAL.pdf

Gibson, Cynthia M. 2006. *Citizens at the Center: A New Approach for Civic Engagement*. Washington, DC: Case Foundation. http://case-foundation.cachefly.net/pdf/citizen_whitepaper_web.pdf

———. 2004. Thinking Outside of the (Ballot) Box: A Broader Political Engagement Strategy for America's Civic Organizations. *National Civic Review* 93, no.2. http://www.ncl.org/publications/ncr/93-2/03_NCR93_2Gibson.pdf

———, and Peter Levine. 2004. The Path to Consensus: Coalition-Building, Advocacy, Research and Communications Converge for Success in Carnegie/CIRCLE Program. In *Gold Book: Success Stories in Nonprofit Management*. Washington, DC: Alliance for Nonprofit Management.

Grantmakers in Health. *2005. Funding Health Advocacy*. Report based on a Grantmakers in Health issues dialogue. Washington, DC. http://www.gih.org/usr_doc/IssueBrief21_Funding_Advocacy.pdf

———. 2000. *Strategies for Shaping Public Policy: A Guide for Health Funders*. Washington, DC. http://www.gih.org/usr_doc/53198.pdf

Guthrie, Kendall, et al. 2005. *The Challenge of Assessing Policy and Advocacy Activities: Strategies for a Prospective Evaluation Approach*. Los Angeles: The California Endowment. http://www.calendow.org/reference/publications/pdf/npolicy/51565_CEAdvocacyBook8FINAL.pdf

Holton, Ruth, and Gary L. Yates. 2002. How Foundations Can Help in Tough Times. *The Chronicle of Philanthropy*, December 12, 2002.

Krehely, Jeff, Meaghan House, and Emily Kernan. 2004. *Axis of Ideology: Conservative Foundations and Public Policy, Executive Summary*. Washington, DC: National Committee for Responsive Philanthropy. http://www.ncrp.org/downloads/PDF/AxisofIdeology-ExecutiveSummary.pdf

Pennsylvania Public Policy Initiative. 2002. *A Report on the Public Policy Work of Eleven Regional Associations of Grantmakers and Five Other Associations* (October 15, 2002). http://www.givingforum.org.

Philanthropic Initiative Inc. 2004. Public Policy, Politics and Philanthropy. *Initiative Newsletter* (February 1, 2004). http://www.tpi.org/resources/initiatives_newsletter/public_policy_politics_philanthropy.aspx

Schambra, William A. 2005 In a World of Bloggers, Foundations Can Expect More Scrutiny. *The Chronicle of Philanthropy* (May 12, 2005). http://www.hudson.org/index.cfm?fuseaction=publication_details&id=3682

Stone, Deborah. 2001. *Policy Paradox: The Art of Political Decision Making*, revised edition. New York: W.W. Norton & Company.

Troyer, Thomas A. 2000. *The 1969 Private Foundation Law: Historical Perspective on Its Origins and Underpinnings*. Washington, DC: Council on Foundations.

Web Resources

Advocacy Institute (now part of the Institute for Sustainable Communities)
http://www.advocacy.org
Many useful ideas and stories for effective advocacy and leadership growth.

Alliance for Justice
http://www.afj.org
Find out about the training and publications available to help your foundation understand the laws governing advocacy.

Alliance for Justice, Nonprofit and Foundation Advocacy Blog
http://allianceforjustice.org/blog/
Provides articles and information about rules governing nonprofit and foundation advocacy.

Center for Lobbying in the Public Interest

http://www.clpi.org

Provides easy to read one-pagers, tools, and stories for foundations and other nonprofits on how to shape public policy, fund policy engagement, and follow the legal rules.

Council on Foundations' public policy web page

http://www.cof.org/action

The Council's public policy web page lists key resources for foundations including information about foundations that have been nationally recognized for their work in the public policy arena.

Domini Social Investments

http://www.domini.com/shareholder-advocacy/index.htm

A great place to learn about the world of shareholder advocacy.

Forum of Regional Association of Grantmakers

http://www.givingforum.org/policy/toolkit.html

Resources for grantmakers about getting involved and taking action on public policy.

Grantcraft

http://www.grantcraft.org

See Grantcraft's informative primer called Advocacy Funding: The Philanthropy of Changing Minds *for information about the why and how of funding advocacy.*

Nonprofit Good Practice Guide

http://www.npgoodpractice.org/Default.aspx

A web-based center for learning about sound nonprofit and foundation practices sponsored by the Dorothy A. Johnson Center for Philanthropy and Nonprofit Leadership at Grand Valley State University.

Northern California Grantmakers Association's Public Policy Grantmaking Toolkit

http://www.ncg.org/toolkit/home.html

The primary goal of this toolkit is to demystify public policy grantmaking with an eye toward building the capacity of funders to engage in public policy initiatives.

NPAction

http://www.NPAction.org/

An all-in-one place to learn about public policy advocacy and to use web-based tools for advocacy directed at government and media.

Robert Wood Johnson Foundation's Connect project

http://www.rwjf.org/publications/connect

Brings together grantees and policymakers for educational purposes and to build working relationships.

Strengthening Nonprofit Advocacy Project

http://www.ombwatch.org/snap

National research on the factors that influence nonprofit public policy participation from OMB Watch, Tufts University, and Center for Lobbying in the Public Interest.

Urban Institute

http://www.urban.org/nonprofits

Shares research and discussion papers on the topic of advocacy prepared for the Urban Institute's Center for Nonprofits and Philanthropy's seminar on nonprofit advocacy. The papers investigate important questions about the basis for and nature of nonprofit advocacy in the U.S. political process.

W.K. Kellogg Foundation's Policy Toolkit

http://www.wkkf.org/Default.aspx?tabid=90&CID=280&ItemID=5000236&NID=5010236&LanguageID=0

Organizations

Alliance for Justice, Foundation Advocacy Initiative

http://www.afj.org

The Alliance for Justice created the Foundation Advocacy Initiative to help increase grantmakers' support for nonprofit advocacy. Premised on the belief that nonprofits play a unique and necessary role in forming good public policy, the Foundation Advocacy Initiative seeks to inform grantmakers about their legal rights to provide resources and support for their grantees' and their own public policy advocacy efforts.

The Alliance for Justice conducts a coordinated program of workshops, technical assistance, and publications to provide private and public foundation leaders and staff with important legal information about the dos and don'ts related to lobbying and other legislative advocacy, election-related activities, grant agreements, building grantees advocacy capacity; and evaluating advocacy.

Alliance for Justice has a number of publications (many of which are free) for foundations interested in advocacy. These include

- *Build Your Advocacy Grantmaking: Advocacy Evaluation Tool & Advocacy Capacity Assessment Tool*
- *Foundation Advocacy Bulletin*
- *Advocacy Advisory*
- *Investing in Change: A Funders Guide to Supporting Advocacy*
- *Myth v. Fact: Foundation Support of Advocacy*
- *Worry-Free Lobbying for Nonprofits*
- *Model Grant Agreement*

Center for Lobbying in the Public Interest

http://www.clpi.org

Center for Lobbying in the Public Interest (CLPI) promotes, supports, and protects nonprofit advocacy and lobbying by all 501(c)(3) organizations. CLPI partners and provides coaching and assistance to foundation grantees and foundations to encourage and enable public policy advocacy including lobbying to occur inside the boundaries of the law. CLPI operates through a national network of advocacy and lobbying trainers and its comprehensive web site. It is the home of letters from the IRS explaining frequently asked questions about foundations, philanthropy, and public policy.

The Communications Network

http://www.comnetwork.org/aboutus.htm

An association of foundations that provides training and resources in public relations and strategic communications.

Council on Foundations

http://www.cof.org

As one of the largest associations of private and community foundations in the nation, the Council on Foundations (COF) advocates and lobbies Congress and the administration on issues affecting the health of philanthropy. COF provides several important means for foundations to learn more about how public policy is and can be part of the many ways foundations strengthen causes and communities. Foundations on the Hill is COF's annual opportunity for foundation leaders to come to Washington, DC to speak with their members of Congress. COF Government Affairs staff also provide legislative and policy information to foundations through their web site and via government relations staff. COF now includes lessons and examples of foundations engaged in public policy and civic action as part of its professional development workshops and workshops on the law, including those for new grantmakers and new board members. If you are with a community foundation, COF's Center for Community Foundation Excellence offers a workshop on community leadership that includes discussion and lessons learned about civic engagement and public policy participation as a function of leadership. Finally, COF's many affinity groups, including associations of foundations by cause area (for example, Grantmakers in Health and Funders Concerned About AIDS), get involved in public policy in their respective areas. One may connect with affinity groups through the COF web site.

Environmental Support Center

http://www.envsc.org

The Environmental Support Center (ESC) was founded in 1990 by grassroots environmental activists, state environmental policy advocates, environmental justice organizations, and environmental funders. These leaders were concerned about the sustainability of environmental advocacy organizations working at the local, state, and regional levels in the United States. A guiding principle driving ESC's mission is the belief that environmental conditions and quality of life are most likely to improve when individuals from communities and neighborhoods play an integral role in finding solutions to environmental problems. ESC fills an important niche in the capacity building field by providing support to environmental groups that are working at the local, state, and regional levels. Groups assisted by ESC's programs range from small, all-volunteer, single-issue groups to large, fully staffed organizations, from start-up organizations to long-standing ones. ESC's assistance includes subsidies for training and consulting, low interest loans, and technological equipment. They match clients with consultants and training and provide direct training, all of which strengthens individual groups and their collective impact. ESC's four programs are Training and Organizational Assistance, Leadership and Enhanced Assistance, Technology Resources, and Fundraising for Sustainable Organizations.

Forum of Regional Associations of Grantmakers

http://www.givingforum.org

The Forum of Regional Associations of Grantmakers is a national network of local leaders and organizations across the United States that support effective charitable giving. The Forum's network focuses on the philanthropy of the city, state, and multistate areas of the United States and encompasses thirty-one regional associations of grantmakers. These regional associations collectively represent more than 4,000 grantmakers and others interested in philanthropy. The forum's web site provides information and resources for grantmakers about public policy strategies, events, and results.

Funder's Committee for Civic Participation

Funders' Committee for Civic Participation (FCCP) works to encourage more attention and support of the broad issues of citizen engagement, both electorally and in society. For more information contact Geri Mannion at Carnegie Corporation of New York.

Grantmakers for Effective Organizations

http://www.geofunders.org

Grantmakers for Effective Organizations (GEO) is a community of grantmakers dedicated to building strong and effective organizations. GEO's mission is to maximize philanthropy's impact by advancing the effectiveness of grantmakers and their grantees. Through research, conferences, its web site, publications, and other activities, GEO highlights knowledge and practices in the field that advance the organizational effectiveness movement.

Grantmakers in Health

http://www.gih.org

Grantmakers in Health (GIH) is an educational organization that works to help foundations and corporate giving programs improve the nation's health. GIH is a leader in encouraging an appropriate and strong role for foundations in the public policy arena. Its web site provides tools for grantmakers that benefit all foundations, not just those in the health arena. GIH's publication *Funding Health Advocacy* is a well-done brief booklet that covers some of the same topics this book does.

National Committee for Responsive Philanthropy

http://www.ncrp.org

Since 1976, the National Committee for Responsive Philanthropy (NCRP) has advocated for the philanthropic community to provide nonprofit organizations with essential resources and opportunities to work toward social and economic justice for disadvantaged and disenfranchised populations and communities. NCRP has encouraged infrastructure development and effective giving for public policy and advocacy, defending the advocacy and lobbying rights of nonprofits and foundations, and educating policymakers and the philanthropic community about key policy issues affecting the charitable sector.

National Network of Grantmakers

http://www.nng.org

The National Network of Grantmakers (NNG) is an organization of individuals involved in funding social and economic justice. The network values individuals, projects, and organizations working for systemic change in the United States and abroad in order to create an equitable distribution of wealth and power and mutual respect for all peoples. NNG works primarily within organized philanthropy to increase financial and other resources to groups committed to social and economic justice.

The Philanthropic Initiative

http://www.tpi.org

The Philanthropic Initiative, Inc. (TPI) is a nonprofit organization offering individuals, foundations, institutions, and corporations a disciplined and results-oriented approach to philanthropy. Since it was founded in 1989, TPI has helped hundreds of donors to have an impact on some of society's most complex challenges through strategic philanthropy.

In addition, TPI encourages a positive climate for philanthropy and actively promotes giving though its work with community foundations, the Regional Associations of Grantmakers, and others.

The SPIN Project

http://spinproject.org/

The SPIN Project provides accessible and affordable strategic communications consulting, training, coaching, networking opportunities, and concrete tools. The SPIN Project's skills and expertise are blended with its commitment to strengthen social justice organizations and help them engage in communications to achieve their goals.

About the Chapter Authors and Contributors

Listed alphabetically

David Abbott, Executive Director, The George Gund Foundation

David Abbott became executive director of The George Gund Foundation in 2003. Prior to joining the Foundation, he served as president of University Circle Incorporated, executive director of the Rock and Roll Hall of Fame and Museum, and executive director of the Cleveland Bicentennial Commission. David was also the Cuyahoga County administrator and, early in his career, a reporter for *The Plain Dealer*. He holds a BA in political science from Denison University, an MS in journalism from Columbia University, and a JD from Harvard Law School.

David F. Arons, Editor

David F. Arons serves the nonprofit sector as an attorney, advocate, and coach. He was formerly codirector of the Center for Lobbying in the Public Interest (CLPI) in Washington, DC. While at CLPI, he directed the Strengthening Nonprofit Advocacy Project, a national research project conducted by three partner organizations—Tufts University, OMB Watch, and CLPI—to understand factors that influence nonprofit participation in public policy. The project produced articles and books including *A Voice for Nonprofits* (Brookings Institution Press: 2003) and *Seen But Not Heard: Strengthening Nonprofit Advocacy* (Aspen Institute: 2007). David taught graduate courses in nonprofit advocacy at Johns Hopkins University and Georgetown University. As an attorney he works with nonprofits and foundations to strengthen their role in public policy. David received a BS in political science from James Madison University, an MA in Urban and Environmental Policy from Tufts University, and a JD from William Mitchell College of Law. He resides in St. Paul, Minnesota and can be reached at dfarons@yahoo.com.

Emmett D. Carson, PhD, CEO and President, The Silicon Valley Community Foundation

Emmett D. Carson, PhD is internationally recognized as a catalyst for progressive social change. A renowned speaker, he has published over seventy-five works on philanthropy and social justice. Prior to his appointment as CEO and president of Silicon Valley Community Foundation, Dr. Carson served as President and CEO of The Minneapolis Foundation. Under his leadership, The Minneapolis Foundation received national recognition for its grantmaking, lending, development and communication efforts as it increased assets from $186 million to over $640 million. Previously, Dr. Carson was the first manager of the Ford Foundation's worldwide grantmaking program on philanthropy and the nonprofit sector. He also has worked for the Joint Center for Political and Economic Studies and the Congressional Research Service.

Dr. Carson serves on several nonprofit boards including Blue Cross Blue Shield of Minnesota, Southern Education Foundation, and the University of Minnesota's Humphrey Institute of Public Policy, among others. He is a former trustee and the former board chair of the national Council on Foundations in Washington, DC. He is the recipient of several nonprofit leadership awards and has been recognized numerous times by *The Nonprofit Times* as one of the fifty most influential nonprofit leaders in the United States. Dr. Carson received his PhD and MPA degrees in public and international affairs from Princeton University and his bachelor's degree in economics (Phi Beta Kappa) from Morehouse College. Married to Jacqueline Copeland-Carson, PhD, he shares the privilege, pleasure, and occasional challenge of raising a teenage daughter.

Hodding Carter III, formerly President and CEO, John S. and James L. Knight Foundation (currently University Professor of Leadership and Public Policy, University of North Carolina)

Hodding Carter III, a native of New Orleans who has spent half his life in Mississippi and the other half in various political, media, and nonprofit enterprises along America's East Coast, was appointed university professor of leadership and public policy at the University of North Carolina at Chapel Hill in January 2006. Hodding came to that post after almost eight years as president and CEO of the John S. and James L. Knight Foundation in Miami. Knight is a $2 billion foundation concerned with community and civic development in selected American communities and the furtherance of press freedom and improvement of press performance at home and abroad. Hodding has written two books and contributed to nine others. A trustee of Princeton University over a fifteen-year period, he is currently on the boards of The Century Foundation, the Center for Public Integrity, the Enterprise Corporation of the Delta, the Foundation for the Mid-South, and seven Dreyfus Corporation mutual funds. Past board memberships include Independent Sector, the Japan Society, the American Committee on U.S.–Soviet Relations, the George C. Marshall Foundation, the American Council of Young Political Leaders, the Atlantic Council, the Center for International Journalists, the Reporters Committee for Freedom of the Press, and the Action Council for Peace in the Balkans. He has been awarded nine honorary degrees.

Stuart Comstock-Gay, Director of the Democracy Program, Dēmos (formerly Vice President, New Hampshire Charitable Foundation)

Stuart Comstock-Gay is executive director of the National Voting Rights Institute, a Boston-based nonpartisan legal center that seeks to make the electoral process equally accessible to all citizens, regardless of race or income. From 1997 to 2004, Stuart worked for the New Hampshire Charitable Foundation (NHCF), initially as vice president for programs and ultimately as chief operating officer. At NHCF, among other work, he oversaw the development of the Entrepreneurial Investing (EI) initiative, a high engagement grantmaking program for rapidly growing statewide nonprofits, and New Futures, a statewide advocacy and leadership organization addressing issues of substance abuse. Prior to his foundation work, he spent fourteen years with the American Civil Liberties Union, the last ten as executive director of the Maryland ACLU.

Stuart earned a master's degree in public administration at Harvard's Kennedy School of Government and a BA in political science from Bucknell University. He lives in Concord, New Hampshire.

Marcia Egbert, Senior Program Officer, The George Gund Foundation

Prior to joining The George Gund Foundation in 1998, Marcia Egbert was vice president of the National Urban Policy Institute, a social policy analysis and lobbying firm in Columbus, Ohio. She also served as government relations director for the Cuyahoga County Commissioners and worked for the speaker of the Ohio House of Representatives.

Marcia is active in a number of local, state, and national organizations of grantmakers including the Early Childhood Funders Collaborative, Grantmakers Income Security Task Force, Funders Network on Reproductive Health and Rights, and the Public Policy Committee of Ohio Grantmakers Forum. She is also a founding board member of the Health Policy Institute of Ohio. Ms. Egbert is a two-time alumna of Ohio State University, having received both BA and JD degrees from that institution.

Cynthia M. Gibson, PhD, Principal, Cynthesis Consulting (formerly Program Officer, Carnegie Corporation of New York)

Cynthia M. Gibson, PhD, is an independent consultant specializing in public policy research and analysis, program development, strategic planning, and marketing and communications for several national nonprofits and foundations. Previously, she served as a program officer at Carnegie Corporation of New York in the area of Strengthening U.S. Democracy, overseeing two national subprograms in Strengthening the Nonprofit and Philanthropic Sector and Youth Civic Engagement, both of which she developed. During that time, she authored two publications—*From Inspiration to Participation: Strategies for Youth Civic Engagement* and (with Peter Levine) *The Civic Mission of Schools*—that became standards for the civic learning field and the basis of a national advocacy campaign and federal legislation for better school-based civic education.

Earlier in her career, Cynthia was a consultant on nonprofit and philanthropy strategic planning, research, and communications for a variety of foundations and organizations including Annie E. Casey Foundation, Nathan Cummings Foundation, Andrew W. Mellon Foundation, Rockefeller Foundation, Open Society Institute, Planned Parenthood Federation of America, National Institute of Health, and Citizens Committee for Children. Cynthia also has served in senior staff positions at the National Family Planning and Reproductive Health Association, the Ms. Foundation for Women in New York, and the Partnership for Democracy (formerly The Youth Project). As an associate at People for the American Way, Cynthia produced several videos with television producer Norman Lear and created the nation's first videotape library on ultrafundamentalism.

In addition to speaking and publishing widely on nonprofit strategy, citizenship, education, philanthropy and social policy, Cynthia teaches at the Robert J. Milano Graduate School of Management and Urban Policy, is a senior fellow at Tufts University, and has served on numerous advisory committees, selection panels, and editorial boards. In 2003, Cynthia was selected by *The Nonprofit Times* among its "Power and Influence Top 50 Leaders."

Lenore M. Hanisch, Executive Director, Quixote Foundation

Lenore M. Hanisch brings expertise in journalism and event management to her triple roles as Quixote Foundation family member, board member, and, since 2003, executive director (aka "The Energizer E.D."). Her activism begins by choosing green, socially equitable, and progressive ways to manage home and office, and it extends to working closely with grantee organizations, promoting their overall health as well as specific initiatives. Lenore's board colleagues have described her as "new and lovely" for her refreshing approach to Quixote Foundation's work. "I am going to save one seven-foot-diameter tree, even if I actually have to hug it," says Lenore of her current priorities.

Jeff Krehely, formerly Deputy Director, National Committee for Responsive Philanthropy (currently consultant with the LGBT Movement Advancement Project)

Jeff Krehely currently works with the Lesbian, Gay, Bisexual, Transgender Movement Advancement Project (LGBT MAP), which provides strategic research services to help advance equality for the LGBT community. Prior to LGBT MAP, Jeff worked for the National Committee for Responsive Philanthropy (NCRP), serving as NCRP's research director (February 2003 until January 2004), as well as its deputy director (February 2004 until he joined LGBT MAP in September 2006). Jeff has also served as the special assistant to the president of The Atlantic Philanthropies, Inc., a multi-billion-dollar international grantmaking organization, and as a research associate at the Urban Institute's Center on Nonprofits and Philanthropy. Jeff has been quoted in and featured on regional and national media outlets, including NPR, *The New York Times*, and CNN. He holds a BA in English from King's College (Pennsylvania) and a Master of Public Policy degree from Georgetown University.

Gara LaMarche, Vice President and Director of U.S. Programs, Open Society Institute

Gara LaMarche is vice president and director of U.S. Programs for the Open Society Institute, a foundation established by philanthropist George Soros to promote open societies around the world. His articles on human rights and social justice issues have appeared in publications including *The New York Times*, *The Washington Post*, *The Los Angeles Times*, *Newsday*, *The Nation*, *The American Prospect*, *The Texas Observer*, and *The Wharton Magazine*, and he is the editor of the book *Speech and Equality: Do We Really Have to Choose?* Gara has taught at New School University and the John Jay College of Criminal Justice. He serves on the boards of Article 19 (the international free expression organization), PEN American Center, and *The Nation*; as a member of the Sundance Documentary Fund Selection Committee; on the U.S. advisory committee for *Index on Censorship* (a London-based human rights magazine); and on the advisory committees for the Human Rights Watch's women's rights division and U.S. programs.

Abby Levine, Foundation Advocacy Counsel, Alliance for Justice

Abby Levine serves as foundation advocacy counsel at the Alliance for Justice. Prior to joining the Alliance, she was the public policy analyst at the National Council of Nonprofit Associations (NCNA). At NCNA, Abby monitored and analyzed issues affecting the nonprofit sector, such as challenges to nonprofit tax exemptions and advocacy, state budget cuts, government grants streamlining, and corporate governance. Before working at NCNA, Abby was an associate in the tax department at Squire, Sanders & Dempsey in Cleveland, Ohio. Ms. Levine holds a BA from American University and a JD from Case Western Reserve University's School of Law.

Patricia S. Lieberman, Chair, A.L. Mailman Family Foundation, Inc.

Patti Lieberman serves as chair of the A.L. Mailman Family Foundation, Inc. She is a member of the board of trustees of Grantmakers for Children, Youth, and Families as chair of the program committee and former co-chair of the GCYF 2004 annual conference. Ms. Lieberman is a founding and current member of the Child Care and Early Education Fund in NYC, for which she was the 2002–2003 chair. She currently serves on the oversight committee of the NYC Early Childhood Professional Development Institute based at City University of New York, on the advisory committee of the HRA/CUNY Informal Child Care Training Project, and on the New York City Department of Education, Office of Early Childhood Education's advisory committee. Ms. Lieberman is a former board member of the New York Regional Association of Grantmakers, for which she served as chair of the committee on directors, a member of the strategic planning committee, and vice chair of the program committee. Ms. Lieberman holds an MSW from Columbia University's School of Social Work and a MBA from New York University Stern School of Business.

Geri Mannion, Program Chair, Strengthening U.S. Democracy Program, Carnegie Corporation of New York

As chair of Carnegie Corporation's Strengthening U.S. Democracy Program, Geri Mannion brings a wealth of experience about the role of philanthropy in challenging, improving, and deepening the civic dialogue. She has chaired the division since 1998, after staffing the Corporation's program of Special Projects for almost ten years. In addition to supporting projects that focus on improving broad civic engagement, the U.S. Democracy Program focuses on strengthening the capacity of nonprofit organizations that contribute to a healthy civil society. Separately, Geri continues to chair the Corporation's Special Opportunities Fund, which allows the Corporation to respond to proposals that are important but not related to the foundation's primary foci. These proposals are by invitation only. A generalist, Geri has spent more than thirty years in the field of philanthropy. Before joining Carnegie Corporation, she worked for the Rockefeller and Ford Foundations. Mannion holds a BA in English and an MA in political science, both from Fordham University.

Lloyd H. Mayer, Associate Professor of Law, University of Notre Dame Law School and Of Counsel, Caplin & Drysdale, Chartered

Lloyd H. Mayer is an associate professor at the University of Notre Dame Law School and Of counsel with the firm of Caplin & Drysdale, Chartered. Prior to joining the Notre Dame faculty in 2005, he practiced full-time with the tax-exempt organizations group of Caplin & Drysdale in Washington, DC, first as an associate and then as a member. Before joining Caplin & Drysdale in 1996, he clerked for two years with the Honorable Lowell A. Reed, Jr. of the United States District Court for the Eastern District of Pennsylvania. Mr. Mayer received his JD in 1994 from Yale Law School and his AB, with distinction and honors, in 1989 from Stanford University.

Maria Mottola, Executive Director, New York Foundation

Maria Mottola is the executive director of the New York Foundation where she served as a program officer from 1994 to 2002. One of the first foundations in the United States, the New York Foundation supports groups in New York City with an emphasis on making start-up grants to new, untested programs that have few other sources of support. The New York Foundation gave approximately $5 million in grants in 2002. Prior to joining the Foundation, from 1989 to 1994 Maria was executive director of the City-Wide Task Force on Housing Court, a housing advocacy organization that promotes the reform of New York City's Housing Court. As the Task Force's founding director, Ms. Mottola managed the group's transition from a volunteer activist campaign to a fully staffed and funded organization. From 1984 to 1989, Ms. Mottola was the director of neighborhood programs and a community organizer at Lenox Hill Neighborhood House, a settlement house on the East Side of Manhattan. Ms. Mottola has taught community organizing at New York University School of Social Work and has been an adjunct professor at the Hunter College Graduate School of Urban Affairs and Planning since 1996. Ms. Mottola is a co-chair of the Neighborhood Funders Group, a national affinity group. She received her undergraduate degree in liberal arts at the University of Toronto and a master's degree in social work from Fordham University in 1984.

Phil Nash, Vice President for Communications, Rose Community Foundation

Phil Nash is vice president for communications at Rose Community Foundation, where he has worked since 1999. Phil has specialized in philanthropic communications since 1992, serving in both staff and consulting roles to Colorado funding organizations. With a background in community organizing and journalism, Nash has been involved in leadership and communications roles in areas as diverse as urban redevelopment, HIV/AIDS, the arts, volunteerism, and human rights. He previously worked for the Downtown Denver Partnership, former Denver Mayor Federico Pena, and as communications manager for Ambassador Swanee Hunt and The Hunt Alternatives Fund, her family foundation. Mr. Nash has served on the Council on Foundations' public affairs committee and has been a presenter at several Council on Foundations conferences. A thirty-year resident of Denver, he has served as a board member and volunteer for numerous civic and community organizations.

Mary O'Connell, Director of Communications, The Joyce Foundation

Mary O'Connell is director of communications at The Joyce Foundation, a Chicago-based philanthropy with assets of over $800 million that works to improve the quality of life in the Great Lakes region. Prior to joining the Foundation, Ms. O'Connell was an editor covering health care reform at *American Medical News* and edited the monthly publication *The Neighborhood Works*, published by the Center for Neighborhood Technology. She is the author of *Welfare to Work: What Have We Learned?*, *School Reform Chicago Style*, *Working Neighborhoods*, and *The Gift of Hospitality: Opening the Doors of Community Life to People with Disabilities*.

Gayle Peterson, Senior Partner, The Headwaters Group Philanthropic Services

As cofounder of The Headwaters Group, Gayle has more than twenty-five years of experience in philanthropy, nonprofit management, and public policy issues involving housing, the arts, community development, and environmental conservation. She is driven by a focused vision, a commitment to social justice, and community action and partnership.

Gayle began her career in policy as a legislative director for the Health and Medicine Policy Research Group and the Chicago Council on Urban Affairs. She later served as program director of the Great Lakes Protection Fund, executive director of the Minnesota Center for Environmental Advocacy, and executive director of Milkweed Editions, a national nonprofit literary press. At Milkweed, she developed Alliance for Reading and Literature for a Land Ethic, both of which promote using art and literature as tools for policy change. Gayle earned a MA in social policy from the University of Chicago and received the Minnesota Award for Excellence for her work in promoting children's literacy. She is a member of the American Evaluation Association and the Grand Avenue Business Association. She and her family live in Saint Paul, Minnesota.

Jeffrey T. Pinzino, Program Officer, Woods Fund of Chicago

Jeff Pinzino has been a program officer at the Woods Fund of Chicago since 2002. He manages grants in the program areas of Community Organizing and Public Policy Advocacy. Jeff is vice-chair of the Chicago Capacity Building Initiative, a funders' collaborative that aims to build the capacity of community organizing groups in the Chicago area. Jeff also cochairs the Community Building Task Force at the Donors Forum of Chicago. Prior to working at the Woods Fund, Jeff worked as an organizer in Chicago neighborhoods for seven years and has worked with the Logan Square Neighborhood Association, the Northwest Neighborhood Federation, and the Interfaith Youth Core. Jeff was a founding member of the Stone Soup Cooperative.

Tony Pipa, formerly Executive Director, Warner Foundation

Tony Pipa earned a masters degree in public administration from the Kennedy School of Government at Harvard University in June 2005. Prior to enrollment, Tony had served as the first executive director of the Warner Foundation, a family foundation focused on stimulating long-term improvements in economic opportunity and race relations in North Carolina. During that time, he was the founding chair of the North Carolina Network of Grantmakers, a member of the 2004–2009 strategic planning committee of the Council on Foundations, and a member of the board of directors of Neighborhood Funders Group. Tony previously served as the first director of philanthropic services at the Triangle Community Foundation in Research Triangle Park, North Carolina, creating a program to help donor advisors strategically increase the impact of their giving. A native of rural Pennsylvania, Tony attended Stanford University and Duke University, graduating summa cum laude from the latter with a BA in English and economics. After playing professional tennis internationally, he also served as the first employee and executive director of Mt. Diablo Habitat for Humanity in Walnut Creek, California.

Helen Davis Picher, Director, Evaluation and Research, William Penn Foundation

Helen Davis Picher is director of evaluation and research at the William Penn Foundation. Helen manages the Foundation's *Focus on Learning* program, which evaluates the Foundation's grantmaking and the performance of grantees in order to contribute to the knowledge base in areas of interest to the Foundation. Prior to becoming director of evaluation and research in 2001, Helen served the Foundation in several capacities, including as vice president for programs and senior program officer. She has played an instrumental role in many of the Foundation's grantmaking efforts over the years, such as restoring the Schuylkill River watershed, preserving culturally significant collections, and developing the Avenue of the Arts. Ms. Picher joined the Foundation in 1983, after serving as a program analyst with the City of Philadelphia's Office of Housing and Community Development and a research associate with the Pennsylvania Environment Council. She is a member of the board of Delaware County Community Foundation and the

Nonprofit Finance Fund Greater Philadelphia Advisory Board and a former board member of Delaware Valley Grantmakers. Helen holds a master's degree in public policy from the Kennedy School of Government at Harvard University and a bachelor's degree from Dartmouth College.

William A. Schambra, Director, Bradley Center for Philanthropy and Civic Renewal and Senior Fellow, Hudson Institute

Prior to joining the Hudson Institute in January of 2003, William Schambra was director of programs at the Bradley Foundation in Milwaukee. Before joining Bradley in 1992, William served as a senior advisor and chief speechwriter for Attorney General Edwin Meese III, Director of the Office of Personnel Management Constance Horner, and Secretary of Health and Human Services Louis Sullivan. He was also director of Social Policy Programs for the American Enterprise Institute (AEI) and codirector of AEI's "A Decade of Study of the Constitution." William was appointed by President Reagan to the National Historical Publications and Records Commission and by President George W. Bush to the board of directors of the Corporation for National and Community Service. William has written extensively on the Constitution, the theory and practice of civic revitalization, and civil society in *The Public Interest*, *Public Opinion*, *The Wall Street Journal*, *The Washington Times*, *Policy Review*, *Christian Science Monitor*, *Nonprofit Quarterly*, and *Philanthropy and Crisis*, and is the editor of several volumes, including *As Far as Republican Principles Will Admit: Collected Essays of Martin Diamond*.

John Sherman, Senior Partner, The Headwaters Group Philanthropic Services

John is a cofounder of The Headwaters Group, with twenty-five years of experience in nonprofit management, grantmaking, and strategic planning. As executive director of the Tennessee Environmental Council, he earned special recognition from the Tennessee legislature and governor for his humanitarian service. As program director and acting executive director of the Great Lakes Protection Fund, John combined his nonprofit experiences with philanthropy. He currently chairs the regional solid waste board for Davidson County, Tennessee and serves on the board of his neighborhood association. John earned a Master of Public Health degree from the University of Michigan. He is a member of the American Evaluation Association and the American Public Health Association. He lives in Nashville, Tennessee, with his wife and three children.

Kelly Shipp Simone, Senior Staff Attorney, Council on Foundations

Kelly Shipp Simone responds to foundations' legal inquiries, reviews applications for membership in the Council on Foundations, and maintains a broad knowledge of legal and policy issues affecting foundations. Prior to joining the Council, Ms. Simone was a law fellow with the Alliance for Justice, providing training and technical assistance to foundations and other nonprofits on the federal tax and election laws governing advocacy by nonprofits. Ms. Simone is one of the authors of *Investing in Change: A Funder's Guide to Supporting Advocacy*, recently published by the Alliance for Justice. Ms. Simone is a graduate of the University of Maryland at College Park and the University of North Carolina School of Law. She also received a Certificate in Nonprofit Leadership from the University of North Carolina School of Social Work.

Brent Thompson, Director of Communications, William Penn Foundation

Brent Thompson is director of communications at the William Penn Foundation, where he provides communications support and counsel to the Foundation's grantees, manages the Foundation's external affairs, and serves as assistant secretary to the board of directors. Previously, Brent was chief of staff at the American Red Cross in Philadelphia, where his responsibilities included public affairs and strategic planning. Before that, Brent was a program manager with Search for Common Ground, a Washington-based NGO engaged in international and domestic conflict resolution. He is vice chairman of the Council of New Jersey Grantmakers and serves on the advisory board of the Regional Foundation Center (a collection of the Free Library of Philadelphia) and the Communications Committee of Delaware Valley Grantmakers. Brent also volunteers with his local United Way as an allocations chair. Brent earned a master's degree from the Fels Institute at the University of Pennsylvania and is a graduate of Drew University. He lives in southern New Jersey with his wife and their daughter.

Index

f indicates figure

More books available from Fieldstone Alliance

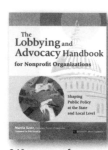